ACADEMIC
LIBRARY
MANAGEMENT

ACADEMIC
LIBRARY
MANAGEMENT

Edited papers of a British Council sponsored course,
15–27 January 1989, Birmingham

EDITED BY

MAURICE B. LINE

THE LIBRARY ASSOCIATION

LONDON

© The British Council 1990

Published by
Library Association Publishing Ltd
7 Ridgmount Street
London WC1E 7AE

First published 1990

British Library Cataloguing in Publication Data available

ISBN 0-85365-839-0

Typeset in 10/11pt Times by Library Association Publishing Ltd
Printed and made in Great Britain by Bookcraft (Bath) Ltd

Contents

Foreword   vii
Editor's preface   viii
The contributors   x

Introductory
1 Current issues in academic libraries *Maurice B. Line*   1
2 The relationship between the academic library and the parent institution *Christopher J. Hunt*   7

Functions and objectives
3 Large university library *James Thompson*   14
4 New university library *Peter J. Tucker*   18
5 Technological university library *Lynne Brindley*   24
6 Polytechnic library *Nigel Macartney*   28

Collections
7 Concepts of stock: comprehensive vs. selective *Brian J. Enright*   36
8 Stock management and disposal: collection building and demolition *Ian Winkworth*   51
9 Acquisitions: Books *Geoffrey Ford*   64
10   Journals *Alan MacDougall*   78
11   Grey literature *David N. Wood and John P. Chillag*   84
12 Preservation and conservation *Peter Fox*   90

Services
13 Cataloguing and subject access *Philip Bryant*   101
14 Reference and information services *John Fletcher*   114
15 Lending services *Geoffrey Ford*   122
16 Services to external users *Lynne Brindley*   133

Cooperation

17 Interlibrary access, national and international *Maurice B. Line*   139
18 Cooperation in collections *Henry J. Heaney*   147
19 Other forms of cooperation *Alan F. MacDougall*   155

Staffing and personnel

20 Management styles and systems *Ian Rogerson*   160
21 Staff structures *Christopher J. Hunt*   166
22 Staff development and appraisal *David M. Baker*   173
23 Training for management *Alan F. MacDougall*   180

Evaluation

24 The concept of 'library goodness': user and library perception of quality and value *Maurice B. Line*   185
25 Performance measurement *A. Graham Mackenzie*   196
26 Monitoring and management information *Lynne Brindley*   206

Finance

27 Financial management systems *John Fletcher*   215
28 Revenue earning and cost recovery *Nigel Macartney*   223

Automation and electronic technology

29 The IT-based manager *Mel Collier*   232

Marketing and public relations

30 Marketing *Nigel Macartney*   237
31 Public relations and publicity *Lynne Brindley*   249

In conclusion

32 Academic libraries: a new generation? *Maurice B. Line*   255

Index   264

Foreword

The Editor notes in his Preface that this volume grew out of a course on Academic Library Management organized by the British Council. The Council sets up about 50 short specialist courses and seminars in Britain each year on a wide variety of topics among which library and information services are a regular feature. Each course aims to provide an opportunity for a small, selected international group of experienced senior professional and academic people to discuss recent developments in Britain relating to their field of work and to participate in a lively exchange of ideas. Both these aims were more than fulfilled with this course which at the outset attracted such a number of applicants that careful selection was then required to ensure a good balance of participants. This was achieved and those who attended mixed and worked very well together. The resulting course − thanks to the outstanding direction of Maurice Line and to his first-class team of speakers − was so well received by the participants that they wrote to the British Council not only to express their great satisfaction with the course but also to recommend that it should be repeated. They will therefore welcome the appearance of this volume for which the British Council is delighted to contribute this Foreword and it is hoped that others will also find these papers of equal interest.

Libraries Department
The British Council
London

Editor's preface

The origins of this volume lie in a course on Academic Library Management organized by the British Council and directed by myself. It was held in January 1989 at Aston University, and attended by 26 senior library managers from 18 countries of widely differing kinds − large and small, highly developed and less developed. The course was very well received by the participants, who expressed a strong wish that the papers be published in one volume. This had in any case been considered when the course was planned, and speakers were asked to prepare their papers with a view to eventual publication.

The papers as published here do not include quite all of those presented at the course. One speaker has left the profession (and the country), and there were no written papers for two sessions that were improvised (one because a speaker was unable to come, one as an extra by special request). All the rest are here, as written up by the authors and edited by myself, largely to reduce unnecessary overlap in content.

The course covered a great many aspects of academic librarianship, but all from a management angle. Some of the papers, for example those on staffing and finance, are obviously concerned with management. The appearance of others may seem surprising at first in a book with this title; but (e.g.) cataloguing and services to users are viewed not as techniques but as operations to be managed.

One of the most interesting and encouraging features of the course was the extent of common thinking among the speakers (and, as the course progressed, the participants, although many of the concepts and approaches were novel to some of them). All recognized not only that the academic library world was changing (that is obvious) but that some major rethinking was needed if librarians were to cope with the changes. My final chapter reflects this; unlike the other papers, it could not be prepared in advance, and in its present form it is a developed version of an improvised lecture. It tries to pull together some of the main threads into a rather different version of the academic library from the traditional one.

All of the contributors were British, and, with the exception of Philip Bryant (a researcher) and myself (retired six months previously) were practising academic librarians. Inevitably the papers reflect British knowledge and experience, but this does not significantly affect the issues considered or the approach to them: these are of universal relevance. It is hoped that the papers in this volume will appear as useful to others as they did to their original hearers.

Maurice B. Line
September 1989

The contributors

David M. Baker Librarian, University of East Anglia, 1985—. MA (music, first class honours), Cambridge, 1973. Fellow of the Royal College of Organists. MLS and PhD (library and information studies), Loughborough University. Formerly worked in the libraries of Nottingham University, Leicester University and Hull University. Has published in librarianship and musicology.

Lynne Brindley Director of Library and Information Services, Aston University, 1985—; also Pro-Vice-Chancellor for Information Technology, 1987—. BA (music, first class honours), and MA (library and information studies), London University. Formerly worked in Bodleian Library, Oxford, Reading University Library and British Library Bibliographic Services. Has published on the future of information services and management issues in librarianship.

Philip Bryant Director, Centre for Bibliographic Management (formerly Centre for Catalogue Research), University of Bath, 1977—. Formerly worked in Bath Public Library and Bath University Library. Has published extensively on cataloguing and bibliographic control.

John P. Chillag Head of Special Acquisitions, British Library Document Supply Centre, 1969—88 (other posts in BL 1963—9). Fellow of the Institute of Linguists. Formerly worked in Australian Atomic Energy Commission and Snowy Mountains Hydro-Electric Authority. Has published extensively on various aspects of grey literature.

Mel W. Collier Chief Librarian, Leicester Polytechnic, 1985—. MA (Arabic studies), University of St Andrews. Formerly worked in libraries of St Andrews University, University College Cardiff, Hatfield Polytechnic and Polytechnic of Central London (Deputy Head of Library Services). Active in research and development of library information technology.

Brian J. Enright Librarian, University of Newcastle upon Tyne, 1972—. MA (history) and DPhil (history), Oxford University. Formerly worked in the Bodleian Library, House of Commons Library, BBC Television Film Library (Head), City University, London (Librarian) and University of Sussex (Librarian). Recently led the British Library review of acquisition and retention policies.

John Fletcher Librarian, Coventry Polytechnic, 1979—. BA (Econ), Manchester University; MA (library and information studies), Loughborough University. Formerly worked in Leeds City Libraries, Bradford Institute of Technology Library and Warwick University Library.

Geoffrey Ford Librarian, University of Bristol, 1989—. BSc (geology), University of Leicester; MSc (information science), University of Sheffield. Formerly worked in libraries of Leicester University, Durham University, Bristol University, Lancaster University and Southampton University (Deputy Librarian). Research officer, UGC Steering Group on Library Research, 1977—9.

Peter Fox Librarian, Trinity College Dublin, 1984—. (Deputy Librarian from 1979—84). BA (German, first class honours), King's College London; MA (librarianship), University of Sheffield. Formerly worked in a number of posts in Cambridge University Library. Member of the British Library's National Preservation Advisory Committee.

Henry J. Heaney Librarian and Keeper of the Hunterian Books and Manuscripts, University of Glasgow, 1978—. MA (modern history), Queen's University Belfast. Formerly worked as Secretary of SCONUL and in the libraries of Magee University College, the New University of Ulster, University College Dublin (Librarian) and Queen's University Belfast (Librarian). Chairman, Working Group on Library Cooperation, National Library of Scotland. Member of British Library Board. President of the Scottish Library Association 1990.

Christopher J. Hunt Librarian, British Library of Political and Economic Science, 1985—. BA (history), Exeter; MA (history), University of Durham. Formerly worked in the libraries of Newcastle upon Tyne University, Manchester University, James Cook University of North Queensland (Librarian), and La Trobe University, Melbourne (Librarian).

Maurice B. Line Information and Library Consultant, 1988—. MA (English language and literature), Oxford University. HonDLitt, Heriot-Watt University; HonDSc, Southampton University; Hon Fellow of the Library Association; President of the Library Association 1990. Retired in 1988 as Director General, Science, Technology and Industry, The British Library. Formerly worked in Bodleian Library, and the libraries of Glasgow University, Newcastle upon Tyne University, Bath University (Librarian), National Central Library (Librarian) and the British Library Lending Division (Director General). Professor Associate, University of Sheffield; Visiting Professor, Loughborough University. Has researched and published widely on many aspects of librarianship and information science.

Nigel Macartney Librarian, Hatfield Polytechnic, 1982–; also County Technical Librarian. MA (history), Cambridge University. Formerly worked in Leeds City Libraries, the Agricultural College in Hertfordshire (Librarian, 1972–8) and Hatfield Polytechnic (various posts).

Alan MacDougall Senior Assistant Librarian, Loughborough University; also teaches in Department of Library and Information Studies. BA, Birmingham Polytechnic; MA, London University; PhD (all library and information studies), Loughborough University. Assistant Secretary to the Library Resources Committee, University of London, 1974–8. Has published widely in the field of library training.

A. Graham Mackenzie Librarian, University of St Andrews, 1976–89. MA (classics), University of Glasgow. Formerly worked in libraries of Durham University, Nottingham University, Leeds University and Lancaster University (Librarian and Director of Library Research Unit). Has published widely.

Ian Rogerson Librarian, Manchester Polytechnic, 1973–. MLS and PhD (library and information studies), Loughborough University. Formerly worked in libraries of Lancashire County, Luton College of Technology, Lancashire Polytechnic and Gloucestershire Technical Information Service. Chairman, Board of Assessors, Library Association Council, 1983–9.

James Thompson Librarian, University of Birmingham, 1987–. BA (English literature, first class honours), Durham University. Formerly worked in libraries of University of East Anglia, Glasgow University and Reading University (Librarian). Author of 10 books on librarianship.

Peter E. Tucker Librarian, University of Warwick, 1963–89. MA and BLitt (English language and literature), Oxford University. Formerly worked in libraries of Liverpool University, Leeds University and Leeds University Institute of Education (Librarian).

Ian Winkworth Librarian, Newcastle upon Tyne Polytechnic, 1983–. (Deputy Librarian, 1975–83). BA (English and philosophy), Durham University; MPhil, Durham University. Formerly worked in libraries of Bristol University and Leeds University. Managing Director of Newcastle Polytechnic Products. Has published widely on library costing and performance measures. Chairman, Northern Regional Library System/Information North.

David N. Wood Deputy Director, British Library Document Supply Centre. BSc (geology), Nottingham University; PhD (geology), Leeds University. Has worked at the British Library in Boston Spa (formerly National Lending Library for Science and Technology) in various posts since 1962.

1

Current issues in academic libraries

Maurice B. Line

Introduction

This paper attempts to identify the main current issues in academic libraries. It is intended as an introduction to the other papers, which take up all the issues in much greater depth. Inevitably it is written from a British viewpoint, but although there are certain particular features about the British scene there is no reason to suppose that most of the issues are not universal.

The main fundamental problem facing academic libraries is their inability to maintain their acquisitions and their services at previous levels. The reasons for this are fairly clear. Even in countries that are relatively wealthy, governments are trying to cut public expenditure, and since higher education accounts for a significant amount of this, it has received reduced government funding over the last decade or two. Since staff account for a high percentage of all recurrent expenditure in academic libraries — in Britain, typically about 55% — savings have had to be made here, not least because staff are a continuing commitment; unlike acquisitions and equipment, they cannot be cut back suddenly if cuts are necessary. If staff were not reduced, they would gradually account for an ever-increasing proportion of library expenditure; if some libraries in Britain had maintained their staff numbers as they were 10 years ago, they would probably by now account for almost all of the budget.

Even if libraries received funding in line with inflation, this would not be sufficient to keep up with the continuing growth and cost of the literature. Books and journals have increased in price a good deal faster than general inflation for several years. If a library were to buy the same proportion of output that it acquired 10 or 20 years ago, it would have needed an increase in acquisition funds of something in the order of 15% per annum on average. It is safe to say that no library has received funds of this kind, and as a result there have been great pressures on acquisitions.

At the same time, there has been an increasing necessity to spend money on automation and the appropriate equipment. The aim has always been greater efficiency in the long run, but meantime extra expenditure has to be incurred. Some automation systems that libraries have acquired have not proved satisfactory, or the firms responsible for them have gone out of business, and new ones have had to be installed, at a large cost.

Finally, accommodation in many libraries is running out or has already run out.

1

The capital funds required for new buildings have not always been forthcoming, and this has created a space crisis in many libraries.

Together, these pressures have brought to the fore some problems and issues that probably ought to have been tackled long before; libraries have been in a position of reacting to circumstances rather than planning well in advance. There are lessons here for the future.

Function within the institution

Academic institutions have had to reassess their objectives, and many of them have produced forward plans which include a clear statement of functions and how they are to be fulfilled. These affect the library fundamentally. If, for example, a university is to spread research thinly over many subjects, this would require a different stock and different services from one that concentrates research in a few specialized areas of high excellence. An academic institution may emphasize teaching, backed up by reading; or it may emphasize self-instruction on the part of students, backed up by teaching. Many more books will be wanted in the second case than in the first.

More fundamentally still, the library needs to determine whether it is primarily a book resource, available for use but not extensively exploited by library staff, or an information service based on collections. Different types of institution may well require different sorts of service; in particular, scientific institutions are much more likely to benefit from an information service than ones in which the humanities are prominent. The first type of library will put all the emphasis it can on extensive acquisitions, while the second will focus on services, which may be highly staff-intensive. This does not incidentally mean that they need spend a higher proportion of the budget on staff, since the processing of large quantities of acquisitions is also staff-intensive, and many information services can be given more or less mechanically, for example by regular computer printouts against matched research profiles.

In some institutions in Britain the librarian's responsibility has been widened to include audiovisual collections and services, and, more significantly, computing services. Responsibility may be at the policy level, in which case the librarian coordinates separately managed services, or it may be operational, with an increasing integration of activities. There may be new services that could be offered. It is essential for the library to keep in very close touch with the institution and its policy, both reflecting and serving policy and influencing it where necessary.

What is absolutely vital is that the library should work out its objectives clearly. This is less simple than it sounds. It is of course possible for the head librarian to state the objectives as he sees them, and in effect impose them on the rest of the staff, but he would be much wiser to consult with his staff. It is very important that all staff are committed to the objectives of the library, and this is much more likely to happen if they are involved in their formulation.

Resources required to run the library

One approach to rethinking the functions and objectives of a library is to start from a zero base. This approach would identify what the institution aims to do and how it aims to do it, and then calculate what information resources (in the form of both books and services) are needed to serve the institution's objectives effectively. For example, a physics department with a research specialism in semi-conductors can hardly operate effectively without strong collections in the field and without keeping up to date with all significant relevant literature. The cost of providing a department with information services can be calculated, as can the cost of literature. Even when this sort of exercise is not 'for real', it is an extremely useful discipline. It may well work out that the resources required are considerably more than the library is given at present; in this case the library can argue for more resources on a very much stronger basis than simply asking for an increase on last year's budget. In effect, the librarian would be saying to the institution that if he gets less than is required to serve the institution, the institution would not be served properly and therefore would not serve its own objectives so well.

Allocation of existing resources

Whatever arguments the librarian puts forward, and however soundly based they are, in the end he receives a certain budget. The question is then how to allocate this most effectively. Ideally he should have virement between staff, equipment and acquisitions; unfortunately, this is rare, and staff in particular are usually treated as a separate budget head. However, the librarian can nearly always switch money from staff to acquisitions and equipment, and he may in due course become able to move money in the other direction. At any rate, he is not excused from working out what would be the optimal allocation of resources.

One main allocation is between collections and services: the equipment to serve either or both is a secondary matter. For this allocation, he needs to know how much different services cost. Many libraries are surprised to discover how much they spend on cataloguing and classification as against direct service to readers. Service costing is essential for effective allocation, as is unit costing – the calculation of cost per unit, whether it be a book catalogued, an item lent or a search conducted.

Within acquisitions, the balance between books and journals needs to be calculated. it is very easy for journals to assume an ever-increasing proportion of the budget, because their costs have risen faster than books and because librarians are very reluctant to break runs of journals once they have started subscribing to them. As a result, the balance may easily switch from 60:40 in favour of books to 60:40 or more in favour of journals; something of this kind has in fact happened in British universities. If this process is allowed to continue, in a few years time nothing whatever will be spent on books.

Allocation has also to be made between subjects. While it is easier to do this using last year's expenditure as a base, adding something pro rata to each subject allocation, it is necessary at least every five years to stand back and re-calculate the requirements. Output in one subject may have grown much faster than in another, or requirements may have shrunk, for example if academic staff or student numbers in a particular subject have been much reduced. Within the journals budget, it is less difficult to allocate funds; ideally, the cost of acquiring each journal should be related to the use made of it, and then compared with the cost of interlibrary access. If the cost of interlibrary access is higher, obviously the journal should be bought on economic grounds. If it is lower but not much lower, it may still be desirable to buy the journal, currently at least, to enable researchers to keep up to date in a subject. Another calculation should be made as to whether each journal should be bound and retained, retained unbound, or disposed of after two or three years; this depends on the relative cost of binding and retention on the one hand and of interlibrary access on the other.

There is a possibility – in the UK a strong one – that with the search for more rigorous control over expenditure, emphasis on the market approach and the creation of cost centres in academic institutions, departments will take control over spending on library materials. Most of the acquisition budget would then be outside the librarian's control; at best, he would merely administer it. Allied with this may be a trend back towards departmental libraries. The implications are profound.

In libraries with a major research or archival responsibility, the balance of expenditure between acquisitions and preservation has also to be calculated. If any substantial portion of the stock needs to be preserved, the cost can be very high, and leave much less for acquisitions. At some point, a policy decision has to be made that preservation (including ordinary binding) should not amount to more than, say, 20% of combined acquisitions/preservation expenditure. The figure would probably be much lower in many libraries, but could be much higher in a major library with a high proportion of valuable or unique items.

Services to internal and external users

Until relatively recently, academic libraries gave a rather limited range of services to their own users, and did little more for external users other than admit them to the library for consultation purposes if they could prove a case for needing to use it. However, the library represents a major capital resource, and its exploitation is both a social obligation and an economic necessity. Academic libraries are usually much the largest information resource in the neighbourhood, and the possibility exists of giving a number of services to local and regional users, particularly in industry, for payment. The payment should of course cover the total costs of giving the service and something more. A good knowledge is required of local industry and business, which is the main potential market, and the costs need to be carefully calculated. Cooperation with the private information sector might usefully be sought, particularly for such activities as publications.

If internal users are to be charged, a clear set of principles needs to be established for charging. Services can be divided into 'basic' and 'extra' or 'premium', but this leaves open the question of what is basic and what is extra. Members of an academic institution are there to prosecute research, teaching and learning, and great care must be taken before charges are made for services to enable them to do so.

Cooperation

A great deal of library literature is concerned with cooperation and resource sharing. Each library needs to decide what it has to gain from cooperation. For example, cooperation in a national bibliographic network means that it has to standardize its own records to fit in with the system; this may incur extra local costs but may also bring greater rewards in the form of cheaper catalogue entries extracted from the national database. Before libraries enter into cooperative schemes they should take great care to ensure that they really are cost-effective. In all the various schemes of resource-sharing, even when they have been going for several years, very rarely does any evaluation appear to have been made of the costs incurred or the benefits received.

Staffing

As mentioned above, staff numbers have been reduced in most libraries, or at least have not kept pace with the growth of collections and services in the library. It is important to ensure that staff money is used as effectively as possible. Some work that has previously been regarded as 'professional' may be more appropriate for a lower level; 'professional' and 'non-professional' duties are in urgent need of re-definition. Libraries should consider conducting a 'skills audit' to identify what skills will be required in a different and changing future, and then preparing a programme for ensuring that they become available over a period of five years or so.

Performance measurement

There is great pressure on libraries to give value for money; in any case, they ought themselves to be aiming to give value for money without external pressure. This means first that they must cost their activities to a level of detail and accuracy they have not done before, and also measure performance, in terms of outputs (such as loans or bibliographic searches undertaken) rather than inputs (such as expenditure per student). Most measures that have been used hitherto are either input measures or rather crude output measures, such as issues per student. As performance measures are developed, it is important they should be standardized across all academic libraries within a country, if not between countries, since much of the value lies in the ability to compare different institutions, as well as different years within the same institution. Work is being done in this, but it is making slow progress, and the need is urgent.

Information technology

Information Technology (IT) is having a big effect on libraries, though to date this has been confined mainly to 'housekeeping' automation − of catalogues, issue records, acquisitions and so on. Again, the costs have to be carefully assessed against the benefits. In any case, if any automation plan is effective, the real needs of the system need to be carefully examined, since it is all too easy to automate a system that has grown up over the years and developed accretions which ought to be removed. Indeed, if the system is simplified, it may sometimes be possible to continue to operate it manually just as effectively and at much less cost than if it were automated.

Forward planning

Few libraries have done much forward planning; instead, they have tended, as stated earlier in the paper, to react to events and pressures, often in rather hasty ways that prove in the longer run to be detrimental to the library. Every library should do some forward thinking. For example, it should consider precisely what it would do if it had a 5% cut in resources, a 10% cut and so on, so that if the time comes a considered plan can be implemented swiftly. This requires a clear identification of priorities, including a list of activities that may need to be sacrificed. At the same time, potential new services need to be considered, even if it means reducing or cutting out some existing activities. Close contact with the user community is necessary if their needs are to be properly satisfied.

The most systematic way of approaching forward planning is to construct a Strategic Plan, looking ahead, say, five years. My own preference is for a long term (ten-year) vision and a five-year plan. This would set out the aims and objectives of the organization, decide where the library wants to be in five years' time, on various assumptions (level funding, increased funding, reduced funding), and then, activity by activity, indicate how to get from here to there. Performance measures would be included after each activity, and targets would be set; these would be more precise

5

for the first year than for subsequent years. Activity targets could then be broken down into individual targets, preferably set by the staff themselves, thus enabling the performance of individual staff to be appraised. Such a plan should be updated every two or three years; best of all would be a rolling plan, with a revision every year.

Management and related skills

If the various issues facing academic libraries are to be properly addressed, there is clearly a much greater need than hitherto for skills that have not traditionally been associated with librarianship. Every activity should be viewed from a managerial angle; for example, cataloguing is not a question of how to construct an ideal catalogue record, but on how to use most effectively the resources allocated to cataloguing. Among the skills required are:

- resource management and optimization
- staff management and development
- finance and costing
- marketing
- negotiating skills
- public relations.

Conclusion

The academic library of the future must be efficiently managed, and be able to prove that it is efficiently managed. It must be much more user-oriented, it must have clear objectives, and it must be planned. The utmost efforts must be devoted to developing staff so as to increase their personal satisfaction and at the same time increase their productivity. Political skills are also needed.

The future will be one of continuing and perhaps accelerating change. To cope with it, and to meet the pressing problems of today and tomorrow, high qualities of vision, managerial ability, flexibility and above all leadership will be essential.

2

The relationship between the academic library and its parent institution

Christopher J. Hunt

By definition an academic library is an institution within an institution. In a statement famous amongst British academic librarians, the University Grants Committee in 1921 described the library as the 'central organ' of a university, by its treatment of which the entire 'character and efficiency' of the parent body might be judged. There are few countries today where so confident a statement would be made by a government funding body, and the number of faculty members who would do more than pay lip-service to the principle is also diminishing. Academic libraries today have no monopoly of information services to their university communities, and funding resources have to be argued for on grounds of material benefit rather than of scholarly principle.

The primary purpose of a university library is to support the teaching and research carried out in the university. To that extent the problems all librarians have in delivering such support services efficiently are common problems, to be solved by drawing on the library and information delivery skills that make up the body of our professional literature. In managing academic libraries, however, the modifications of approach dictated by the particular institutional environment are fundamental to success. There are chasms of difference between an academic library serving a population of 2,000 students, and one serving 20,000; between a single site university, and a multi-site one (particularly if compounded by distance); between universities in the same country serving one ethnic or religious mix, and one serving another. There are also obviously fundamental differences when an institution sees research as its prime purpose, and one where teaching is paramount (with prestige, unfortunately, normally being attached to the former only). There appear to be cycles in the national funding of universities. Fortunate is the librarian who is in office during a rising phase, and the corollary is also true. To change the metaphor, all things seem possible when the cake is growing bigger but, when it is diminishing, university life is a messy squabble over the teacups. In the United Kingdom in the 1980s librarians are finding to their cost that serving a state-funded institution, where the pursuit of knowledge in a spirit of free enquiry (the traditional role of universities) is regarded as their legitimate role, is very different from working in an institution that is expected to fund itself within a market, competing for both students and research funds.

All this leads fairly easily to the subject of money. The ideal funding arrangement for a library manager might be to receive a single block vote, which could be spent

7

as wished on books, staff, computers and everything else that makes up a modern library. This grant would increase every year by rather more than the rate of inflation. Every few years would come, reliably, a capital grant to enlarge and otherwise modernize the library building.

This beautiful dream unfortunately is just that; fighting for funds, and spending wisely the inadequate money that does come, is the central job of a chief librarian as it is of any manager. The rules of the game, i.e. the academic library budgetary process, differ markedly from country to country. In some countries libraries receive earmarked funds from the state, separate from those provided to support the parent university. In the United Kingdom this is not the case and the academic librarian argues for funding almost entirely within the parent institution, and thereby against all the other internal supplicants for their share of the pot.

There is a considerable body of literature on how to measure adequacy by formula in a university library. By and large the formulae are useless, giving an appearance of universality to local circumstance. This literature pretends to be empirical, but is entirely country-dominated. Germany, the United States and Australia have very different standards. Use of these formulae is almost invariably political in nature rather than scientific; it is special pleading to match the particular circumstances of time and place, and not to be confused with true performance indicators. The librarian picks and chooses formulae that support the case and ignores those that do not, trusting (usually correctly) that university administrators will not know of their existence. Comparisons with competing institutions are always very strong arguments. University x does not wish to be seen to be spending less than University y on library support for, say, law because it fears loss of prestige and scholarly reputation. These are the traditional arguments of librarians seeking funds within their own institutions. In Britain they are currently losing much of their cogency. Unfortunately, there appears to be no research from anywhere in the world that decisively proves that academic excellence is dependent upon library excellence. There are only too many examples where there is clearly little relationship between the two.

Virement, i.e. freedom for the librarian to transfer money from budget head to budget head within defined rules, is vitally important for the efficient running of a library. Rigidity in budgetary lines makes change and reform intensely difficult. The librarian who is expected to cut down the number of staff employed by the library without cutting back services, a very common circumstance all over the world, will do so more easily and efficiently if allowed to keep some savings for expenditure in other ways. If cash savings have to be made it is better for the university to set targets, and leave the librarian to achieve these by whatever means seem best; crude staff or purchase freezes can cripple an entire library service. Similarly, if income generation by the library is desired, it is rarely possible to do this without increasing expenditure on staff and other facilities, with the intent that the increase in revenue will more than compensate for the additional costs. A budgetary system allowing the librarian maximum flexibility in transferring resources from one area to another is as much in the interest of the parent institution as it is for the library.

Another fundamental principle, which university administrators do not necessarily like, is that money earned by the library should remain within it, without resulting in an automatic matching cut in the grant from the university. The capitalist principle, that people will work harder if thereby they benefit themselves, applies forcibly to libraries. Universities which want their libraries to sell services and publications profitably outside the campus, must allow the libraries to benefit at least partially from the proceeds.

The greatest proportion of library expenditure, as in the university as a whole, goes on staff. In terms of pure financial efficiency this is inconvenient, leading to inflexibilities. It is not so easy to sack a staff member to make a cash saving as it is not to buy a book, or even to cancel a journal subscription. Hence, in both Britain and Australia, there is current legislation by government to abolish tenure, enabling universities to dismiss staff on grounds of redundancy as well as for disciplinary offences. Such measures are clearly undesirable, and may be poisonous to the morale of the organization. But the chief librarian would do well to ensure the maximum flexibility in staffing without resorting to draconian action, such as the use of fixed term appointments, part-time labour and student labour, wherever possible. This results in the inconvenience of a frequently changing labour force at some levels in the library, but the flexibility gained is almost certainly worth this.

Faculty members, even those who are heavy users of the library and are vitally dependent on services offered, are normally far more concerned with expenditure on books than with the nature and pattern of staffing. Control of money for books and serials is normally vested in the library but in many universities in the United Kingdom a system of departmental allocations exists, whereby proposals for acquisition come almost entirely from faculty members rather than from library staff. One British vice-chancellor has recently suggested that the library should be divested of all its book funds; these should be incorporated in faculty departmental grants for faculty members to use for books, chemicals, computers, travel or wherever their priorities lie.

The (preferable) alternative is that new books and serials should be chosen by library staff, according to a defined acquisitions policy and on the basis of advice from academic colleagues. Continuity and flexibility in collection building are much easier to achieve when the acquisition responsibility is firmly in the hands of the librarian. But academic support is crucial to the success of the library. The librarian must be seen to be exercising legitimate authority, within the framework of the governance of the university.

In most institutions a library committee forms the central matrix for this relationship. If, however, it is the *only* place of contact between the librarian and the institution it is very unlikely that the relationship is a happy one, and the library is almost certainly a bad library. The library must be concerned with all areas of the working of the university if it is going to function efficiently, and provide the services required of it. Academic governance is pervasive in its variety and level. If the library is represented in as many forums as possible, the more influence and information (in both directions) will pass to improve it, and to educate people outside the library in its direct importance to them. Participation in the work of a wide range of committees, formal and informal, academic, administrative and social, is necessary not only for the chief librarian but for all professional members of staff. Effective liaison arrangements with all academic departments are most important. Merely by being present, without necessarily opening one's mouth, ensures that the library is not forgotten, as it so easily can be when academic decisions are made. Information is gathered which can be put to good use and, of course, when necessary, battle can be joined. The need to argue a case will arise at least as frequently in the staff club or senior common room as it will in senatus academicus.

The constitutional position of the chief librarian differs fundamentally between

9

university and university. To whom is the librarian responsible in terms of reference for the management of the library – to the university president; to his deputy; to senate; to a library committee? There is no doubt that it is normally best to report directly to the university's chief executive, as the ultimate managerial authority. Management equals control of resources. Who chooses library staff? Does the librarian control staff wherever located, money for books, money for other purchased items, the proper maintenance of the library building? Who represents the library outside the institution? The librarian needs authority in all these areas not as personal aggrandisement, but because it is the only way effectiveness in management of the library can be achieved. A fundamental error, however, is for the librarian to take this principle of being manager in his or her own house too far, and use the library as a power base from which to influence the direction of the entire university. Very strong librarians can fall into this error, particularly in a university where authority is very diffuse and the librarian, by virtue of membership of many committees including academic appointment committees, is able to exert greater influence than any single professor. While a librarian seen to be using all his authority to run the library to the best of his ability on behalf of the university is generally trusted by faculty members, one perceived to be using his powers to influence academic decision making in areas other than the library will quickly unite opposing academic factions against him, and thus do the library harm.

One of the biggest threats to the successful management of a library is academic indifference. If faculty members do not see the library as their own they cannot be expected to support it. If they expect a service to be always unresponsive to their individual needs that is what they will get, because the library will lack the information needed to construct services to meet these needs. The library committee is not the only point of governmental contact between the librarian and his academic colleagues but it is a vitally important one, a forum where the audience is captive and the subject of debate has to be the library. The library committee is an excellent sounding board to test new ideas, but it is also a warning bell for the librarian, where faculty members (and students) can indicate what is not working properly.

Management committees are now rare as controlling bodies for academic libraries. Most library committees are advisory, to the librarian as to the needs of the academic community, and to senate and the university president as to the needs of the library. A productive and successful committee rarely comes into being by accident. There must be effective representation from all the recognized academic areas of the university, and from the organized student body. At least some members must be influential figures in the university. There needs to be some continuity of membership from year to year and, most importantly, members should be persuaded to turn up to meetings. All these things rarely come about without some manipulation on the part of the librarian and his chairman. An enthusiastic chairman, with whom the librarian has a close understanding, is a vital figure in the administration of an academic library. Poor relations between these two individuals can cause much harm. A supportive chairman makes the job of chief librarian very much easier.

Constitutions are a very poor guide as to how an administrative structure actually works. Ambiguity is normally the most significant feature. The powers of officers and committees in universities are rarely defined in sufficient clarity to satisfy a constitutional lawyer. Almost any structure can be made to work. In academic life, however, committees are very unwilling to make authoritative decisions in such a way that members collectively are prepared to accept full accountability for them if they later turn out to have been wrong. Thus even when the constitutional wording suggests that the library committee rather than the librarian is sovereign, in practice it is the individual rather than the collective body who must make the running. But the library committee is the legitimizing body. Overall library policy and the laying down of library regulations must be done according to correct forms. The librarian however is well advised to see that it is he who writes the minutes!

The librarian is not usually an academic but nor is he only an administrator. Many American universities go to considerable trouble to ensure that running an academic library is seen as a legitimate branch of scholarship. In the United States, it is most unusual for anyone to become director of a major academic library without a PhD in librarianship, as distinct from a doctorate in some more mainstream academic discipline. Some libraries have academic structures parallel with their management structures, to ensure that their faculty status is perceived. Such an approach is not in the British academic library tradition; this particular American situation is like that of Hans Anderson's emperor, the academic clothing is imaginary rather than actual. But the librarian with recognized scholarly competence, if not distinction, does have a considerable advantage in achieving peer recognition from his academic colleagues.

Managing a library is also a branch of university administration, and the view of the library taken by university administrators is very different from that taken by faculty members. In an excellent short article, 20 years old but still very applicable, with the evocative title 'The bottomless pit, or the academic library as viewed from the administration building', Munn graphically describes the picture that many (most) professional university administrators have of the library.[1] They tend to be very unsympathetic towards 'motherhood' arguments, as to why the library should be funded without reference to demonstrable and quantifiable benefits to the institution as a whole. In any case, in times of reasonable financial stability, the basis for the distribution of funds around an institution is almost invariably by crude formula. You get what you got last year, plus or minus a fraction according to circumstances and the quality (or lack of it) in your arguments. The need for a librarian to have good working relationships with his administrative colleagues cannot be too highly stressed. As in the case of relations with academics it is only too easy to create resentments which, at their worst, can be poisonous and last for years. The librarian's acceptance as a full or quasi-academic does not necessarily endear him to administrative colleagues, who frequently have to put up with the insolence academics can so easily show towards those they regard as their administrative servants, and the administrator may see the librarian in a position of unjustifiable privilege. These prejudices can be overcome by proper give-and-take in relations, or 'you scratch my back and I'll scratch yours', an attitude which will create alliances, however uneasy and ephemeral, in finding solutions to problems.

The cooperation of administrative colleagues is particularly vital for success in those areas where the management of the library is part of the wider processes of administering a university. The most central of these is, of course, the budgetary process, bidding for money, normally on an annual basis. The librarian who is actually a member of the university finance or budget allocation committee is fortunate, but not all that common. Almost as crucial are the formal procedures necessary to hire new staff, promote old ones, and occasionally to fire them. The library with its unique

11

mix of professional, non-professional and technical staff, many service points requiring continuous manning and long opening hours, is a nightmare to manage if overall university staffing policies do not take its peculiarities into account. In its need for equipment and frequent modernization of physical plant the library is more akin to a scientific department than a humanities area. Unfortunately it is frequently seen as the latter in the allocation of equipment funds. Lastly, even if run as a steady state collection, with new acquisitions being matched by the discarding or despatch to store of older material, the library is in constant need of major and minor building alterations to provide new or changed services.

All of these seemingly insatiable demands are a strain on the university committee system and on officers responsible for resource allocation. In bad financial times the library may come to be seen as a luxury rather than a necessity, or even as a fat pig costing more to feed than its market worth. There are times when the position of university chief librarian appears a singularly thankless task with little to offer but 'lurching from crisis to crisis', as Brian Enright has put it. Librarians 'have an enormous span of responsibilities ... The work ranges from the very unlikely to the completely impossible. It is not at all clear precisely what academic libraries are expected to achieve. The freedom of action of the new appointee seems remarkably limited by the need to clear up the inherited messes of the past and to avoid leaving even worse ones for the future'.[2] Working to a defined strategy is perhaps the most useful discipline one can apply to avoid being overwhelmed by feelings of hopeless inadequacy. Setting realizable objectives for each segment of the library as an organization is a fundamental principle in getting the best out of staff. The principle applies even more forcibly to the chief librarian. He must know where he wants the library to go; these views must be projected to library staff, to faculty members, and to administration at every opportunity. Traditionally this has been through the medium of an annual report, but as this also necessarily serves as outright propaganda, to impress people outside the immediate university community, it is inadequate and unclear on its own. In Britain today every university is required by the University Grants Committee (now the Universities Funding Council) to publish an academic plan; a strategic plan for the library falls easily into such a framework, and can be developed in greater detail as required. It should emphasize achievable objectives rather than vague or over-idealistic goals.

The job of chief librarian of a university is highly political in nature, with politics at least as important as library professionalism on the one hand and the techniques of scientific management on the other. To quote Richard De Gennaro, 'The library operates in a political environment and nearly all the really important decisions that we make at the highest levels have an overriding political component. They are rarely the product of cost benefit analysis or Operational Research where the various factors are weighed and compared, and the 'best' or most cost-effective course is 'chosen' ... A good deal of the quantitative research that is done in the library field is unintelligible, irrelevant, or too complicated and theoretical for any practical use in libraries.' As a manager, he says 'My real problem has nearly always been to correctly assess the political rather than the economic or quantitative factors. It is fairly easy to determine the most cost effective course of action with or without detailed data. It is much harder to map out and implement a successful strategy for achieving it, to assess how the various persons and groups affected will perceive the manager's intentions, and how they will react to the decision'.[3] Library managers should read

Macchiavelli as well as Ranganathan and Max Weber.

One of the most dangerous 'actions' a chief librarian can take is inaction. He must act as leader, not only to his staff, but to the university as a whole in library matters. His role is different from that of head or chairman of an academic department where leadership is indeed necessary but of a rather different kind. Members of a department of chemistry, or of history, should work together in a proper collegiate spirit, serving the same ideals, and needing similar administrative support, but leadership by a head of department, in the sense of precise direction, would be resented and ineffectual. The chief librarian must be concerned with the detailed organization of the whole library. To do this he must know what he is doing professionally and organizationally; but he must also display good judgement and common sense and, when the odds are right, be preparted to take risks. A sense of humour helps, too.

It is crucially important for a chief librarian to be identified with his institution, to fight for it honestly and publicly, to be perceived by his staff and academic colleagues to be vitally concerned with advancing the institution's interests. There are excellent academic librarians who spend months every working year away from their libraries, but it is very much more difficult to be successful in these circumstances. Conflicts within the parent university concerning the role and funding of the library are inevitable and will occur frequently; winning these conflicts, or at least isolating them and thus living to fight another day, is almost the most important part of the job. But continually using these military analogies is unfair. We are not all so badly treated by our academic colleagues that we go off to start a Great Cultural Revolution. In spite of everything an academic environment is a rewarding and enjoyable place to work.

References

1   Munn, Robert F., 'The bottomless pit, or the academic library as viewed from the administration building', *College & research libraries*, **29**, (1), January 1968, 51–4.
2   Enright, Brian J., 'Academic library ideals and reality: the library practitioner and introgenics', *in* Line, M. B. (ed.), *The world of books and information: essays in honour of Lord Dainton*, London, British Library, 1987, 59–73.
3   De Gennaro, Richard, 'Library administration and new management systems', *Library journal*, December 15, 1978, 2477–82.

3

Functions and objectives: large university library

James Thompson

A large university is not, primarily, a teaching institution. Its main purpose is research and scholarship. That is not to say that large universities do not have large numbers of students − of course they do; but servicing the needs of those students, though it is the most visible of our functions, is not our main objective.

Sometimes the sheer volume of work involved in dealing with large student numbers obscures our real objective. Our large library buildings have to be as large as they are because, as at Birmingham, we have 10,000 students coming through our doors, and, in examination times at any rate, we appear to have all 10,000 seated at our tables. Our building is awash with hordes of young people in T-shirts, chattering, chewing gum, and clutching lecture notes and paperback textbooks.

On the library side, we match these hordes of young users by a large number of library assistants. Indeed, sometimes these two groups appear interchangeable; when a library employs student helpers, they actually are interchangeable. We need a large number of junior staff just to process the numerous loan and other transactions. To this end also most of our automation systems are directed: computerized book issue systems; and on-line public access catalogues, for ease of use. Though students are not the only reason for the long hours we keep our libraries open, students are the most vociferous in demanding long hours. They greatly occupy us also in terms of the large number of general enquiries we handle, and they are the largest consumers of the most basic levels of any reference services we offer. They also are the reason why academic libraries in the United States and the United Kingdom have committed themselves to open access systems, with all the problems and man-hours that entails in shelving, keeping order, instituting and installing and operating security checks, stocktaking, and organizing the replacement or repair of missing or vandalized items.

However, having said all that, if you look at the costs of running a library, our service to students, despite their large number, represents the least demands on our overall expenditure, and in particular, the least demands on our expenditure on books and journals.

It is easy to describe an ideal academic library in student terms. You need a very large building, with tables and chairs and a heating system, equipped with a cafeteria and many lavatories. You need a portering staff and a junior staff. You need long hours, preferably 24 hours a day, seven days a week. You need a huge battery of self-service photocopying machines. You need about 15,000 textbooks, covering all undergraduate courses, in multiple copies.

You will immediately appreciate however that whatever I have described, I have not described what you or I would regard as an academic library. This is not to say that we should not provide the best and most effective service to students possible. Indeed, one reason for our present emphasis on student provision, in the United Kingdom at any rate, is that 30 years ago we provided such a poor one. My generation of librarians, having suffered from an indifferent service in our own student days, have made sure that the generations under our care have not had to suffer likewise.

Another sign of this emphasis on student provision is the elaborate consultation machinery which exists in most library systems, so that there is a formal student input influencing all of our decisions. Some kind of Student User Group exists in most libraries. In most libraries also, though the reasons are more general than just to do with library management, there are student members on the main Library Committee.

A further sign is the spread and prevalence in recent years of elaborate schemes of user education. It is a familiar sight, at the beginning of every session, to see cavalcades of students being trouped around our libraries by harassed members of the senior library staff. Quite a few librarians of my generation have made their reputations on the basis of devising and promulgating a variety of dubious and often impractical schemes of user education.

Unfortunately, the reverse of the coin over the past several years has been, to some degree, the neglect of the research staff and scholars in our universities. It is one thing to turn our backs firmly on the unlovely tradition that the professor is king, but it is altogether a bad alternative not to consult him much at all, and to ignore the true objective of a large academic library.

To move on now to this true objective. What makes a great university great is certainly not the size of its student body. It is its reputation for research and scholarship. It is because it can number among its academic staff several Fellows of the Royal Society, and maybe a Nobel prize-winner or two. Its status relates to how many researchers and scholars it has with an international reputation; how many of its departments, schools and institutes are national and world leaders; and in how many fields the name of the university is synonymous with excellence. Along with this goes a major provision of research and scholarly facilities: well-equipped laboratories, with a sufficiency of technical and support staff; and, of course, a good library.

By a good library plainly is not meant a library with 15,000 student texts in multiple copies. Nor is meant a museum of ancient volumes, gold-tooled and leather-bound. Nor is meant necessarily a library large in numbers of volumes, though sometimes the effect of greatness can be achieved by overkill. What is meant is a library which in scale and depth and range and service provides the necessary support for the pursuit of front-line research and advanced scholarship.

Achieving this by overkill *is* possible. If you and I could provide a library of 20 million volumes, with 50,000 periodical subscriptions, unlimited access to on-line services, and unlimited interlending and fax and photocopying services, and keep the place open and staffed all hours, we would have few problems in meeting any of the demands of research and scholarship.

Our true range, however, as large libraries in the United Kingdom, is between 1.5 and 3 million volumes, with fewer than 10,000 periodical subscriptions, with under

200 staff, and with only limited funds for all other services. Our objective has to be to match that level of resource as optimally as possible with our university's research and scholarly profile.

Until recently in the United Kingdom this was very difficult, because to rationalize a large academic library is to assume that the activities of the parent institution are rationally organized also, and this was never the case.

Even so, some sort of match has always been possible. If a university was strong in English and history and agriculture, so tended to be its library; and if it had no theology, it was perverse of its library to develop a strength in theology of its own — though there have always been wilful and idiosyncratic librarians who would do just that, especially in being willing to house almost any collection offered free.

However, these crude matches are now becoming much less crude. In the United Kingdom the University Grants Committee has been pursuing an increasingly firmer rationalization of research in the institutions under its care. Research selectivity is now the goal. Not every and any university institution can now teach and research in earth sciences or archaeology or classics. Whole departments are being shunted around, or amalgamated, or closed; likewise their attendant library collections.

But it now goes even deeper than that. Even when a large university and its large library have identified what they aim to be selective in, a level of resource has still to be established.

I can say, from personal experience of having been a librarian of both a medium-size university and (more recently) of a large university, that at least it is easier in a large library to convince oneself that one can achieve an acceptable level of provision.

The fact is that to pursue research or scholarship in any subject one can think of is expensive. It may already be beyond the reach of some very small academic libraries. To start with, consider periodical subscriptions. In scientific research you are always talking big money for periodicals, even if you have applied every method and every measure known to librarians to sieve out only what is essential and relevant. I have to mention expenditure on periodicals, because nearly every academic library in the United Kingdom now spends more on periodicals than it does on books, and has been doing so for the last several years. At the frontiers of research you are now also nowadays talking of the cost of electronic information services; and again you are talking of a significant financial outlay, both capital and recurrent.

I must add that in respect of scholarship in the arts, as opposed to research in the sciences, we are in a different and even more difficult game. It is conceivable that one could buy in almost immediately, if one had the money, the library provision needed to support scientific research in specific fields, because by their very nature the texts required are up-to-the-minute; but in scholarship in the arts I do not think it is possible to start from scratch over any range of subject areas. The advantage of a large library here is that by virtue of it being just that — a large library — it will have all the necessary foundations of the collection strengths required in the arts areas selected for excellence by its university.

I have so far identified the paramount objective of a large university library as being to support research and scholarship. I have not denied or decried the responsibility to service efficiently, effectively and thoroughly the needs of its large student body. I take it for granted that such service to students should be constantly checked, measured and reviewed on almost a daily basis. Likewise I think there is a need to keep an eye on comparisons with other institutions providing much the same sort of service: it should always give you pause for thought if what you are doing seems to cost more than it is costing elsewhere. Having said that, I would like briefly to examine the paramount objective in more detail.

Providing for selected areas of research and scholarship will account for the greater part of one's acquisitions budget. To make best use of that major share of one's resources a variety of mechanisms are required. Primary among these is a framework of consultation with one's university and with academic faculties, schools and departments, and with individual academic colleagues. For the chief librarian and his or her senior staff that means formal and informal involvement in discussions of academic policies. You do not really want your university or one of your university's departments to launch into an ambitious programme of high-level research or scholarship without everyone being aware of what resources the library can or cannot offer.

You then need a second level of consultation which gets down to which periodicals to subscribe to, which books to buy, and which services to invest in. My own preferred approach to this is to develop a team of subject librarians who construct strong liaisons with their academic counterparts. These subject librarians must have the main say in their respective areas as to the resources and services required.

To state this is to signal a quite specific strategy on the part of the chief librarian. He or she is then directing a library in which the considerations of selected areas of research and scholarship count more than everything else. If that is the stated management objective, it affects every decision; it puts every request for staff or funds or facilities into an automatic order of priority. I could perhaps put it more colourfully than accurately by saying that the purchase of a special collection would take precedence over refurbishing some part of the building; that a programme of preservation would take precedence over a desired upgrading of a system of automation.

All of this, I must conclude ironically, is very much against the ethos and philosophy which informed most of my generation of librarians. We were dismayed by a previous generation of specialist scholar librarians, who counted themselves as one with their academic colleagues, who built up astonishingly good research and scholarly collections (but in dingy dilapidated buildings), who preferred the safety and certainty of closed stacks to open access, and who barely recognized the existence of students.

I do not think that, in meeting the objectives now more explicitly set for us by our institutions in respect of concentrating on specific research and scholarly needs, our professional pendulum will swing quite as far back as that, but certainly for large academic libraries the most traditional of the definitions of our role has been externally reiterated and reinforced.

4

Functions and objectives: new university library

Peter E Tucker

Background

Facing the question of fundamental objectives is very rarely an attractive prospect; for the librarians of the new universities in the 1960s the confrontation was stark indeed. There were seven of them in all, gallant or foolish enough to undertake to provide a university library within a measurable time-span with very little to rely upon other than their own experience, an insufficiency of money and − rather more attractive − joint consultations. I write as the only survivor of that group still in his original post and have the clear sense of describing a past epoch. The new universities are no longer new, not only because of the movement of time and general feelings about them, but also because the kaleidoscope situation of British universities in the late 1980s has shaken up everyone's assessment. Not only did one or two of the new institutions quickly overtake some of the smaller established ones, but in the mid-1980s Sussex and Warwick occupied positions half-way down the hierarchy of institutions in order of size, a hierarchy related basically to student numbers and University Grants Committee allocations. Warwick, in particular, is one of the tail runners among the universities, 15−20 in number, which have by some observers been sized up as potential 'research institutions'. I make this point in order to explain that my own viewpoint is that of a librarian in an institution which has embraced the concept of the university as a place primarily for research rather than for teaching, and which has so far successfully raised funds and attracted the talent to enable it to sustain that position. The newness of the seven institutions was not simply the coldness of starting from scratch. It should be seen in the context of the spirit of making things new and of revising old practices and principles which swept upon us in the 1960s. The contrast with what had been going on in the 1950s was very marked for those of us who experienced those epochs; in retrospect the 1950s was a period of dullness. But from about 1960 a decade of discovery and rediscovery set in. In broad brush terms, the 1960s in the United Kingdom are comparable with the 1920s. I am thinking here particularly of the arts − music, painting and the theatre and the new enthusiasm for television. A new affluence added for us the important spicing of exploratory visits to the United States and friendship with American academic librarians.

Perhaps because they were part of this movement, the new universities achieved for many years, certainly until the calamities of 1969/70, great prestige on the national scene. Sussex was the popular forerunner in the new euphoria for university education. The new places attracted leading academics, for instance Asa Briggs, subsequently Lord Briggs, and the author-to-be of the standard history of the BBC − itself an institution of great prestige and as important as any single university in the cultural history of the twentieth century. At Warwick the school of pure mathematics quickly took second place only to Cambridge, and its leader, Christopher Zeeman, founded an international centre for his subject, made it popular, and appeared on television with a dramatic programme which illustrated his catastrophe theory. Many of the academics welcomed the opportunity to go to a new institution and to introduce changes in the approach to university studies, particularly in the development of what we then called 'area studies'. In several universities the idea of the single subject honours degree was regarded as old-fashioned, though in fact Warwick was not one of these. There were changes in teaching styles; the development of teaching in seminars offered a mode of exchange between tutor and students which could challenge the Oxbridge superiority in tutorial methods. Such developments were undoubtedly invigorating, as was the shared life on a new campus; they were reported extensively in the new popular colour supplements of the Sunday newspapers. Of equal interest to the outside world was the flowering of new architectural styles in the universities. The architect of Coventry Cathedral, Sir Basil Spence, began to build Sussex in a graceful style, though it was apparently related to early theories predicting that the new universities would have populations of not more than 3,000 students. Other places experienced the 'new brutalism' of shuttered concrete or became known as the 'plate glass' universities. But however easily these institutions acquired prestige, they genuinely intended to be better than the traditional places. The librarians also planned to do it better, and they were equally happy to tackle the problems of fresh architectural ideas.

Provision for students

The librarians had to accept, to a large extent, the basic objectives of their institutions, which are best considered under the traditional headings of teaching and research. It may be revealing to look at these divisions in terms of just whose objectives were being followed. To begin with teaching, the official view was that the new institutions had been founded largely because more student places were needed for an expanding population, the result of the increase in the birth rate immediately after the end of the war. Because of social developments under the Labour governments and in the 1950s, this plan was linked with a demand for better means of access to higher education. Among supporters of these developments there was probably some confusion between the two objectives; among opponents it was darkly said of the increased numbers that 'more means worse'. However, each new university accepted with enthusiasm the notion of increasing ease of access for students and plunged into new methods of attracting them, in some cases drawing them away from the older institutions. For the reasons already mentioned it became rather fashionable to go to a new university, and there was no difficulty in the early days in attracting as many students as could be accommodated. Only later, when the money began to give out, and grants were strictly related to student numbers, did competition with the older institutions − themselves undergoing a revitalization by this time − bring problems.

The librarians of the new institutions firmly intended to do things better as far as students were concerned. I had myself been involved in the late 1950s in a survey of the use of the Brotherton Library in the University of Leeds, which had the slightly unreal intention of discovering exactly how academics and students used their libraries. Perhaps the only clear information that came out of this lengthy exercise was that insufficient copies of books were being provided for students, given an assumption that the institutions were expected to cater for their students' textbook needs. The Deputy Librarian at Leeds at that time was Dennis Cox, who then became the first librarian of a new university at Sussex. There extraordinary efforts were made to cater for a great influx of students who were on a campus university and had virtually nowhere else to look for their resources. Sufficient finance was available to provide the means, which were three: multiple copies of textbooks (from specific reading lists), multiple copies of articles photocopied from journals using the new photocopying machines to the full, and sufficient funds to appoint an adequate staff both at subject level and for clerical support, with extended hours of opening. This new policy was an enormous success. It went with the provision of a new style building. One walked not into an enormous reading room, reminiscent of a classroom, with a dislocation between reading and the bookstock, but into open areas on a human scale, where bookshelves and readers alternated and where the gangways were often occupied by rows of armchairs and students relaxing over their work. It was the 'sixties style and it marked the full-scale arrival, so far as Britain was concerned, of the student-orientated library.

The other new institutions followed this model, looking to the United States for inspiration on the design for buildings and to the changes in social style for the running of them. Virtually all of them embraced the attractive and relatively novel idea, in general libraries, of the subject librarian who took a close interest in the welfare of the students in his subject. This approach to the subject side of librarianship was a strong attempt by many of us to provide in the central general university library the facilities and attention to readers which in the red-brick universities existed on the whole only in faculty or 'special' libraries, to use the terminology of that period.

Thus the first objective was met: full-scale provision for student needs in a positive and welcoming style, with all resources bought to bear upon it.

Provision for research

Provision for student reading and for academic success in the new terms had to be successful in the new institutions, whether it was regarded as a *raison d'être* or not. In looking at objectives under the heading of research there is more variance to be discerned in different approaches. I have little doubt myself that in official circles it was the provision of student places that really mattered. In this connection I may relate the story of how two senior officials, one from the Treasury and one from the Department of Education and Science, came on an official visit to Warwick. In a tour of the buildings and facilities, which were then only in the preparation state, they observed a growing set of the newly-printed catalogue of the British Museum Library on the shelves and asked whether it was necessary for a new university library to have such things. The individual universities were of course determined on research from the outset. The Civil Service had perhaps not appreciated that hardly any academic in the country would go to a new university institution without the recognition of his research interests and requirements. This was self-evident for scientists, for whom laboratories clearly had to be built, but it was equally true in

20

other subjects. However, no statements of principles were available from an official source or indeed even within individual institutions − I mean statements of the kind that would give a librarian specific guidance over the kind of library he was to develop. No-one knew how big the institutions would be or how much money in the end would be either required or available. There was apparently an undergraduate requirement and there was a research requirement, but these vaguenesses had to be turned into the titles of books and journals and something called 'non-book materials'. In Sussex, and to some extent elsewhere, there was the impediment on the research side that some authorities expected scholars in the humanities to make use of the facilities in London for their research. Others launched a long official campaign to urge upon universities the economics and virtues of an improved interlibrary loan system. We needed a better system, but it could not be the universal solvent. The ordeals of research by interlibrary loan were rapidly brought home to scholars for whom materials could not easily be provided on the spot and for whom travel was very necessary and increasingly costly.

Each university had its new research enthusiasms. American Studies became popular and biology turned into something much bigger, also with popular appeal, called life sciences. I have already mentioned the example of pure mathematics in my own institution and the general development of area studies, e.g. for Africa or Latin America. The social studies area proved very fruitful for the new institutions, not only in sociology but in the extending role of economics (meaning applied economics) as a discipline of national value and in the new enthusiasm for business studies or management and its related subject, industrial relations. To begin with, the librarian was expected to deal with all subjects equally. As to the means available, the demand for more scholarly material in greater quantities, seeing that other countries were also expanding in higher education, led to increased output from the scholarly presses and the benefits of larger production runs. Equally, the demand fuelled a programme of reprinting. Here again, improved photocopying methods came into play, and the production of roll microfilm, microfiches and microcards also soared. In spite of the drawbacks of microtext for the users and the lamentable quality of the means of reading them, these developments gave institutions with sufficient money the means of providing 'complete' research collections in such areas as nineteenth century government publications for the United Kingdom, or three hundred years of British drama, all packed on a few shelves. Rapid progress nevertheless depended upon the flow of a considerable amount of money, and here the universities which were successful in launching financial appeals, or found themselves in relatively supportive parts of the country, had a considerable advantage. There were plenty of instances of gifts of small research collections and of earmarked gifts of money which helped to build up such collections by purchase.

Selectivity and specialization in acquisitions

Nevertheless, the librarian found himself without much freedom of manoeuvre, and certainly in some difficulty over objectives, if they entailed favouring the areas likely to be most easily provided for. Provision for research in universities is evidently of several different types. For the scientist it is first of all in terms of laboratories. For a second group of scholars the *sine qua non* is the living person; the medical and educational disciplines will have such material at hand wherever they are established. In mathematics and law such materials as are used − long runs of printed records of the work of other mathematicians and the work of the law courts — must be provided on the spot if the subject is to take root. In such subjects large scale expenditure on materials, from a librarian's point of view, is indispensable. For the humanities at large, and this is particularly true of history, the provision of a universal library is hardly within the sphere of human possibility, and the decision of the historians at Warwick to teach history on a world-wide scale was enough to damp the prospect of being even moderately helpful to them. Many researchers in these subjects, though they can be helped by a good general library in their subject and related areas, expect to go to other places to use primary materials, meaning in effect either unpublished materials or materials so voluminous — like those for the French Revolution — that few institutions can find the wherewithal to acquire them even when over many years they are ultimately republished in some form or other. The new libraries could however aim for exceptionally good collections of bibliographies, catalogues and reference works.

All subjects cannot be treated 'equally' by the librarian because each one has to be given at least the basic library materials without which it is not viable. However, in terms of objectives a kind of independent objective for the library emerges when there is nothing to start with and there is everything to be won or lost in certain areas. This objective is to develop areas in which materials can be obtained free or at least on deposit terms and thus create potentialities for research. Such developments are likely in early days to receive formal approval from the institution, if it is required, so long as they are within the general framework of the institution's interests. Acquisition of this kind, of course, is well beyond the scope of seeking gifts to the library in a general way. Many such gifts swell the volume of generally useful material, but they very rarely create the kind of solid core on which continuing research can be founded. Some variation is possible in the style of acquiring such materials. The 'blanket' approach to acquisition is exemplified in the development in my own institution of a collection of statistical material ranging back over the past 100 years and published in something like 5,000 different serials, which usually come from governments and official organizations. These provide the basis for research in economics and related areas and at the front edge have provided the essential material for mounting an information service relating to business enterprise. This information service, offered outside the university, then becomes a means of raising income. In a more specific area, Economics Working Papers, the collection is again international and is one step more esoteric in research level, representing the draft papers which may subsequently find their way into economics journals or books and are much sought after at this stage in their development. Having identified this area and this need at Warwick, it proved feasible for our economics librarian to create an international centre for the collection of the working papers and to operate a loan system within the United Kingdom. With commercial partnership, we established the basis for a published bibliography and sets of papers reproduced on microfilm. This again produces enough income at present to pay for itself in terms of everyday running. My third example is of the blanket kind but is in terms of deposit rather than outright gift. This is the collection of trade union and business records which we identify as the Modern Records Centre. Here the essential starting point was the identification of vast quantities of records which were actually in the process of being thrown away in the 1970s as unions amalgamated. These archives, and those of bodies like the Confederation of British Industries, are voluminous, but they offer essential information for the historians of British labour and industrial development over the past 100 years.

It will be seen that these collections, which I cite from my own institution, favour the social sciences. (Instances from other places are the Latin American collection at Essex and the Institute of Development Studies collection at Sussex). A library is able to take the initiative in this field in particular because it can collect material which is not only available, but also obtainable at virtually no cost. There is a price to be paid in terms of staffing, which can only partially be carried on external funding or by the generation of income. When things get difficult such costs may be looked at askance by the institution, which tends to forget that it has acquired virtually for nothing a research resource of unique value. Since all three of these projects at Warwick were supported at their outset almost entirely by grants from official or independent fund-giving bodies I would not feel too bad myself at expecting the institution to sustain staffing and housing costs when such funds are no longer available. The institution has to run the risk of suffering in its library provision, as in all other kinds of provision, from the present reluctance to dispense funds centrally for certain purposes, in particular the preservation of archives of national value.

Conclusion

This paper is devoted almost entirely to the question of fundamental objectives, since I think there is virtually nothing specific to new universities in terms of functions to be described. New ground was broken with the very varied and generous provision for students in the early days of the new universities. On the other hand, it could be argued that the arrival of the student-orientated institution as it appeared in the 1960s caused in the end a great deal of damage and has left to this day an assumption that universities are intended first of all for students – an assumption which has to be challenged, I think, if research activities are to be funded as they require. The new institutions also broke fresh ground in developing the concept of the subject librarian, seen not only as an aid to offering services which were badly under-provided for students in most places, but also to take initiatives in building up research collections. On this last point again, the amount of activity which can continue after the initial build-up period depends very much upon good financial support, including staff maintenance costs for relatively large collections of material. To a large extent I believe that success in the development of research collections depends upon the library identifying its own objectives and having sufficient prestige, funds and knowledge to seek out such collections and to develop them. The fight to support them thereafter, particularly in terms of staffing needs, is regrettably part of the picture of universities' difficulties today. The final result of creating for each institution just two or three areas in which a centre of excellence or a unique research collection is established is perhaps in the end no more than what a long-established institution would regard as one of its own objectives. To that extent also the new universities are no longer new.

5

Functions and objectives: technological university library

Lynne Brindley

Introduction

The nature and character of an academic library cannot sensibly be considered in isolation from its institutional context, the mission and culture of the parent body. Technological universities grew out of existing Colleges of Advanced Technology during the 1960s, a period of major expansion in higher education. The government was keen to increase the attractiveness of technology and science courses to potential students and thus ensure a swing to science and technology from the most able students, to the benefit of the UK economy and industry in general. (This objective was in fact not achieved and the 1970s saw the diversification of the technological universities into the social sciences and the arts.)

The distinctive feature of technological universities thus created was (i) their emphasis on technology and (ii) their close links with the industrial world, especially through 'sandwich' courses, in which students spent some time working in industry as an integral part of their degree course.

Aston is one such technological university. Aston's charter, granted in 1966, defined the university's purposes as being 'to advance, disseminate and apply learning and knowledge by teaching and research for the benefit of industry, commerce and the community generally, and to enable students to obtain the advantage of a university education'.

It follows that Aston is a modern, technological university whose ethos derives from this commitment, which determines the distinctiveness and relevance of the Aston University community. Its academic disciplines and programmes are chosen for their evident relevance to this outside world and in that sense its Modern Languages department is 'technological' in orientation by concentrating, not on literature, but on the modern history, politics and socio-economics of the relevant country, combined with its language. The university has three faculties, Engineering, Science, and Management and Modern Languages, with a student population of some 4,000.

University strategy

Since suffering major financial cuts in 1981, Aston University has undertaken a comprehensive restructuring programme. It has followed a quality-driven, demand-led strategy through restructuring of its academic programmes, merger or closure

24

of half its departments, and the departure of half of its academic and non-academic staff.

The university's first consideration has been financial: to balance its budget and to live within its means. Now, its academic programmes are highly attractive to well qualified candidates, selective research strengths are being pursued, and a major physical restructuring and relandscaping programme is almost complete. It is an important element in Aston's strategy to strengthen academically challenging links with industry and commerce, and to contribute to the economic regeneration of the West Midlands. The Aston Science Park is flourishing and now employs some 500 people, and the West Midlands Technology Transfer Centre, housed on campus, is well under way in promoting technology awareness and facilitating access to research expertise in higher education in the region.

A central and distinctive part of the university's strategy is a commitment to the use of Information Technology across all its activities. Aston has been investing significantly of its own resources to build up a powerful IT infrastructure to support the entire range of its teaching, research, and administrative programmes. Included are powerful central computing facilities, video-based education, widespread use of personal computers and electronic mail, and most recently a major networking project to wire up every room on the campus.

Library and information services strategy

The LIS environment is characterized by the very fast pace of change, the need for continuing change, the applied nature of the academic programmes and the emphasis on widespread use of information and information technology. In this context, after a fundamental review of operations of the library in 1985/86, it was decided that the model of a traditional, collection-focused university library would be inappropriate and indeed unachievable at Aston (hence the re-naming as LIS). So what is the strategy for the LIS?

By 1985 the library had the advantage of being well automated, including the use of external bibliographic services. It shared with other younger institutions the lack of significant historical collections, both in depth and breadth.

Taking this into account, together with the size and subject orientation of the academic programmes, and our view of longer-term trends in electronic publishing, we are pursuing a rather distinctive approach. All opportunities are being taken to develop the LIS as a proactive information service of the kind more usually associated with industrial and special libraries than with academic libraries. This is particularly true in support of research, and increasingly true in support of advanced project work in undergraduate programmes. We do not have the benefit of large research collections but this has advantages in that it enables us to move more easily and quickly to an information-led strategy, relying on access to provide relevant research support in fast-moving areas. These priorities are reflected in resource distribution, where we spend minimally on binding and preservation, while spending three times as much on external document supply services and online database searching.

Further characteristics of the service include collection policies which aim to serve immediate needs of teaching, with some emphasis on weeding of older and less used material, and in-depth purchasing only in areas of particular research strength, and in relation to demand and usage at teaching level. Catalogue records are mostly derived from external sources, and most processing work is done at a para-professional or clerical level. The core collection is supplemented by unrationed document supply services, primarily from the British Library Document Supply Centre. There is a team of information specialists who are attached to faculties, providing an extensive programme of information services, ranging from information skills programmes at all levels, online searching of databases and databanks, end user searching services, and current awareness and alerting services. In all these activities use of IT is vigorously pursued.

Functions and objectives

The general objectives of the LIS are expressed in the Forward Strategy as follows:

1 To provide quick and easy access from its own stock to a specialized and limited range of material in support of the university's teaching, research and service programmes.

2 To provide ready access to a much wider range of material and recorded data from outside its stock.

3 To provide a range of information services in support of research groups and other academic needs.

4 To develop personal information handling and management skills, to promote an understanding of LIS capabilities, and to encourage informed use of its resources and services.

These general objectives are then supplemented by more specific objectives, spelling out, at a more detailed level, support for teaching, research, and other groups. Examples from these include the following:

1 Wide reading lists will be encouraged and the LIS will stock each item on a reading list. Textbook and multiple copy provision will be de-emphasized in order to provide a wider range of materials, more suitable for independent study and project work.

2 Priority will be given to the needs of Research Groups in line with the University's Academic Plan. Comprehensive research collections will not be attempted. Rather the emphasis will be to build on selective research strengths, concentrating on better provision of research awareness, state of the art material, reviews of research, current research monographs and journals. In all areas the provision of access tools, in hard copy of electronic access form, will continue to be given priority.

3 The information needs of the Science Park companies are important and steps will be taken to allocate time to serve these needs.

More specific objectives are then articulated in support of these service objectives. Examples are as follows:

1 To maintain a programme of staff development and training to ensure the best possible staff support for services.

2 To ensure the efficient management of LIS financial and other resources, and their optimum use in support of objectives.

These overall aims and objectives provide a framework for setting priorities and action. However, in themselves they are too general for most purposes and are amplified by more specific targets, usually reviewed and prioritized on an annual basis.

Examples of such targets from recent years include the following:

1   Information Skills Workshop. Plan phase two of the development of the Suite, to include provision of a lecture space, with demonstration facilities, for 70 people, a workshop of 12 microcomputers and a reception area. This is required in outline to input to building refurbishment plans by January 1989.

2   In the LIS Factsheet series, develop general service descriptions, aiming this year to complete them on use of statistics, law reports and standards.

3   Evaluate options and purchase one relevant electronic database on CD-ROM to assess potential for services, user response and operational issues.

These more tangible targets may be the responsibility of an individual or a group, and should be monitored for progress and for review on a regular basis.

Relations with other groups
For a library such as that described above which is at the forefront of use of Information Technology and electronic databases, the most natural relationship is with the Academic Computing Service of the university. Indeed there is an increasing overlap of interests which have potential for conflict if not handled sensitively and cooperatively. Areas of common interest include database creation and access, use of networked facilities, desk-top publishing and so on.

Conclusions
From the descriptions above it can be seen that the strategy and functions of the LIS at Aston are guided by its organizational context and culture. The emphasis on IT across the institution makes it important that the LIS has a high IT profile. The subject coverage of the academic programmes suggests high use of current material, and not a significant archival collection. Research is in fast moving areas, again requiring an emphasis on information and current awareness material. Thus we aim to match the needs and style of the university.

6

Functions and objectives: polytechnic library

Nigel Macartney

Introduction

This paper has as its terms of reference to suggest what the objectives of a polytechnic library *should* be, but this will be difficult as much of our way of working is being increasingly laid down by Government; the more satisfying and ambitious professional objectives we might set for a library service are becoming mere pipe-dreams. Many polytechnic libraries have evolved carefully researched and reasonable aims but some of us are having doubts now about how far our institutions are interested in libraries achieving their own professional objectives. As I shall show, polytechnic management is now dominated by the need to reach financial and performance targets, often unrelated or hostile to good quality library services.

What is a polytechnic?

I must begin by defining the term 'polytechnic', which can have different meanings in different countries.

A polytechnic is an institution of higher education in England and Wales which offers undergraduate and postgraduate courses. Some polytechnics undertake sponsored research; Hatfield, for instance, earns £2 million per annum in research, almost all in applied research projects, which compares with the research income of a small or medium-sized university; but many polytechnics do not undertake a substantial amount of research.

The features of polytechnics which distinguish them from universities include

- validation of their courses by an external body, the Council for National Academic Awards
- local government control, though this is tempered by some central direction from the National Advisory Body for Public Sector Higher Education (now superseded by the Polytechnics Funding Council)
- lower cost per student (largely because university costs include a substantial allowance for research)
- a strong direction in favour of the non-traditional student (for instance, part-time, sandwich, mature and short course students)
- a strong connection with their local and regional areas

28

- a tradition (inherited from their earlier existence as local colleges) of teaching rather than lecturing, and of encouraging less academic students
- concentration on vocational courses, notably in science and technology but also in the professions
- close links with industry and commerce
- innovative course structures (for instance, modular courses, combined studies, sandwich courses)
- lower level courses, notably Higher National Diploma, from which students can transfer to degree courses, or vice versa

The polytechnics were designated by the British government in 1967 and expanded rapidly until the mid-1970s. They have also enjoyed a second era of growth in the 1980s when they took in the majority of the extra school leavers who sought higher education following the rise in the UK birthrate in the 1960s.

There are 29 polytechnics in England and one in Wales. Scotland has a separate education system, but in its five largest 'central institutions' (which are funded by the Scottish Education Department) it has colleges which are similar to polytechnics. The one polytechnic in Northern Ireland merged with the New University in Coleraine to form the University of Ulster. There are also 376 other colleges in England and Wales which offer higher education courses; the large majority are relatively small institutions of further education.

The emergence of polytechnic libraries

Written statements of aims for polytechnic libraries in their formative years are rare. It is clear that they concentrate on two areas, firstly building up their book and journal collections as rapidly as possible, and secondly on developing their institutions' general commitment to helping students by making their libraries student-oriented. Detailed statements of aims and objectives were not produced until the middle or late 1970s. The example from Huddersfield Polytechnic is dated 1979 and gives broad general aims typical of the times (Appendix 1); the commitment to co-operation with local libraries is a hallmark of many polytechnic libraries which wished both to retain connections with the local community and to recognize their interdependence with other libraries.

This new breed of academic library made several distinctive contributions to library innovation. This achievement was partly because small collections (they averaged only 100,000 books each in 1973) were easier to experiment with than the very much larger collections in research-oriented universities. Some of the areas in which polytechnic libraries have made important contributions are set out below.

(a) *Audio-visual and non-book materials*

Apart from collecting substantially in video, film, audiotape, slide and other materials libraries also found themselves working closely with the audio-visual aids or media service; some also were directly managing television units and educational development services, notably Brighton Polytechnic, and expounding a much wider approach to information and materials than the traditional library. More recently electronic media (online databases, CD-ROM and videodisc systems) have found an important place in polytechnic libraries, and there are growing links with computer centres. Currently about half of the 30 polytechnic librarians are responsible for media services in their institutions.[1]

29

(b) *Automation*

Having comparatively small library stocks, polytechnics moved enthusiastically into computer systems. Currently all polytechnics are using computerized cataloguing, and all but two, automated circulation systems. OPACs and computerized acquisitions systems are now in operation in half these libraries.

(c) *User education*

At least some of the interest in library user education during the 1960s and 1970s stemmed from earlier work in the further education sector, notably in the Hertfordshire college libraries where Gordon Wright invented the term 'tutor librarian'. The new polytechnic libraries were keen to develop information skills and to train students to use a wide range of local libraries, not least because of the inability of these libraries to meet the needs of their users in the way that the larger more self-sufficient collections in universities could.

It is also noteworthy that the Travelling Workshop Experiment packages, developed in the late 1970s with British Library funding, had strong polytechnic connections.

(d) *Buildings*

While the several new buildings housing polytechnic libraries were not on the scale of those for universities, they pointed the way forward to the modern concept of open access collections in simple buildings, often with substantial provision for audio-visual services. That at Preston (now Lancashire Polytechnic) is in my opinion one of the most successful polytechnic library buildings but those in Coventry and Birmingham are also of interest.

(e) *Council of Polytechnic Librarians (COPOL)*

The early establishment of COPOL soon after the opening of the first polytechnics did much to assist the development of an open-minded and adventurous approach by their librarians. COPOL meetings provided that vital opportunity for colleagues in similar situations to compare notes and swap ideas. Some of its successful publishing ventures reflect this function, notably the Working Papers series,[2] which consists of collected volumes of the better internal documents written by polytechnic librarians and their colleagues on various themes.

Much discussion and many new approaches were also stimulated by the problems facing librarians. Inevitably inflation in the cost of academic libraries, and reductions in local government and central government funding were the main difficulties but almost all polytechnics continued to be involved in mergers with other institutions during their first two decades. These mergers and the original constituent colleges gave an inheritance of multiple sites many of which required library services. While the operation of multi-site libraries has brought substantial management difficulties it has also given young staff opportunities to prove themselves and emphasized the importance of automated systems, staff development and good communications.

At the end of the first two decades of its existence, the following picture of an average polytechnic library is gained from looking at COPOL statistics:

Bookstock	293,346 volumes
Additions to stock	12,334 volumes per year
Periodical titles currently taken	2,245
Audio-visual items held	12,961 (excluding slides)
Issues	300,667 per year
Interlibrary loans borrowed	6,042 per year
Interlibrary loans made	976 per year
Online searches	331 per year
Total library expenditure	£979,878
Percentage of polytechnic budget spent on library	4.78%
Number of library readers	9,542
Number of readers per library staff	166

(Mean figures for all polytechnics. Source: *COPOL statistics of polytechnic libraries 1986/7*).

The changing nature of polytechnics

Polytechnics are now facing major changes following the Education Reform Act, 1988. The 29 polytechnics and the 56 largest colleges in England became independent of their local authorities on 1 April 1989. Their freedom will be tempered by having to negotiate with a new Government body, the Polytechnics and Colleges Funding Council. The Council intends to allocate funds for courses to polytechnics on the basis of contracts; the contracts will be awarded according to the price per student offered by the institution as well as the quality of its courses and student demand.

Performance measurement, staff appointment systems, and the earning of extra income through commercial activities are also to be features required of polytechnics by the Council; the director and the governing body (which must now include many more business and industrial representatives) will have more powers and more responsibility.

These changes should be seen against a background of a substantial decline in the school-leaving population of the UK between 1989 and the mid-1990s, perhaps by as much as 30%. Inevitably open competition for students will be a feature of this new system, with institutions' management concentrating on costs and efficiency.

Trends and new aims for polytechnic libraries

To some extent one can only guess at the implications of this new world for academic libraries. However, the following issues are almost certain to be at the forefront in the minds of my colleagues and myself in the next few years.

Independent study Polytechnics will try to reduce the amount of teaching carried out by lecturers in order to free them to undertake commercial activities and to reduce their numbers. Consequently courses will make more use of independent learning. While this is good news for librarians it also brings problems, notably the increasing use of group projects where students work in teams; such groups use libraries and are entitled to do so, but they need areas where their discussions will not disturb others.

31

Performance measurement   The Funding Council and polytechnic managements are looking to performance measures to identify services which are efficient or inefficient. Academic librarians from both SCONUL and COPOL are working urgently to produce their own measures, since it is likely that non-librarians will concentrate on indicators such as cost per student which do not adequately measure a library's outputs. The long term implications of performance measures on academic libraries must be a matter for speculation and concern.

Income generation   Like all my colleagues I am being asked to increase substantially the income my library earns through commercial activities. Again, as such activities are at an early stage of development, the degree of success which is possible in such ventures is not clear.

Collection building   In most polytechnic libraries traditional collection building will become unsustainable. Besides expressing concern about the costs of purchase of stock, institutions will be wary of sanctioning significant growth in their libraries because of the cost in accommodation. Performance measures will also militate against collection growth.

Library staff   Staff costs will be kept under a tight rein in all departments, and once again efficiency measures will undermine cases for increases in staffing. I suspect we shall also see staff structures becoming more hierarchical, at least at first, as section managers are given more responsibilities.

Services and environment   What the customer (that is, the student) wants will become the guiding principle. Libraries will seek to attract users by providing refreshment facilities, better opening hours and more copies of student textbooks. They will speed up their interlibrary loans and reservations services. They will attempt to provide more comfortable seating and other improvements to the study environment.

Cost centre approach   Some polytechnics have already experimented by allocating the library book fund to the faculties who then decide to what extent they will spend the money on library materials. Encouragingly, early experience suggests that many faculties will actually add to their book funds although some others will seriously consider diverting the money for other purposes.
  Some library and information services in industry and commerce are 'charged out' to the other departments but operate successfully. It remains to be seen whether academic librarians could meet the challenge posed by this cost centre concept; it is an idea that has already been suggested for polytechnic libraries.[3]

The aims and objectives of a library in this type of environment will change significantly. The Aims document for Hatfield Polytechnic Library reproduced here (Appendix 2) was written before much was known about the Funding Council, but you will see several reflections of the new ideas and pressures there.

Conclusions
It is clear that the directors of polytechnics are under increasing pressure and in some instances it may be even a question of the survival of the institution. Librarians should

not take for granted the idea that libraries are a good thing: polytechnic management may well think the unthinkable. I suspect that because of this situation, polytechnic libraries will become the test-beds of library cost-effectiveness, much more so than those in universities, colleges and the public service.

References
1 Thompson, A. H., 'Relationships between academic libraries and audiovisual production services'. Part One. *Audiovisual librarian*, **14**, (3), 1988, 136–141.
2 Revill, D. H. (ed.), *Working papers on objectives and planning*, COPOL, 1987.
3 National Advisory Body for Public Sector Higher Education, *Management for a purpose*, London, NAB, 1987.

Bibliography
Revill, D. H., 'The polytechnics and their libraries', *in* Fletcher, J. (ed.), *Reader services in polytechnic libraries*, Aldershot, Gower, 1986.
Cowley, J., 'Polytechnics and central institutions', *in* McElroy, A. R. (ed.), *College librarianship: the objectives and the practice*, London, Library Association, 1984.

Appendix 1

THE POLYTECHNIC, HUDDERSFIELD

ACADEMIC BOARD: LIBRARY COMMITTEE, March 6, 1979

Terms of Reference of the Committee
"To advise the Academic Board on broad library policy; more specifically to advise the Board on (i) Annual Estimates as submitted to the Finance Committee; (ii) allocation of budget; (iii) changes to library regulations."

Source: Revision of existing statement in the light of Academic Board Minute 78/118 (1)

Library policy objectives proposed for the Academic Board
1. To collect and organise resources of recorded information in accordance with the academic aims and needs of the Polytechnic.
2. To promote the use of these materials in the best interests of learning, scholarship and research.
3. To provide advisory and enquiry services to assist staff and students in the pursuit of these aims.
4. Accordingly, to provide an integrated library service throughout the Polytechnic, based on a single management structure, with centralisation of library services on each site or campus.
5. To cooperate with other libraries and information agencies in order to further objectives 1–3, and to make a positive contribution to inter-library cooperation locally, nationally and internationally.

Sources: a. policy implicit in planning of Central Library
b. Librarian's paper "A Polytechnic Library Service" accepted in principle at the May 1976 meeting of the Library Committee (LC 76–11)

Appendix 2

Aims for The Hatfield Polytechnic Library

1. **Fundamental principles.** There are three main principles
   1.1 The role of the library is to support and contribute to the aims of the Polytechnic
   1.2 The function of a library service is the storage, retrieval and dissemination of documented and recorded information and ideas
   1.3 The Library is inter-dependent with other libraries and information units in the region and as such plays an important role in the community and in the profession

2. **Aims**
   2.1 To identify user needs, individual or group, expressed or unexpressed and respond to them. Changing circumstances in the Polytechnic require this identification to be a continuing process
   2.2 To provide information media and services to support the activities of the Polytechnic
   2.3 To make Library services as simple to understand, easy to use and economical of users' time as possible
   2.4 To promote the use of Library services and facilities
   2.5 To develop awareness and understanding of information sources and the library within the Polytechnic
   2.6 To provide comfortable and well equipped study and reference facilities
   2.7 To co-ordinate the work of the Library with that of other Polytechnic staff, and to maintain formal links with all bodies in the Polytechnic at various levels, and especially other support services such as Media Services and the Computer Centre
   2.8 To plan for the use of the Library's resources by the regional community and for drawing upon the information resources of other libraries in exchange
   2.9 To maintain access by the regional business and industrial communities to the Library and to provide specialised services for them, at least recovering all costs, through the HERTIS Information for Industry
   2.10 To maintain an innovative approach to new information technologies and techniques and to contribute to their development in the information professions
   2.11 To manage the staff, financial resources and other assets of the Library with efficiency and an entrepreneurial approach.

Adopted 1988

7

Concepts of stock: comprehensive vs. selective

Brian J. Enright

Comprehensiveness

British academics recently attracted an exasperated ministerial criticism for 'cowering in the secret garden of knowledge'. Academic libraries, like the institutions they serve, cannot 'ivory-towerlike' be exempt from natural physical and economic laws: 'Every physical quantity growing in a finite space must eventually exhibit one of three basic behavior modes: a smooth transition to steady-state, oscillation around an equilibrium position, or overshoot and decline'.[1] Libraries are not alone in having to struggle with problems of near-infinite aspirations from finite resources, sharing this mismatch dilemma with such areas as health, housing, food, and defence.

The assumptions underlying academic library development during the expansion of higher education in the 1960s of open-ended, comprehensive collection-building now, from the vantage point of the 1980s, appear naive and even perhaps irresponsible. Conditioned by the 'All and forever syndrome', deriving from nineteenth century 'imperial overstretch' aspirations of national libraries (when it may have just briefly appeared to be a realizable dream), academic librarians were encouraged to act as if self-sufficiency was a possible objective and that the larger in volume-count a university library became the better it would be. The Alexandrian library sought to achieve infinite comprehensiveness − to acquire everything it possibly could and keep it forever 'lest something of inestimable value perish from the earth through negligence or misvaluation'.[2]

The book has become invested with a semi-sacred character. 'Print was not just a new means of communication, of learning, of art − it changed the nature of man's mind, the basis of thought, the meaning of meaning. Print changed history, indeed practically created it . . . and a book, irrespective of its contents, is a holy object'. Libraries have been looked upon as 'Treasurehouses of books' 'Temples of knowledge' and 'Repositories of civilization'. To retreat from a comprehensive, aspirational approach can be particularly perilous for a librarian, attracting charges of cultural subversion and iconoclasm, as well as the risk of subjective prejudice and even censorship. The year 1989 will be noteworthy for having provided chilling reminders of the power of the printed word to arouse passions and of the validity of Heine's dictum in *Almansor*: 'Wherever they burn books they will also, in the end, burn human beings'. Those librarians not totally convinced about the comprehensive goal argue

36

from expediency about the dangers of opening up the debate. Generations of librarians have relied on the power of studied procrastination and inertia to survive the neglect and even hostility of funding masters. It was said that during the First World War the main threat to the British Museum Library 'came from the conduct of the government [i.e. funding inaction], not from enemy action'.[3]

For academic librarians the comprehensive goal was a comparatively easy way to win bonus points and even bogus reputations, maintaining that the standing of their universities would be enhanced by the size of their library collections. The excitement of the bibliophilic hunt or the chase for fresh acquisitions was for many librarians far more satisfying than the less spectacular role of organizing services and maintaining collection relevance. Some academic librarians constantly gave the impression that if universities could just be a little more generous the library's problems could be met. Their annual reports bewailing the shortage of funding generally contained accounts of fresh collection conquests calculated to make the resources mismatch worse but to keep the academic appetite fuelled, and at all costs it was necessary to maintain that eternal growth was axiomatic and inevitable. The concept was perhaps cherished warmly because it was unattainable. Blame for the inevitable failure could always be pinned elsewhere, generally on miserly administrators. There was no need for controversial decisions or judgements, indeed it was the duty of the librarian to remain neutral. Every book was to be considered equal, and distant memories of Ranganathan's laws from library school days provided reassurance that each would meet its appreciative reader, and given enough time would have its day.

It is undeniable that the totality goal was and always had to be a theoretical objective. A completely comprehensive printed archive has not been achieved even by a national library and 'is likely to be less so in the future'.[4] It is surprising that in institutions committed to rational pursuits such an irrational and illogical library aspiration should have survived. Ironically while the university acclaim was welcome, particularly if acquisitions came by means of what was often termed a free gift or bequest, the rising cost of maintaining the expanding collections in a condition suitable for use was less generally acceptable, especially if the library's bids for funds or buildings conflicted with faculty requests for more academic staff or a new laboratory in the university buildings queue − a not uncommon case of universities willing the ends but not the means. This ambivalent approach soon became reflected in the views of a new generation of acute and numerically brutal university administrators who instinctively realized that as libraries grow larger they inexorably become more expensive to maintain and come to be seen as an economic liability.[5] They were not slow to point out that even the wealthiest nations find themselves obliged to review and rigorously weed their public records to avoid being swamped in paper.

In a prescient paper of 1951, Keyes Metcalf pointed out that 'one of the easiest things we could do was to make our libraries grow rapidly. Library growth reminds me of the Sorcerer's Apprentice, who turned on the water but didn't know the combination with which to turn it off and so was swamped by the results . . . Sooner or later we shall find that there is a limit to the percentage of the funds in each university that can be properly spent for the library', and he added, 'As far as I know there has never been an adequate study made of this problem'.[6] More, as in other parts of academic life, may not have meant 'worse' but it certainly means 'different'. There appears to be an ominous, almost conspiratorial silence on what could be considered an obvious, if embarrassing, subject. A moment's thought and reflection, based on the most primitive housekeeping economics, should bring awareness of the dangers of over-commitment: that libraries like families will bankrupt themselves if they indulge in over-vigorous adoption policies without making provision for the growing demands of the acquired progeny in the future. Inevitably the provision of adequate academic library buildings has always tended to lag behind need. The librarian has had, as one administrator put it, 'to achieve a desperate congestion problem' before relief would be provided, by which time yet another building would be needed. Yet many of the academic library problems seem somehow to be self-inflicted, a classic case of librarians 'shooting themselves in the foot and then scoring an own goal'. What has been termed the 'academic library eternal growth dilemma' has tended to create instability, to render libraries inflexible and difficult to control, while making backlogs, arrearages, and congestion (necessitating ad-hoc emergency double-decanting stock-moves) a regular feature of academic library life. It seems not a little bizarre that a profession so committed in its traditions and skills to the creation of order and discipline should by its unbalanced ambitions succeed in achieving 'out of control' and 'inheritance mess' situations which at times threatens to consume the bulk of available resources, to imperil current acquisition intake, and to open up an alarming gulf between library ideals and library realities.

Equally damaging, perhaps, has been the fostering of the obsolescent, if not obsolete, notion, more in tune with nineteenth century concepts than those called for on the eve of the twenty-first, of an academic library as a book-hoarding warehouse instead of a service providing access to the books and information needed by their clients regardless of source. The 'piling Pelion on Ossa' approach has also had the unfortunate effect of perpetuating the wretched image of librarians as scrooge-like biblioklept figures, constantly acting the Oliver Twist role in mendicant moaning and dignified reproach, acting as a sort of institutional hairshirt or doormat, the modern equivalent of the medieval court jester only retained because the post happens to be mentioned in the university's charter. The unkind have suggested that the basic qualification required for academic librarians is to have undergone 'charisma bypass operations' so as to endure with equanimity lives devoted to shoring up ruins, indulging in eloquent soliloquies about how badly they are treated by the world, and particularly hating the prospect of being deprived of their complaints. One university pro-vice-chancellor described his own role as that of a 'mouse aspiring to be a rat'. It would be unfortunate if academic librarians were to be judged largely for their pack-rat characteristics and appetites, for their libraries to become 'mausoleums for dead books', and for the word 'library' like 'museum' most unjustly to become a term of abuse.

Academic library realities: escalating publishing output
In a paper to IFLA in 1988 entitled 'The end of all and forever', Bendik Rugaas maintained that a comprehensive approach cannot be sustained and is 'no longer a self-evident truth' even for the national libraries of the wealthiest countries. Since 1950, when output of titles in the UK was under 20,000, the total rose by 1988 to over 62,000, and by the year 2000 is estimated as likely to reach 90,000 titles. Paradoxically, computerized information technology has not led to the paperless society which some predicted, but it has made it very much cheaper to publish than it would have been by conventional means. In the past the traditional publishing mechanism to some extent tended to act as a filtering process; now most restraints have disappeared. Desk-Top or Self-Publishing promises to snowball and to produce social

changes as momentous as those resulting from the invention of movable type — the 'soldiers of lead' which Gutenberg said would 'conquer the world'. It is now not so much a question of the publishing of manuscripts but of 'manuscript publishing'. The warning issued by the seventeenth-century Quaker, George Fox: 'Take heed of printing anything more than ye are required of by the Lord God' is likely to remain unheeded in the 1980s, especially by academic authors under dire pressure from their universities and the Universities Funding Council to lengthen their publication lists, and compete in the bibliometrical race-stakes, perhaps by dividing scholarly work into as many 'Least Publishable Units' (LPUs) as they can contrive.[7]

The hope that a solution to such accumulation problems would arrive in the shape of a quick and cheap 'technological fix' has not materialized so far. There appears to be a significant bill to pay either in money, staffing, equipment or space to secure partial benefits from technological developments which of their very nature are based on 'planned obsolescence' and regular replacement. Paul Fisher summed up the situation when he concluded that 'the paperless library remains about as likely as the paperless lavatory'.[8]

Rugaas pointed out that 'the completeness fixation' related to print on paper and conventional library material has made us 'forget the raison d'être ... [even for national libraries] which, as I see it, is not to collect printed material per se, but rather to collect important information regardless of form'. This tradition comes from a time when 'the printed word on paper dominated the scene as the one and only information carrier', whereas not only is it now possible for there to be a print shop in every basement, but the real information explosion 'has been in the field of new media and new technology'. It is surprising how those prophesying the demise of the printed book continue to send out their anti-lineal messages in print, but there is a growing quantity of 'hybrid media' being published and finding its way through legal deposit into national libraries, and the British Library Act 1972 made provision for collecting materials 'whether printed or otherwise'.

Over the past hundred years 'libraries have been fighting a losing battle with costs'. In the 1880s they spent about three-quarters of their budgets on acquisitions and a quarter on personnel and operating costs; a century later the ratio has almost been inverted. Libraries 'are faced with a three-front battle in managing their overall costs: the exponential growth of the materials they must acquire, the exponential growth of the salaries of their personnel, and a growing need to provide more access-per-item to their collections due to their increased size'.[9] During the past ten years there has been a rapid escalation in journal prices, the average increasing by 245%. At this rate the single remaining journal costing £1m can be envisaged similar to the defence predicament: 'When computers project that on the present basis (of price escalation) we will only be able to afford one warship by the year 2010 and one aircraft by 2036, decisions need to be taken of a fairly fundamental nature'.[10] The UK Universities Pay and Prices Index, considered to be conservative and in arrears, gave a value of 235.6 at 1 July 1988 (Nov.1980=100) for books, periodicals and binding compared with 160.9 for all other non-pay items.

The academic library has no control over market forces or currency fluctuations. There has been a tradition of academic librarians expecting proportional increases in all inputs so as to acquire and hold large collections indefinitely, but as 'this projection calls for exponential increases in both material and personnel costs, libraries can expect to be even harder pressed in the future to devote all available resources to the maintenance of programs which offer little promise of fundamental innovation. Indeed the larger the scale of operations the more difficult it is to foster innovations'.[11] The only 'method that society has found for increasing productivity exponentially is by increasing use of mechanization',[12] and great strides have been made by academic libraries in automation. Yet the high costs of system and equipment maintenance, the size of the ever-growing files, and the inevitability of expensive regular replacement or upgrade give cause for considerable concern. To make matters worse, UK universities suffered a 17% fall in net income between 1979 and 1984/85, and the libraries' share of university expenditure fell by 6% during this time. It seems inevitable that for the foreseeable future academic libraries will be severely under-resourced and subject to uncertainty, arbitrary and disruptive costs together with 'freezing' of staff posts when vacancies occur, if not wholesale redundancies and premature retirements. What is completely new − and in stark contrast to the expansionary expectations taken to be the norm in the early careers of many academic librarians − is the near-total lack of hope that the situation will become any more favourable in the future.

Traditionally it has been assumed that capturing material from possible destruction − 'brands snatched from the burning' − and acquiring it for potential future research was for the academic librarian the supremely virtuous act of supererogation. The relatively sudden awareness of conservation problems and of the high, near-bankrupting costs necessary to achieve the newly developed 'principle of maintainability' threatens to dent Schopenhauer's image of libraries as 'the only secure and permanent memory of mankind'. Libraries, like museums, are becoming vulnerable to mounting public criticism for irresponsibility in acquiring and hoarding rarities *for* rather than *from* destruction and for 'dog-in-the-manger' attitudes while materials inexorably disintegrate on their shelves.[13] The problem with paper is that it self-destructs, and if handled it self-destructs more quickly. The National Audit Office reported on the collections 'of enormous size' at the British Museum and the Victoria and Albert Museum that 'though acquisition policies are selective the legacy of past acquisitions places a heavy burden on storage, conservation, staffing and other costs' and that 'there is a potential conflict between maintaining and enhancing the size, range and comprehensiveness of the collections, and meeting increasing storage, conservation and other costs from limited funds'.[14] What appear to be assets rapidly become liabilities. Acquisition and retention policies need to be linked far more closely than in the past and their potential conflict identified.

Academic libraries cannot be exempt from biological and chemical laws. The penalty for over-commitment, mismatch of resources to workload, and lack of control is that library materials will rot and decay in backlogs or they will rot and decay after acquisition − fairly indiscriminate but also fairly comprehensive decomposition. They will also be subject to all the natural and man-made catastrophes, from intrusive insects in hot climates, or in more temperate zones, from floods, defective plumbing and leaking library roofs and, of course, from the universal enemy, fire, all of which threats the current emphasis on library disaster planning is designed to combat. The selection process by librarians which is so vigorously criticized and castigated in some circles is likely to be far more arbitrarily applied and imposed by natural causes than by librarians. Books like battleships and vegetables must be recognized as being perishable goods. Many publishers issue forth their products in ways which suggest that they do not wish them to last, and their wishes are amply fulfilled by the treatment they receive in libraries. User behaviour to books and libraries worldwide has deteriorated, as though war has been declared in a new type of Battle of, or for, the Books – an unholy alliance of publisher and library-user. Theft is on the increase, and costly security and policing counter-measures often provoke outbreaks of mutilation, book-vandalism and desecration.

It became clear with the decline in political and emotional support for universities in the 1970s that government would not fund buildings to house ever-expanding stock in all higher education institutional libraries. Indeed, most countries, regardless of ideology, are looking for economic justifications in the various operations run or funded by the state. Rugaas remarked that 'all over the world the scalpel of economy seems to be preparing for operations which could easily lead to cultural lobotomy'. A vigorous restructuring of university decision-making in the UK had been taking place within the framework established by the Jarratt Report, which promises to alter profoundly the place of the library in the university.[15] Universities and their libraries have not been helped by the behaviour (and how it has been presented by the media and perceived by the general public) of a minority of the student body 'part of the miasmic foam on the breaking crest of the higher education wave', which has led to public disillusionment and the collapse of political and emotional support for universities.[16] While there is widespread and insufficient awareness of the importance and value of universities and their libraries to society, there is positive contempt for university handling of 'the stony world of industrial relations'.[17] Their strait-jacketting effect within academic libraries, leading to 'fossilization of inefficiency ... truculence, slackness and readiness to enter into industrial dispute',[18] has produced a new and insidious form of 'tyranny from below' which virus-like limits the library's ability to reorganize itself even when it wishes to do so in the interests of its own staff members and threatens to turn the librarian into a 'galley-slave on his own ship'.[19] Keyes Metcalf recommended librarians to forget about 'inter-library rivalry' (and librarians have not always been innocent here), pointing out that 'no one library can have everything and that unnecessary duplication of little-used books among libraries reduces the total research resources of the country and just does not make sense'.[20] The Atkinson Report, *Capital provision for university libraries*, of 1976 was well in advance of the times and introduced the 'finite, working academic library concept' aimed at producing a rational library buildings policy, balancing strong, relevant local core collections with access to national and international library and information networks. It liberated academic libraries from the impossible and even undesirable mission, the 'university librarian's burden', of being expected to create locally some sort of latter-day instant Bodleian. Even well-endowed national libraries realize that they cannot be comprehensive but must increasingly be seen as 'an integral part of the nation's library and information system', as Kilgour aptly remarked, 'the national library is the nation's libraries'. They are also part of a world library and information ecology, required to operate as Rugaas pointed out in 'an international context which more and more influences every nation and its national library'. Hence the widespread interest in Conspectus and similar arrangements for mapping collection strengths worldwide. In the age of the satellite and the global economy, knowledge knows no frontiers.

Academic libraries and university reorganization

During the period of expansion of higher education in the UK the university system could be steered relatively painlessly 'by adding desirable developments in what were thought to be the right places. But no serious thought had ever been given to the possibility that ... growth might actually have to go into reverse. To have foreseen or provided for such a contingency, say in 1964, would have seemed not only absurd but in a way morally wrong. Just the same, it is one thing to restrain a growth deemed to be unsound, and quite another actually to demand the excision of established fibre: for the excision had to be done, in the last resort, by the very bodies of which the fibre was a part. The principle of autonomy imposed the act as well as the pains of amputation on the patient himself.[21] The unthinkable has now happened. The future in higher education certainly is not what it used to be.

It is clear that the academic library 'can no longer afford to take its relationship with the university for granted at a time when universities are in the midst of probably the most drastic restructuring in their history. The whole future of the library within the university depends on the library's response to these challenges'.[22] Universities themselves are now undergoing continuous programmes of rationalization and selectivity largely because of the escalating cost of scientific and engineering plant, academic staff and no doubt academic libraries. A massive redistribution of intellectual resources is currently taking place − perhaps the largest in Britain since the sixteenth century Dissolution of the monasteries. Academic librarians have been accustomed impotently to bewail their plight when their institutions have been either unwilling or unable to indicate academic priorities.[23] Now their prayers have been granted in full with regularly revised academic and strategic plans, selectivity evaluation, and reviews of subject teaching and research ratings (monitored by bibliometric and citation counts often provided by the library itself), and whole departments being dispersed or even closed. The fiction of local university autonomy appears sometimes to be preserved as a screen for increasing central direction. The practice of posting of academic staff by Whitehall has not yet totally followed the pattern of the armed services but, after the experience of staff diaspora from dismantled departments, it may be too tempting to be resisted by the centre for much longer. It certainly seems likely that all university library books will be considered to be government property and available to the national library system as a whole.

It is possible that some universities will 'eventually become no more than teaching institutions, while others will only carry out research in a limited range of subjects'.[24] The universality dream for each university has gone for the foreseeable future, and with it the justification for a university library to attempt comprehensiveness in an effort to anticipate expansionary developments of an uncertain future. 'We must educate our masters' was the cry over the 1870 Education Act, and the need now is even more pressing in relation to university academics, libraries and the Great Education Reform Bill of 1988/89. The past record of academic influence and treatment of the central library has reflected a somewhat mixed, Janus-faced, love-hate relationship. There has been a seemingly almost irresistible and widely practised custom of using the library as a battleground on which to damage academic opponents and rivals, and the shape of the collections often reflects the record of historic power struggles. The battles may have been glorious, but battlefields have a habit of being left permanently devastated, mere passive memorials to past conflicts. Little consensus exists about what an academic library should be or do. There appear to be as many, sometimes more, opinions about the library as there are academic staff − five professors, six views. At times they seem less concerned at what is not in the library than in exercising a veto over the disposal of what is already in and is no longer used.

Many academics could hardly claim to have been genuine believers in comprehensive libraries, otherwise they would have been less disingenuous and more self-denying when it came to devoting more resources to them. They often seem to find it difficult to understand libraries or, if they do, fail to succeed in putting the library and the general interest before that of their own sectional advantage. The construction of personalized 'bulge' collections by the enthusiastic, sometimes tending to reflect personal interests of a book-collector manqué posing as research, provoked Maurice Line to suggest some years ago that many of these should be peripatetic and follow their creators around, a new form of mobile, travelling library – a prophecy which with rationalization is now being fulfilled. While there has been lip-service within universities to the UGC's 1921 concept of the library as the 'heart of the university', more often than not the neglect and Scrooge-like resourcing by academics in power have reduced the library to a condition where it is more likely to be in need of joining the hospital queue for a transplant operation. The interminable, internecine, and sterile debates in library committees reflect an unrewarding search for equity in the allocation and distribution of library resources which cannot ever be achieved. The fruitless search for an absolute fair formula seeks to provide for academics a cosmetic, psychologically comforting, but nonetheless illusory feeling of justice and fairness. Books are all too often seen as status symbols. It has been a common ploy for librarians preparing for UGC or CNAA visitations to buy or recall books written by visiting members hoping to flatter their egos, whereas logically they should be more pleased if their literary effusions and scientific offspring were being used. Censorship or blackmailing pressure from academic factions and lobbyists is not unknown. One group of Maoists at a progressive university complained that the university library contained only Trotskyite works and none of theirs, and it required very fast thinking on the part of the librarian to suggest that their books were so popular that they were always out on loan. Others tend to regard the library staff merely as passive order agents for departmental requests, confusing service and servility, and see the university library as a series of individual segments, at most a confederation of distinct departmental collections and interests.

Books tend still by many academics to be considered, particularly in their departmental collections, as property, things to be possessed, even as archival assets – virtually immortal entities subject to a kind of eternal mortmain in a type of semi-national library while the liabilities and obligations which their possession involves are frequently ignored. The primary aim of a university library is to operate as a working collection. Working collections of their very nature are liable to suffer from wear and tear in their working life – indeed, the more successful they are in carrying out their function the faster they are likely to deteriorate. In addition to wear and tear there is a rising tide of book-abuse – tearing out of pages, illustrations, journal articles, and complete contents of volumes, leaving the empty husk-cases (sometimes containing different innards) behind on the shelves. Inevitably, it is the most heavily used items and those in greatest demand that tend to suffer most. Despite electronic security measures, books are stolen. The intensity of student competition for good results to provide for life salary benefits and for academic career advancement, combined with penurious grants making it impossible in the foreseeable future for the majority to purchase books (many of which have too high a rate of obsolescence to be good investments), is likely to add to the pressures on academic library stock.

There always appears to have been tension between the teacher and the librarian

— perhaps symbolic of the old rivalry between the oral and the written word, for from the time of Socrates it was feared that 'writing would create forgetfulness in men's souls'. Sadly, a relatively low priority appears to be given to the construction of course reading lists by academics — a depressing example of the lack of 'pastoral' care, which creates unnecessary and demoralizing work for both students and the librarians to whom they go for help.

There is a real risk that just at the moment when imagination and vision is required, academics may almost by accident foster a resurgence of a traditional and backward-looking role on the library. The reason for acquiring an item for an academic library seems often to be taken as a reason for keeping it for ever.[25] A particularly misleading but dangerous heresy, just at the moment when the library needs to be liberated from departmental interference, is a distorted application of the popular concept of consumerism where departments are seen as the library's consumers; 'treating library materials as an overhead to be charged out to departments' would endow them with dominant control of the library's destiny and budget.[26] The university library has always been concerned with use and with users' needs, but its consumers or customers are, and come to it as, individuals who do not necessarily follow departmental guidance or expectations.

At a time when there is increased need for more precise targeting of library resources to match university selectivity and priorities and there is a desperate requirement on academics to publish in the competitive 'bibliometrical' survival battle,[27] the library's unique ability to analyse and assess use, evaluate document delivery and exposure, and provide information regardless of where or how it is stored, could make an invaluable contribution to the effectiveness and competitiveness of a university. There is now a greater emphasis on multi- and inter-disciplinary collaborative approaches in which the academic library also has much to offer. Academics by abandoning some prejudices and traditional beliefs such as theoretical library comprehensiveness might be enabled to achieve greater productivity through library support and skills, saving their time and providing the necessary bibliographical awareness and precision. The special role of libraries in relating 500 years of printed sources with information in multi-media and electronic formats opens up the possibility of their participating in assisting academic staff and postgraduates in publishing academic works and research reports using high quality desk-top publishing systems, an interesting revival of classical and medieval library traditions.

Information technology developments now and in the future are likely to provide greater scope for cooperation with other academic services (e.g. audio-visual and computing) to enhance facilities for academic work.[28] At present there is a growing rather than diminishing requirement for concentrated work-spaces and work-stations, community and group learning, in a place with long opening hours and good heating and lighting (given the current and anticipated levels of student grant impoverishment), together with some supervision and help facilities. The facilities for transferring and delivering information to remote sites and individual offices will also draw attention to the library as a source of relevant and up-to-date information, enabling researchers and scholars to become aware of gaps in the literature as well as to avoid expensive and wasteful duplication. The implications of developments in the 'wired up campus' are under active investigation at a number of UK universities, and the library is unlikely not to have a role to play as a major access point or node for information.

Crisis or opportunity for transformation?

Changes affecting universities and their libraries have been so monumental that few of the old approaches, concepts and attitudes are likely to remain appropriate. Optimistic hopes that policies which might have been successful in the past, such as discreet inertia, the rousing, ringing clarion call to do precisely nothing, or the equivalent of dormouse hibernation to sleep the crisis out, will prove ill-advised if not positively dangerous. The option of electing not to reorganize or of seeking to defend the indefensible cannot be recommended. Making no decision is in fact a decision which is likely to encourage other agencies to set the agenda for reshaping the library and its future. Within universities now there will be even more vigorous competition for funds and in the new hard and bitter gradgrind context the old compassionate arguments for library budgetary stability and enhancement will cut little ice — and there will be a lot of that around. While it will be necessary for the university not to bankrupt its library, it will be even more vital for the library not to bankrupt its university. Inevitably here will be escalation in a library's materials and operating costs (including staff), and needs — particularly automation. In the past the value of a well-stocked library in strengthening a university by attracting students and research was widely recognized. Yet this cost commitment, at a time when the concept of 'contracting' for resources based on student numbers is under discussion, could now be seen as a threatening overhead for each full-time student bid and a potential handicap in the competitive university survival stakes.

Now there is a great opportunity to turn a predicament into an advantage and to undertake a re-examination of the academic library's role; to attempt to provide an answer to the challenging question posed by Rugaas: 'What is our business?' The task now (as it probably in reality was before) for the academic library is to achieve 'stock management' balance, to be in control of its operations (avoiding demoralizing backlogs and costly commitments which threaten to outstrip available funds), to treat space as a resource, and above all to maintain 'working' collections and network access arrangements which are relevant and responsive to the institution's teaching and research needs. In attempting to demonstrate their utility in maximizing document exposure for the user, it will be essential for libraries to 'differentiate carefully in their statements of institutional goals between archival responsibilities with one set of values and library information system responsibilities with a different set of values'.[29]

Academic librarians might even feel relief at being liberated from an impossible and unachievable comprehensive mission and from spurious special collection building. They might consider welcoming the redistribution of bookstock to follow academic rationalization rather than squabble and resist it, and joyously abandon local non-standard cataloguing together with the non-standard cataloguers. The university librarian is now presented with challenging opportunities to demonstrate those qualities of judgement and selection (and selection implies rejection) which are, and always have been, central to the profession in order to achieve control and balance of library collections and operations. Not all books are of equal value though they take up equal space according to their mass on library shelves. It has been said that the library is older than the book, and librarians have traditionally graded books according to their potential importance, contents, characteristics and anticipated use, and have not adopted a bibliodemocratic approach. Any reluctance to indulge in selection and grasp at retaining complete neutrality by librarians must seem strange since they have no hesitation in going to great pains in selecting staff — a very chancy and costly form

45

of 'multi-year subscription' — and they have to make myriad decisions about access and arrangements for use. In any case, against the background of conservation problems every library item is under sentence of death unless the librarian makes a selection decision to reprieve it, and this is perhaps the most critical act of selection for which the librarian is responsible.

The validity of the *laws* as distinct from the *lore* of librarianship must be recognized, for example that it is impossible to satisfy 100% of demands (certainly from local holdings), tht 80% of demand may be met from 20% of the stock and to satisfy the remaining 20% would consume disproportionate resources and draw the library into the zone of diminishing returns. Other reassuring precepts are that a relatively small percentage of the university's population makes the major use of the library, that recent materials tend to be most heavily used, and that a Gresham staffing law applies where poor and inefficient colleagues will tend to drive out the competent.

Inevitably there are, and will remain, many anxieties. Who will make the rules about what to keep and discard? Will, as one commentator exclaimed, Posterity ever forgive us? Why bother with non-printed materials when there are insufficient resources for print? Undoubtedly operating a balanced library 'with the stock-discarding virus' is likely to be more demanding and arduous than the accumulating one. As one research report laconically put it: 'Weeding the stock is the ungrasped nettle'.[30] It is not only generally an extra activity but a risky one. To add a book to the library generally needs the suggestion of only one faculty member; to withdraw it may require the concurrence of all who could claim any conceivable interest in it.[31] Recognized as being a librarian's prerogative, it has sometimes been considered a menial activity (which it most certainly is not): referring in the early eighteenth century to the Royal and Cotton libraries (now the jewels of the British Library's collections), Sir Christopher Wren declared: 'I confess both these Libraries may be purged of much uselesse trash, but this must be the drudgery of librarians'.[32] One librarian remarked that 'weeding is an old-fashioned term in library management, but there is still no process so painful to librarians. I have known several who could fire people more easily than they could discard books and journals'.[33] Yet libraries cannot go on growing exponentially: 'In terms of the long term perspective responsible judgement suggests that there is no feasible alternative before libraries other than a wide and continuous programme of selective book retirement' and that it 'must become as routine as acquisitions and other library operations'.[34]

Academic librarians can take some consolation from their unique position in being able to make informed assessments about usage levels. Management information from automated library systems provides the mechanism for reinforcing decisions and in evaluating library use as distinct from demand predicted, desired or anticipated by academic colleagues. 'It continues to be true that many of the books in a large research library are seldom used, that being the nature of a large research library'.[35] Such information sources should enable the librarian to reduce the considerable percentage of acquisitions which tend never to be used, to establish balanced and economic satisfaction/disappointment levels as well as effective ownership/access policies. Librarians are also in a special position as arbiters in assessing the physical condition of library stock in relation to current use and in keeping it available for future use.

Compared with the rest of the university, the academic library is in a comparatively strong position in being able to produce output in addition to input measures in the academic quest for realistic performance indicators and for the level of accountability (not just financially living within the budget but management accountability in achieving objectives) which is now required. It can demonstrate value for money (VFM) and the key qualities of economy, efficiency and effectiveness in its operations such as winning discounts through multi-year subscriptions, currency fluctuation awareness, and revenue generation through fees, charges and provision of external services. Above all it must be able to show that it is an asset to the university in its competitive struggle for survival and not a bankrupting burden which the academic library's traditional open-ended comprehensive mission could entail.

The technique of life cycle costing, used in connection with the procurement of military and defence equipment, where the costs of maintaining items of equipment in a condition to enable them to be used is often found to be many times the cost of original acquisition, appeared to provide a not unsuitable pattern for the academic library to use in its age-old, perennial battle against ignorance and prejudice (both not entirely foreign to or absent in the academic world). Academic libraries must ensure that maintenance obligations do not become such as to limit the scope for current acquisitions and equally that the scale of acquisitions is not such as to impose impossibly expensive maintenance liabilities which may weaken the library's ability to make its crucial contribution to university needs in the future.

The Atkinson report identified the type of problem which the life cycle costing approach addresses when it described the dilemma of indefinite accumulation and overcommitment facing academic libraries as likely to 'pose a threat to the university library system'. The adoption of a life cycle costing model should enable the academic librarian to demonstrate the real and genuine requirements of the library in terms of space, services, and staff to achieve a balanced operation, together with the scale of any mismatch between the level of recurrent resources received and the obligations and responsibilities which the institution the library serves expects it to discharge. The approach can also prevent academic libraries becoming threats both to themselves and to their institutions, since in university libraries, as in other enterprises, the 'costs of owning physical assets can be substantially hidden because of the time scale over which costs are incurred ... The visibility of life-cycle costs can be compared to that part of an iceberg as seen from the sea. Just as the destructive force of an iceberg is a function of its total mass, so the visible costs of physical assets obscure the force and power of underlying costs that propel its owner towards or away from prosperity' – and, it could be added, survival.[36]

Logically every acquisition to an academic library should carry an overhead charge either to ensure its continuing availability or pay for its eventual relegation (rather like the suggestion for a special levy on cars to meet the cost of their disposal when they are no longer capable of giving service).[37] For the university administrator there is no point in providing more resources for more library acquisitions when this merely adds to the library's space and conservation problems and provides a further rod for the funding body's back by creating an even bigger mess and mismatch.[38]

Emphasis on the academic library's educational role

Concentration on a selective rather than a comprehensive, open-ended approach by academic libraries draws attention to the educational purposes of the academic library as a means rather than an end in itself, with a key contribution to make in relation to learning and to 'independent intellectual fulfilment'. The library is both a service agency and a kind of academic department, a discipline in its own right, not merely connected with an educational institution but an integral part of its teaching and research operation.

It is interesting to note the surprising neglect of the library's influence in the taxonomy of learning. Bruner pointed out that 'the single most characteristic thing about human beings is that they learn'[39] and noted that what learners find out for themselves is more readily retrievable, better retained, and more capable of application to new situations.

A curious notion is prevalent in universities that no learning is happening unless teaching is going on, and yet sadly the very opposite is often the case. Surprisingly little attention has been given to investigating independent study, even though students probably spend the greater part of their time at university engaged in it. The purpose of formal higher education courses is not merely to pass examinations but to develop students' ability to think for themselves and work on their own. It has been suggested that one of the main aims of a university education is to teach how to learn, to give students a means of updating their knowledge and continuing their education (as they will need to do) by independent learning for the rest of their working lives. Paradoxically a university course should enable students to emancipate themselves from dependence on the lecturer, to wean themselves from oral teaching, and to become equipped to combat the built-in-obsolescence of much of what they are being taught — an obsolescence which it is the avowed purpose of research and technology to produce. In addition to an ability to maintain specialist competence in a world committed to continual change, the student must develop the facility for acquiring multi- and inter-disciplinary knowledge in areas in which there is no time to obtain formal education. Above all, students must learn the skills of how to control and use information, for this will be the essential common-core requirement of whatever work they undertake after leaving university. What will be increasingly needed will be the art of critical selection — the ability to distinguish between what must be learnt and what can be safely left to be found out from reference works and sources; skills in consulting and evaluating authorities and in conducting search strategies; and precision in keeping notes and personal records and in citing references. Above all discrimination will be essential 'since an instinctive respect for the printed word makes it difficult for most people to appreciate that it is occasionally completely false'.[40]

The exploitation of existing knowledge is often as important as the discovery of new knowledge. Here the library has a significant contribution to make in helping the researcher before selecting a topic for enquiry to discover work which has already been completed and also to keep under review what is in progress in the specific field of study or adjacent fields. It is hardly an exaggeration to maintain that one of the main purposes of a university education is to learn how to use the resources of a well organized, effectively arranged, well guided and signed library which will present major opportunities for discovery, creative enquiry and serendipity through browsing.

The transmission of these and other information skills figuring in academic library orientation and education programmes will assume greater importance as pressures on academic time to deliver research findings and publish make it necessary to leave more time for students to chart their own learning routes and to develop confidence in handling pertinent sources of information and gaining access to library and database networks which will be of such key importance to them during the rest of their lives.

Selective and finite academic libraries (Maurice Line's Model A (conveyor belts) as opposed to his Model B (accumulators)), lean muscular libraries as opposed to fat, bloated ones, at least have a chance of achieving such targets within the budgets likely to be available to universities in the decades to come.[41] The academic library that refuses to face reality and continues to pursue the myth and the mirage of comprehensiveness is fated merely to consume an ever-increasing amount of resources in the self-defeating quest merely to demonstrate extravagances rather than economies of scale. Academic librarians have nothing to lose but their (self-manufactured) chains. There can be no doubt that their libraries are 'in a crisis of funding, like their parent institutions' and that an attempt to follow conventional goals will inevitably lead to 'a gradual but steady, and largely improvised, erosion of facilities and services'.[42]

A radical reappraisal with librarians not administrators setting the agenda could hardly be worse than an 'uncontrolled decline'. In their classic work on universities, Ashby and Anderson maintained that 'An institution is the embodiment of an ideal. In order to survive, an institution must fulfil two conditions: it must be sufficiently stable to sustain the ideal which gave it birth and sufficiently responsive to remain relevant to the society which supports it'.[43] There could be no more fitting summary of the need for control and balance in the governance of the university library to enable it both to survive and to be relevant to the needs of the twenty-first century and beyond.

References

1 Meadows, D. L. et al., *Dynamics of growth in a finite world*, Cambridge, Mass., Wright-Allen Press, 1974, 561.

2 Gore, D. et al., *Farewell to Alexandria*, London, Greenwood Press, 1976, 166.

3 Miller, E., *That noble cabinet*, London, Deutsch, 1973, 323.

4 Green, S., 'Steady-state and national libraries', *in* Steele, C. (ed.), *Steady-state, zero growth and the academic library*, 1978, 138.

5 Cronin, B., 'The uncontested orthodoxy', *British journal of academic librarianship*, 3, (1), 1988, 1–8.

6 Ellsworth, D. J. and Stevens, N. D., *Landmarks of library literature 1876–1976*, Metuchen, N.J., Scarecrow Press, 1976, 297–9.

7 *New scientist*, 19 Nov. 1987, 64.

8 Fisher, P., 'The links that speak volumes', *Guardian*, 24 Feb. 1989.

9 Dolby, J. L. et al., *Computerized library catalogs*, Cambridge, Mass., M.I.T. Press, 1969, 15.

10 Pearce, E., 'Last word', *Sunday Times*, 4 Sept. 1988.

11 Leimkuhler, F. F., 'Planning university library services', *in University of Lancaster Library occasional papers*, 3, 1969, Session 6,1.

12 See ref.9, 15.

13 Press reports, *The Times, Guardian, Daily Telegraph*, 5 Aug. 1988. See also Jenkins, S., 'A treasure-trove rotting in the attic', *The Times*, 10 Apr. 1988; and Ratcliffe, F. W., *Preservation policies and conservation in British libraries*, London, British Library, 1984. (Library & Information Research Report 25).

14 National Audit Office, *Management of the collections of the English national museums and galleries*, London, HMSO, 1988, 1.

15 Committee of Vice-Chancellors and Principals of the Universities of the United Kingdom, *Report of the Steering committee for efficiency studies in universities*

[Jarratt report], London, Committee of Vice-Chancellors and Principals, 1985.
16 Carswell, J., *Government and the universities of Britain, programme and performance 1960–1980*, Cambridge, Cambridge University Press, 1985, ix.
17 *Ibid.*, 101.
18 Barnett, C., *The audit of war*, London, Macmillan, 1986, 154–5.
19 Kerr, C., 'The idea of a multiversity', *in* Reynolds, M. M. (ed.), *Reader in the academic library*, Washington, Microcard editions, 1970, 23.
20 Ellsworth and Stevens, *op. cit.*, 301.
21 See ref.16, 160.
22 Burrows, T., 'Funding and governance of British university libraries', *British journal of academic librarianship*, **2**, (3), 1987, 165–76.
23 Ellsworth and Stevens, *op. cit.*, 305.
24 See ref.22, 173.
25 See ref.2, 171.
26 See ref.22, 170.
27 'Computer check irks dons', *The Times*, 7 Oct. 1988.
28 See *British journal of academic librarianship*, **3**, (3), 1988: issue devoted to convergence of academic libraries and other information services.
29 Burns, R. W., 'Library use as a performance measure', *Journal of academic librarianship*, **4**, (1), 1978, 4–11.
30 University of Durham, *Project for evaluating the benefits from university libraries*, [PEBUL report], Durham, University of Durham, 1969, A 3, 1.
31 Swank, R. C., 'The cost of keeping books', *in* Reynolds, *op. cit.*, 136.
32 See ref.3, 3.
33 See ref.2, 122–3.
34 Ash, L. (ed.), *Yale's selective book retirement program*, Hamden, Conn., Archon Books, 1963, 63, 67.
35 Ellsworth, R. E., *The economics of book storage in college and university libraries*, Washington, Association of Research Libraries, 1969, 14.
36 Department of Industry, Committee for Terotechnology, *Life cycle costing in the management of assets*, London, HMSO, 1977, 53.
37 *Daily Telegraph*, 28 Dec. 1971.
38 National Audit Office, *op. cit.*, 1988, 1.
39 Bruner, J. S., *Toward a theory of instruction*, Cambridge, Mass., Belknap Press of Harvard University, 1966, 113.
40 Noltingk, B. E., *The art of research*, Amsterdam, Elsevier Publishing Company, 1965, 28.
41 Line, M. B., 'The survival of academic libraries in hard times: reactions to pressures, rational and irrational', *British journal of academic librarianship*, **1**, (1), 1986, 1–8.
42 *Ibid.*, 3.
43 Ashby, E., in association with Anderson, M., *Universities: British, Indian, African: a study in the ecology of higher education*, London, Weidenfeld and Nicolson, 1966, 3.

8

Stock management and disposal: collection building and demolition

Ian Winkworth

Introduction: stock management defined

Stock management is about balancing additions and withdrawals, and about the storage, display and accessibility of collections, what Buckland describes as 'managing the physical availability of books'.[1] I take 'books' to include periodicals, audio-visual items, electronic and other media, and 'access' as being to materials not held locally.

Studies have repeatedly shown the traditional belief of academic librarians — that there will eventually appear a reader for any book stored in any location — to be substantially untrue. Meanwhile accessibility, display and costing of the benefits achieved have been generally neglected.

Academic libraries need a better stock management rationale, one which links what we do much more closely with the current, specific purposes of the institutions served, produces real outputs, balances the conflicting demands on the library from researchers and students, and does not result in apparently limitless claims for money and accommodation.

Such a rational approach, involving the notions of limitation and weeding, runs into problems to do with the symbolic and emotive value of books, especially in an academic institution. For these reasons a rational approach to stock management must be cautious, is not easy to implement and has to be combined with skilful presentation and timing. The importance needs also to be stressed of the interrelationship between stock management and other library functions. Although this paper is concerned with the content, storage and display of stock, it is essential that other functions such as loan regulations and interlibrary loans, classification and cataloguing, information services, and photocopying services are all regarded as part of the stock management policy, if a series of sub-optimal systems — of which stock management is the most expensive — are to be avoided.

Objectives of stock management

Woven through the library lore is a confusing network of criss-crossing and overlapping trains of thought about the objectives of library stock management. However, Buckland and Hindle provide a helpful analysis in which six major variations are identified:[2]

completeness
document availability
browsability
circulation
reading
awareness.

Completeness

'Completeness' is not necessarily the uncritical pursuit of quantity of stock; it may alternatively refer to completeness in the sense of representing 'quality literature'. However, the main emphasis in such views inevitably tends to be on increasing the number of titles in a collection. Certainly withdrawal of titles once added is wholly alien. The library stock is seen as an independent work of art in itself. A rather lower priority is accorded to the expressed needs of actual users. Apart from sheer size, the performance measure for such comprehensive collections can only be a comparison of holdings against lists of 'desirable' titles which are based on academic judgement at a particular time.

Document availability

The concept of document availability was invented to deal with the difference between theory and practice in the comprehensive collection, where all the required titles are in theory available but, if lending is allowed, a very large part of the potential demand is never met because of the uneven distribution of demand and insufficient duplication of high-use titles. The performance measure is usually phrased in terms such as: the probability that an actual user will find available in the library the books which he seeks when he wants them. This immediately places an emphasis on consideration of loan regulations and on duplication of titles in order to bring the stock holdings more in line with the actual (short-term) pattern of demand.

Browsability

In browsability the 'representative' nature of the complete collection and the hard-headedness of document availability are combined. The appropriate performance measure has been called 'collection bias'. This is defined non-technically as the extent to which the books most in demand are likely to be unavailable. A 'good' collection would always have a reasonable selection of these to offer and a lower proportion of little-used or unused titles. Browsability is perhaps the objective that most nearly fits the goals of the classic open access subject classified library. It is arguably the case that a reference collection would better achieve the browsability objective than a lending collection.

Circulation and use

Circulation is probably the objective for which performance is most easily measured and understood. Data is cheap to collect and the concept being measured is simple. One disadvantage is that additional, and much less easy, analysis of reference use is required for a full picture. Secondly, maximum measured performance could be achieved by increasing purchases of cheap, high-use books (conceivably of little or no relevance to the academic objectives) and by shortening loan periods.

Reading

Reading tends to be defined for this purpose as 'document exposure': the hours of use of a book by the reader. This is nearer to an assessment of the value to the reader of the book, but is difficult and labour-intensive to measure, requiring detailed information about the behaviour of readers over long periods. The 'value' is still only represented by a surrogate quantitative measure — hours of reading — which clearly may not represent in any real sense the value to the reader: one key idea or fact can be worth more than 300 pages of text. It may therefore be that the extra effort is of doubtful value for a measure of library performance.

Awareness and document supply

Lastly, there are the notions of 'awareness' and 'document supply', which are perhaps the traditional objectives of many industrial libraries: to achieve the maximum knowledge of relevant literature by readers, whether or not the library owns the stock in question, and then to provide access to any items requested by loan from stock, purchase or inter-library loan. This objective represents the ultimate 'access' approach and the complete antithesis of the 'completeness' objective. There is deliberately limited effort put into building up stock in advance of need, and reliance on a network of information provision agencies is essential. The performance measure is perhaps the proportion of users' information input which is gleaned from the library and then the efficiency and economy with which requested documents are supplied.

Specimen stock management objectives

To be practically useful, objectives need to be phrased as targets against which performance can be measured. A statement such as 'Supporting the teaching and research of the university' is an adequate formulation as a stock management objective. How is success defined? Is it simply lack of complaints? But in that case, is it known what standards the readers are using to judge the adequacy of the stock? And do they not adjust their demands to the supply? Certainly this is what research, for example at Lancaster University and at Newcastle Polytechnic, suggests.[3,4] To be practical, objectives must be conceived in terms which allow performance measurement. The appropriate measure of performance depends on the objective or balance of objectives selected. A library whose objective is primarily document availability might adopt:

To make available to readers the literature or information they require:
  60% immediately
  90% within one week
  99% within one month
all at least cost.

If completeness were the goal, then the objective might be something like the following:

To attain as representative as possible a collection of the literature of
lasting importance, within the constraints of the resources available
and the priorities established in the collection policy statement.

The critical features of the objective are, however, the same: clarity, relevance, and measurability.

Stock management policy issues

Size

Traditionally size has been regarded as a measure of the excellence of an academic library. It seems common sense that a library with one million volumes is better than one with 500,000. Yet how big should a library be?

In 1975 it was estimated that the world output of book titles to date was 35 million to 40 million.[5] By 1989 that figure had probably passed 50 million. How far can the holdings of one library, be they 10,0000, 100,000, 1 million or more, go towards 'representing' this world of knowledge? And how are you sure that you really have the right selection? If libraries have chosen the right books, why is it that stock overlap surveys (for example, as reported in Ford) repeatedly show such low overlaps of stock between academic library collections?[6] Perish the thought, but could it be that much of the library stock building has been haphazard, idiosyncratic and self-indulgent? This might be particularly the case where selection has been left in the hands of the academic staff, who have little knowledge of the actual use of the stock, and whose selections quite understandably tend to reflect personal research specialisms to the detriment of representativeness and more general utility.

In the last two decades it has become clear that there are severe operational penalties for size, to do with the administrative structure needed to operate and the higher proportion of unused stock, which offset economies of scale. Users of large libraries have to come to terms with the sophisticated systems needed to organize a large library. But is there any optimum effective size? On what basis are academic institutions to decide how much of their resources to put into their libraries? Is there any limit on what it is sensible for them to invest in libraries? These questions have become steadily more urgent as the volume of publications produced has continued to grow and it has gradually become clear that for an individual library the goal of independently achieving a comprehensive collection is moving further away rather than nearer.

Professional bodies have sometimes sought to set standards for size of library stock based either on a list of desirable titles;[7,8] or numbers of books per student;[9,10] or in the UK Atkinson Report's metres of books per student,[11] which can also be turned into a figure of 'books per student' if an average number of books per metre is applied.

Thus, assuming an average width for a book of 30 millimetres, each, linear metre of books would contain an average of 33 items.[12] On this basis, the stock of UK university libraries varied at that time between 30 and 195 books per student, with an average of 114. Were some libraries six times better or worse than others? Were some over-provided or some totally inadequate? Since 1976, all those libraries will have grown by several hundred thousand volumes. Some will have doubled in size. Are they now proportionately better? The research provides no ready answer to what is an optimum size.

Perhaps this is because 'how big?' is an inappropriate question. To define the optimum library in terms of size or books per student is to measure only inputs, and that very crudely. Such a measure says nothing about local objectives, collection organization, performance or quality, and it provides no guarantee whatever of a good library service. It is suggested here that it will be more profitable to concentrate on defining clear operational objectives and focusing on the outputs of the library for which some real measurement of the degree of achievement is possible.

Obsolescence

A second issue which disturbs the status quo has been the growing recognition of the applicability of obsolescence to library holdings and of the costs of retaining obsolete material. Surveys such as those reported by Ash, Fussler and Simon, and Urquhart and Urquhart have repeatedly confirmed that at an aggregate level use of books is related to their age.[13-15] But the definition and rate of obsolescence varies greatly between subject areas and there are difficulties of comparison arising from different techniques of measurement.[16, 17] However, whatever definition or measuring technique is used, it seems clear that, as a library becomes bigger over time, the obsolete stock becomes a steadily larger proportion and the newer and more used titles a smaller one, if no steps are taken to weed the stock. Libraries, like books, can become obsolete.

Storage and display

There is also evidence that the way in which books are stored and displayed in a library may affect the amount of use.[15, 18, 19] This seems common sense. Indeed, the whole rationale of open access libraries is that open access display increases use of collections.

Potential use of books may also be lost in large libraries because of poor physical arrangement, inadequate signposting, sheer size and users' inability to navigate to the right spot. Thus a survey at Newcastle Polytechnic Library showed that 15% of items which users reported being unable to find on the shelves were actually available in the correct place at the time concerned and a further 23% were available in the library in places such as the Set Text (Short Loan) Collection.[20] The larger the library the more complete and precise the information needed for a successful search. Thus in large libraries display and promotion become very important.

Libraries might reflect on what lessons can be learnt from the retail business. Libraries have a great many more 'product lines' than shops of an equivalent size, but some of the same problems of stock management, storage and display of large amounts of goods as a large store. The retail approach introduces notions such as matching supply as closely as possible to demand, achieving a rapid turnover of stock (selling five times the value of stock held in a year is better than selling four times the value), and layout and display which is both easily understood (without the use of a detailed catalogue!) and promotes higher levels of use for both low-use and high-use stock.

Related to a library context, this approach suggests a much greater emphasis on high-use stock and on physical arrangement for easy comprehension. How many different subject sequences are there in most of those libraries which claim to have stock arranged by subject? While signposting is no substitute for good arrangement, it, too, is important for new users of the library or those using an unfamiliar section. Why not make more use of full-face display of books, as practised in bookshops, to promote unused books which are thought to have some potential use? There should be a greater emphasis on classification and cataloguing as tools for display rather than as abstract intellectual concepts. Finally, the effect of consigning stock to closed access remote stores should not be overlooked. Use of these books as substitute titles becomes very unlikely: future use depends almost entirely on specific recommendation.

Security

A growing concern, as in shops, is the security of open access stock. Electronic security systems appear now to be essential and are effective in reducing theft and unofficial borrowing. However, such systems do not deter the determined thief. Increasingly the books and periodicals parts which are in highest demand by students have paradoxically to be put on closed access, thereby limiting use to some extent, in order to prevent theft.

Costing stock management policies

Rational stock management has been hindered by the absence of proper consideration of the costs of alternative policies. Firstly, it is rare for any library budgets to show the *total costs* of any activities. Building costs and overheads are rarely known, and serious attempts to *allocate* full costs to activities, including stock management and collection building, are almost unknown. *Marginal direct costs* (i.e. additional costs above the existing) of some courses of action may be assessed, as may the *chargeable costs* (i.e. what an institution elects to charge to departmental budgets), but these can sometimes provide a dangerously incomplete picture. Thus additional projects in a library, even if they bring marginal funding, will tend, for example, to occupy space and management time that would otherwise have been devoted to different activities. A concentration on chargeable costs can distort decision-making: librarians would perhaps be more cautious in their demands for ever more space in which to store unused books, if the cost of building the space were to be directly deduced from an annual total grant for library provision. Another costing concept to which I would wish to draw attention is *external* costs. By external costs are meant those costs that are part of the operation but that are borne outside the accounting unit. Thus library costing usually takes no account of the costs to the library user, usually in time, of one policy or another. Finally, there has been almost no concept at all of the *opportunity costs* of various courses of action, i.e. what other use might be made of the same resources. Once a proposal has been judged worthwhile, attention has usually moved directly to raising the money needed. These are all important concepts for proper judgement of stock management policies.

Before looking at the costs of alternative policies such as high-density storage, cooperative storage, weeding, relegation or disposal, it is important as a baseline to try to establish the costs of holding stock, between countries and between times. A useful model for determining the cost of holding stock or alternative policies was put forward in 1980 by the UK economist Richard Brown.[21] This is based on the concept of a 'cost per book per year', derived from adding together the annual cost of:

1 Initial cost of the building which houses the stock — infrequent capital cost to be spread over many years
2 Cost of heating, lighting, maintenance — revenue cost
3 Cost of buying and cataloguing the book — normally funded as a revenue cost but arguably a book is a capital asset like a building, whose cost should likewise be spread over its useful life.

With the costing method established it is then possible to compare the cost of holding stock with relying on interlibrary loan (ILL). The average costs for issuing a book and for obtaining an interlibrary loan are calculated. From these by simple subtraction it is possible to calculate the *extra* direct cost of one ILL, compared with the cost of issuing a book already in stock. This cost per ILL can then be compared with the annual cost of maintaining stock to arrive at a frequency of use which justifies stock-holding. The model also allows, if required, calculation of which books are worth stocking, based on the purchase cost. The model can also be used to compare the costs of stock retention versus withdrawal, once a book has been acquired and held in stock. In addition, the model provides a useful means for calculating an appropriate charge by a lending library to a borrowing library for an ILL which is acceptable to both borrower and lender.

Books as capital assets

A final benefit of the Brown approach is that it begins to regard books as capital assets rather than consumable revenue supplies. The collective bookstock of an academic library clearly fits a normal accountant's definition of a capital asset: a long-range investment, with maintenance costs attached. It is therefore very appropriate to consider the purchase and processing costs of a new book as a capital investment which is consumed over a long period and therefore to be 'written off' in depreciation over a long period. The mechanism of cost per book per year gives precise form to the concept.

Collection development policies

It is not part of the purpose of this paper to consider the issue of collection development policies *per se*. However, the existence or not of such a policy clearly will affect stock management. The aim of policies such as those advocated by the American Library Association or the US Research Libraries Group is to make collection building more consistent and systematic by allocating each subject area a collecting level (e.g. comprehensive, research, study, basic, minimal).[22,23] Such policies are, however, of doubtful value in the average college library, because they usually contain no economic dimension, because of the emphasis on collection building rather than use, and because it is difficult to avoid the implication that an 'A' library is better than a 'D' one, when in reality the 'D' library may be better fitted for its purpose.

Weeding and relegation

Reasons for weeding

The reasons for weeding or relegation centre mostly on two considerations: saving space (and thereby money) and 'improving' the main collection by removing unwanted stock. These possible benefits are offset by the costs of withdrawal and the potential costs of borrowing or reacquiring the small minority of items that will attract use in the future which cannot be predicted today. Costs of withdrawal have tended in the past to be overestimated. Computerized systems can provide sophisticated data about book use and users and make 'uncataloguing' easy and practical in large libraries. In smaller libraries manual methods are quite feasible. However, the real basis of decision-making is much more likely to be in the acceptance or rejection of the notion that a collection can be improved by removing less relevant items of stock. Here the empirical evidence is not conclusive, but it suggests that most academic libraries should weed more freely.[19] However, there can be no right or wrong answer in general terms: the answer has to lie in the objectives of the institution served by the library and the resources the institution is prepared to commit. There is, however, a danger for the librarian in being caught between grandiose, woolly objectives and severely constrained resources.

Hell or purgatory?

If the removal of less-used items from the main open access collection has been accepted as a policy, the next question is whether to relegate to Purgatory or to Hell: to move to some kind of secondary store, or to weed irrevocably from the total collection. The benefits of retaining unused or little-used material in a local secondary store have most to do with the emotive and political issues relating to the goals of the library and the expectations of teaching and library staff. Both groups tend to be very cautious about final withdrawal, for reasons discussed at the beginning of this paper. It is hard to admit that a purchasing mistake has been made. The funds relating to purchase and cataloguing costs are more tangible than, at the margin, the hidden costs of retaining one more book in a library which may not be totally full. There is also an understandable fear that the item withdrawn might not in future be available from another source. Relegation to a secondary store, which makes some savings but defers the final decision, is therefore an attractive choice politically. It has to be said, however, that experiment shows very few redemptions. In Newcastle Polytechnic Library, for example, a relegation programme in the humanities area produced a redemption rate within two years of its relegation of less than 1% of stock relegated. As the volume of publications flows on, librarians may have to harden their hearts and face up to taking firm decisions first time round.

An alternative approach is donation to another library or cooperative store from which the book may be retrieved at a later date if needed while incurring little or no ongoing cost to the original purchaser. The attraction of this approach is that greater savings can be made, if it is accepted that the shared store will not retain duplicates. Such schemes also offer a rational answer to the reasonable expectation that libraries collectively should take steps to ensure the preservation of a few copies of any book published.

Criteria for weeding

A major difficulty in weeding or relegation in the past has been finding criteria and methods which are both cheap to apply and effective. Several major research projects have sought to investigate and provide answers to these problems.[13, 14, 15] However, for reasons discussed above, take-up of the methods developed has been slow and cautious.

The literature boils down to around five approaches plus combinations of criteria. The five approaches are: subjective judgement; age; date of acquisition; use/circulation; shelf time period.

Subjective judgement

Subjective judgement would, of course, be the only method if the objective of the weeding exercise was to retain in the main collection the books which are in some judgemental sense 'the best' rather than the most used. It has, however, generally been poor at predicting future use and is very expensive in staff time.

Age and date of acquisition

Both age of book (or date of publication) and date of acquisition are reasonably predictive of use at an average level: the more recent the higher the use. However, the rate of fall-off in use varies greatly between disciplines and, possibly, libraries. Neither criterion is a good predictor of use of individual titles in individual libraries.

Patterns of past use

Use tends to be concentrated on a minority of titles (the '80/20' rule) and past use has been shown to be a good predictor of future use of individual titles.[13,24] The essence of the 'rule' is depicted in figure 1. Approximately 80% of the use of any collection is provided by around 20% of the books. In addition, research in academic libraries has repeatedly shown that up to 40% of the holdings remain unused, offering a large group of readily identifiable candidates for weeding.[14,25] This is illustrated by the right hand half of figure 1, which is based on Urquhart's formulation.[26]

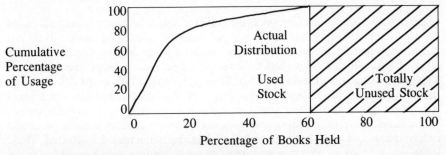

Fig. 1   **Distribution of usage of books held**

Since it is usually not difficult to obtain data on past use of titles from both manual systems (via a book card or date label) and computerized systems, this relationship has attracted considerable interest. The main problems are that the predictions become least reliable in just the area where they are most needed for an academic library: those books that might be used once in 5 or 10 or 15 or more years;[15] and that use data is difficult to collect for in-library, reference and browsing use where there is no record as an automatic by-product of the activity. Fortunately, where comparative research has been done between borrowing and in-library use, while there has been considerable divergence in the reported ratio of in-house to borrowing use, with the obvious exception of books that are available only for in-library use, the two patterns of use do not differ greatly.[15,27] This means that the relative distribution of use of different titles recorded from circulation records is a reasonable proxy for overall use of any particular collection of books. But where should the cut-off date in weeding be placed? How many books can or should be weeded and what is a sensible period of non-use to allow before a title is weeded?

Shelf time period

It is in answering these last questions that the 'shelf time period' method and research of Slote is distinctive.[18] Slote, Hardesty, Williams and others have demonstrated that it is possible to predict which books are most likely to be used in future on the basis of the length of time *between* circulations or consultations, the 'shelf time period' as it is called.[18,28,29] The relationship is depicted in generalized form in figure 2. An analysis showing the last previous date of use of books borrowed or

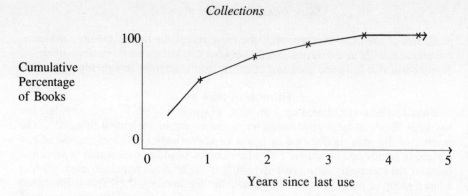

Fig. 2 Period of time since last use for those books that are used

returned over a period of a few weeks provides the data. The theory provides a model for predicting from this data how much potential use of existing stock will be lost and what proportion of the stock would be weeded if a weeding criterion like 'remove all the books which have a shelf time period longer than x years' were adopted. Typically, using a shelf-time period of three years might risk losing 5% of future use of the existing stock, whereas choosing a shelf-time period of five years might risk losing only 1% of future use. Comparison of the table of shelf-time periods with a sample use profile of the whole stock also allows reasonably accurate prediction of how many books will be withdrawn if a given shelf time period is selected. Thus, if the aim is to create a certain amount of space rather than achieve any particular use profile for the current stock, or if there is concern at removing too much stock at once, the criterion can be adjusted in advance of beginning the actual weeding. The weeding can be carried out by clerical staff. The method also has the benefit of having been thoroughly researched. Hardesty and Williams provide independent exemplifications of the method in use.[28,29]

Thorough application of the Slote technique would effect a drastic reduction in the stock size, one that academic staff would find hard to accept. For these reasons most academic libraries that have used the technique have added one or more further sifting stages to provide reassurance, and there has been a preference for relegation to secondary store in place of the outright disposal which the theory would indicate. Williams shows how the Slote method can be combined inexpensively with exposure of the books which are candidates for weeding to subjective review if for political or other reasons it is felt unnecessary.[29]

Disposal

If it has been decided to dispose of weeded stock, what are the alternatives? Wood provides a concise but thorough account of practical experience of disposal in a large academic library.[30] The first option is to pass the books on to another library. Alternatively local, regional or national cooperative stores might be used, in the context either of gift or of deposit, where the original owner retains some agreed special rights. Thirdly, books can sometimes be sold, either on the commercial market or through book sales. The experience seems to be, however, that it is rare for either type of sale to raise much income — unless rare and valuable books are being sold deliberately to raise money — and does not cover the staff effort involved. The book sale may nevertheless be worthwhile as a public relations exercise as an alternative to pulping.

Conclusion: achieving the reader's ideal

For the individual library user, the optimum library stock is one that has all the books one is likely to want, located close together on its shelves, where one expects to find them and when one wants them. The problem for the librarian in such a specification is that it is loaded with contradiction, unpredictability and expense. We operate a community service with finite means. Such a service must be imperfect, but may also be more or less so.

Stock management must be related, first of all, to the particular objectives of the library and its parent institution. There is therefore no one magic recipe for all academic libraries. It would be foolish to assert that a nation does not need any comprehensive, archival libraries, but neither does the UK, for example, need 100 or more academic libraries all pursuing the Bodleian holy grail. Moreover, in the steadily harder times that seem to be afflicting most academic institutions, more and more institutions will be forced to re-examine cherished ideals to see how they can be modified to match the resources available. In this climate it is hard to see how the continued acquisition and storage of never-used library materials, because they might, one day, be used and are deemed inherently valuable, can be sustained. There is an alternative library model, which can support research activity adequately, which approximates to the 'self-renewing' library of the Atkinson Report. For such a library it is not size of stock but relevance to current and foreseeable near-future activity that counts.[31]

It is interesting to witness the collection rationalization between UK university libraries which is currently accompanying the implementation of the University Grants Committee scheme to bring two or more small teaching departments together in one location. These pressures, and the steady growth of regional, national and international stock management plans, will serve to make the abandonment of stock management based on the concept of the self-standing library both less painful and more inevitable, even for inveterate traditionalists.

References

1 Buckland, M. K., *Book availability and the library user*. London, Pergamon, 1975, 3.
2 Buckland, M. K. and Hindle, A., 'Acquisitions, growth and performance control through systems analysis', *in* Gore, D. (ed.), *Farewell to Alexandria: solutions to space, growth and performance problems of libraries*. Westport, Greenwood Press, 1976, 44−61.
3 Buckland, M. K., *Book availability and the library user*. London, Pergamon, 1975, 119−31.
4 McDowell, E., *Book availability survey October/November 1986*. Newcastle upon Tyne, Newcastle upon Tyne Polytechnic Library, 1987. (Planning and Research Notes, 72).
5 Slote, S. J., *Weeding library collections*. Littleton, Libraries Unlimited, 1975, 20.
6 Ford, G., 'Stock relegation in some British university libraries', *Journal of librarianship*, **12**, (1), 1980, 52.

7   Lunsford, E. B. and Kopkin, T. I., *A basic collection for scientific and technical libraries*. New York, Special Libraries Association, 1971.

8   Voigt, H. and Treyz, J., *Books for college libraries*. Chicago, American Library Association, 1967.

9   Clapp, V. W. and Jordan, R. T., 'Quantitative criteria for adequacy of academic library collections', *College and research libraries*, **26**, (5), 1965, 371 – 80.

10 Library Association, *College libraries: guidelines for professional service and resource provision. 3rd ed.* London, Library Association, 1982.

11 University Grants Committee, *Capital provision for university libraries: report of a working party*. London, HMSO, 1976.

12 Ibid., 29.

13 Ash, L., *Yale's selective book retirement program*. Hamden, Archon Books, 1963.

14 Fussler, H. H. and Simon, J. L., *Patterns in the use of books in large research libraries*. Chicago, University of Chicago Press, 1969.

15 Urquhart, J. A. and Urquhart, N. C., *Relegation and stock control in libraries*. Stocksfield, Oriel Press, 1976.

16 Line, M. B. and Sandison, A., 'Obsolescence and changes in the use of literature with time', *Journal of documentation*, **30**, (3), 1974, 283 – 350.

17 Buckland, M. K., *Book availability and the library user*. London, Pergamon, 1975, 12 – 13.

18 Slote, S. J., *Weeding library collections II*. Littleton, Libraries Unlimited, 1982.

19 Roy, L., 'Does weeding increase circulation? A review of the related literature', *Collection management*, **10**, (1/2), 1988, 141 – 56.

20 McDowell, E., *Book availability survey, Main Library, March 1982*. Newcastle upon Tyne, Newcastle upon Tyne Polytechnic Library, 1982. (Planning and research notes, 38).

21 Brown, A. J., 'Some library costs and options', *Journal of librarianship*, **12**, (4), 1980, 211 – 16.

22 Perkins, D. L. (ed.), *Guidelines for collection development*, Chicago, American Library Association, 1979.

23 Research Libraries Group, *RLG collection development manual. 2nd ed.* Stanford, Research Libraries Group, 1981.

24 Trueswell, R. W., 'Growing libraries: who needs them?'., *in* Gore, D. (ed.), *Farewell to Alexandria: solutions to space, growth and performance problems of libraries*. Westport, Greenwood Press, 1976, 72 – 104.

25 Kent, A., *et al., The use of library materials: the University of Pittsburgh study*. New York, Dekker, 1979.

26 Urquhart, J. A., 'Should books be burned?', *in* Storey, C. (ed.), *Stock relegation practice in major academic libraries in north-east England. Proceedings of a seminar held at Teesside Polytechnic Library 1982*. Newcastle upon Tyne, Library Association, University College and Research Section, Northern Group, 1982, 49.

27 Harris, C. G. S., 'A comparison of issues and in-library use of books', *Aslib proceedings*, **29**, (3), 1977, 118 – 26.

28 Hardesty, L., 'Use of library materials at a small liberal arts college: a replication', *Collection management*, **10**, (3/4), 1988, 61 – 80.

29 Williams, R., 'Weeding an academic library using the Slote method', *British journal of academic librarianship*, **1**, (2), 1986, 147–59.
30 Wood, S., 'Retention and disposal of stock: Edinburgh University Library policy and practice', *Scottish Library Association news*, no.190, December 1985, 3–6.
31 Winkworth, I. R. and Enright, B. J., 'Relevance and reality in academic libraries', *Library review*, **35**, (2), 1986, 79–90.

9

Acquisitions: books

Geoffrey Ford

Introduction

This paper deals with three topics: the formulation of acquisitions policy, procedures for book selection, and the management of acquisition systems.

If we think about it we see that an acquisition policy is in fact only part of a collection development policy. It is not enough to state principles which will govern the selection of books; it is also necessary to decide on policies for keeping books and/or discarding them and for ensuring that those books which are kept are kept in a usable condition.

We can see from figure 1 that the acquisition policy goes alongside a relegation or weeding policy and a conservation policy as components of an overall collection development policy. Figure 2 illustrates the relationships between various parts of the acquisitions process in academic libraries.

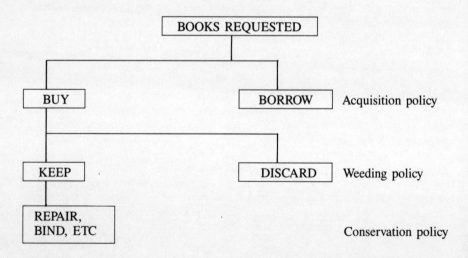

Fig. 1

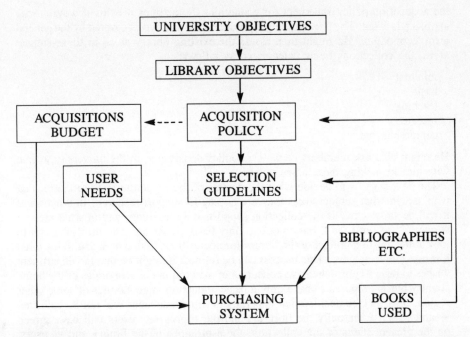

UNIVERSITY OBJECTIVES

LIBRARY OBJECTIVES

ACQUISITIONS BUDGET ← - - - - ACQUISITION POLICY

USER NEEDS   SELECTION GUIDELINES

BIBLIOGRAPHIES ETC.

PURCHASING SYSTEM   BOOKS USED

Fig. 2

The acquisition policy must be determined in relation to the policy and objectives of the academic institution which the library serves. The acquisition budget determines what it is possible to achieve within that policy, and the policy itself leads to guidelines for use when selecting materials for the library, whether they be books, periodicals or other materials. The selection process may be aided by the use of various bibliographic tools and works of reference which help the person selecting the books to keep up to date with what material is being published. However, the book selector must also be aware of the needs of the users of the library, and these may be determined by a number of means: the users may suggest books for purchase, or they may request items for loan through the interlending or other document supply system, and such requests may suggest to the book selector that items should be purchased rather than borrowed. Finally the usefulness of the books acquired may be judged, and this process may feed back into the guidelines for selection or into the acquisition policy.

Acquisition policy

It is desirable for a library to initiate a fairly detailed acquisition policy. This is important so that librarians can refer to it and publicize it to try to ensure that the users of the library do not have false expectations of the library service. The goal of the academic library must be to facilitate access to materials for learning, teaching and research.

Formulation of the policy is best done as a cooperative task by the librarians and the users. For example, the librarian responsible for the economics section of the library would discuss with a professor in the economics department in order to produce the acquisition policy statement for economics. Sometimes it helps if a systematic approach is taken. The librarian might produce a list of subjects covered by the general term 'economics'. He might then assess the existing library stock in those subject areas, the collections being categorized as follows:

minimal
basic
teaching
research
comprehensive.

He might also ask members of the economics department in the university to join with him in making these assessments.

The next stage is to decide what the desires of the academic institution are: that is to say, in what subject areas they are hoping to support research; in what areas it will be satisfactory if the collection supports only teaching; and in what areas it is possible to limit the library stock to only basic provision. The third phase is to look at the existing budget of the library for acquisitions in that area and to say what it is possible to achieve. This process can be refined: it might be that the department wishes to have a comprehensive collection of material in the economics of the home country but is prepared to have only a basic collection in economics of some other region; or it may be decided that materials in some languages will not be collected – and so on. Eventually the librarian and the appropriate users will have agreed on the present status of the collection, the aspirations of the library and its users, and what it is possible to achieve. This approach has been used in a number of academic libraries in the United States of America for a number of years, and the Conspectus system is one implementation of it. The systematic evaluation of collections in this way is a good way of opening up dialogue between librarians and academic staff, and of educating users – important points which are sometimes missed by administrators remote from the user community. The process does require some labour, and systematic data collection is assisted by the use of forms and guidelines: those used at Southampton University since 1980 are reproduced in Annex 1 to this section.

Book selection

In academic libraries there are usually two different kinds of people who select books: the librarians and the users. I think it is true to say that usually it is only the faculty or teaching staff of the university or polytechnic who have any real influence on book selection. Students can exert pressure only by trying to use the library: if there are insufficient copies of a book which many students must have the library will become aware of this and may have money to help to satisfy those needs by buying additional copies. This is not always the case, however. In the ideal situation the librarians have freedom to choose the stock for the library; academic staff will be free to make recommendations for purchase also, but if the librarians are doing their job properly it will be found that most of the books recommended for purchase by the teaching staff will already be in the library or on order. It is clear that the selection process must be heavily influenced by the amount of money available to the library. When budgets are limited it may be desirable to make more systematic approaches to the task of selection. When a book is considered for selection the librarian might ask a number of questions either of himself or of the user who requests the book. For example:

- Who will use this book? Will it be students following a course, and if so how many?
- What kinds of book are suitable for student use? Should they be such as to aid the process of study, with summaries and aids to memory?
- What if the book is intended to support the private research of one member of the faculty? If the book is likely to be of limited use to only one person would it be possible to acquire the book on interlibrary loan instead? If the book is to be of continuing use to only one member of the faculty could that person buy it for himself or herself instead?
- If the books are to be acquired to support research, what kinds of book are suitable for faculty members, who are by definition specialists in the subject matter? Can we say that the way in which the author puts over his argument is less important than the content, or that the validity of the argument depends on the authority of the writer or the way in which he/she uses methods appropriate to the subject?
- Are the ways in which librarians select books affected by different perceptions? Would a librarian be looking for books from which information is easily discovered, or which are suitable for library use? Books which are well arranged for information retrieval, with good indexes perhaps, but not loose-leaf productions which are labour-intensive to maintain and liable to vandalism?

If a librarian is to select books on behalf of different user groups, he must be able to see books from their perspective, which may mean suppressing his own values.

If we assume that librarians are selecting books, how do they go about discovering what material is available for selection? In an ideal world the librarian will have a good knowledge of a book before he decides to purchase it for his library — he may have read it or looked at it in a book shop or have read a number of reviews of the book or be relying on the recommendation of someone whom he has come to trust. To be effective the book selector must keep in touch with the subject fields in which he is selecting; he may do this by receiving material from publishers or by scanning bibliographies such as the national bibliographies of various countries. It is important to do this systematically and to keep it as a regular activity in the working day or working week. Once one loses time it is almost impossible to catch up.

In some cases where budgets are large then approval plans may be operated. In these cases the library specifies the subject areas, countries of interest, and languages of interest to a supplier of books, who then supplies books on approval. It is important that the conditions of the approval plan are carefully worked out and understood by the librarians. The suppliers will want to ensure that most of the books they send on approval are actually purchased by the library and so it is important for the library to ensure it has specified its subjects of interest very carefully to eliminate wastage. For most academic libraries however, approval plans, except in very limited circumstances, are just not possible because budgets are inadequate. It may be possible to arrange with a local supplier to have a limited number of items on approval: this will usually depend on the library having a good amount of trade with that supplier.

Acquisition systems management

Selection leads naturally on to ordering, or the acquisition process itself. We are concerned here not with the *minutiae* of procedure, but with the manager's role.

Buying books can be an expensive process. There is not just the cost of the book itself but there is the cost of ordering it, of verifying when it arrives that it is the correct one, and of ensuring that it is swiftly processed and paid for. Accurate records have to be kept so that wasteful duplication is eliminated and that the progress of a book which has been ordered can be traced at all times. It is the manager's responsibility to design procedures that are effective and efficient.

The functions of an acquisitions system are:

to acquire materials as quickly as possible
to avoid unwanted duplication
to answer queries from suppliers
to answer queries from users
to keep track of items acquired or wanted
to pay for items purchased.

These functions are not unique to library book purchasing systems; similar functions are found in systems for acquiring stationery, furniture and spare parts for cars.

The flow chart in Appendix 2 shows some of the processes involved in a typical acquisition process. The process starts with a form − perhaps hand-written − which identifies the author, title, publisher and so on of the required book. This may be completed by the librarian or a user of the library. The librarian may check these details using various bibliographies and then an order is produced which can be sent to the bookseller. A copy of this order must be retained in the library and it might be helpful if this were included in the catalogue; if the library has a card catalogue then this copy of the order has to be on a catalogue card sized card which can be filed in the appropriate place in the catalogue. The library will maintain another file using some other arrangement (such as order number) to keep track of orders and their progress. When a book arrives in the library it must be matched with a copy of the order to ensure that it is the correct item, the invoice must be passed for payment and the book passed through the system for processing − cataloguing, labelling, etc. When the book has been catalogued then the record of the order which has been in the catalogue will be replaced by the final catalogue record.

The same principles apply when the library has an automated system, only there it is much easier to organize. An automated acquisition system integrated with or linked to an automated cataloguing system makes it very easy for details of books on order to appear in the catalogue, whether this is produced on microform or held online.

An important aspect of an acquisition system that is often overlooked is the provision of management information. Most libraries count the number of books they acquire and account for the money they spend, but comparatively few have a more comprehensive overview of the efficiency of their procedures or the effectiveness of their policies. This paper concludes with some examples of the use of management information from an acquisition system.

Average price

In none of the academic libraries in which I have worked have the published indexes of book price movements proved useful except at the gross level. For detailed budgetary allocation, it is necessary to monitor the average price of books bought in each subject category.

Cost per item

The cost of purchasing books, in terms of labour, computer time, equipment, stationery, etc., is a measure of efficiency in the use of resources. Most systems acquire inefficiencies over time, and a thorough analysis every few years is likely to yield worthwhile savings − anything from 10%−30% in my experience.

Cost per level of acquisition

The different levels of acquisition discussed in the section on acquisition policy (above) clearly have different cost implications. The costs associated with acquiring only the most basic items are low, but when collecting comprehensively in a subject, the marginal costs of acquiring items are likely to rise, as the library seeks out more obscure items, and buys out-of-print materials from secondhand dealers. Some appreciation of these costs is required for budgetary allocation between subjects, since no library will attempt to collect comprehensively in all fields.

Supply times

It is important that a librarian has some idea of the efficiency of the suppliers from whom books are acquired. This is very easy to arrange if the system is automated, since computers are very good at providing numbers: for example, the time taken by suppliers to send books once they have been ordered. It is possible to make similar checks even when the system is manual; this may be done on the basis of sampling the order file every now and again or by examining a sample of completed orders and comparing the performance of different suppliers. Where two suppliers seem to be behaving differently an analysis of the type of material they are supplying may reveal reasons for this and may suggest alternative courses of action.

Timeliness

A measure of effectiveness of the system as a whole: do the books arrive in time to be used when they are wanted? This measure includes within it elements reflecting the effectiveness and efficiency both of the library and of the supplier.

Cost of timeliness

Acquiring and processing books in a hurry can cost more than acquiring them at the 'normal' rate; most libraries find it necessary to have a priority stream for such items as are suddenly discovered to be necessary 'immediately' − usually when a faculty member is late with preparing a lecture course. The costs incurred in speeding books through the system are usually opportunity costs: other items get held up. It is necessary to have some idea of the effects of a priority stream on the general system; as a rule of thumb, if less than 10% of items receive priority treatment, then the delays to other items are not too serious.

Use per item, percentage of books found to be useful, acquisitions cost per use

These three measures may be appropriate for items which are expected to be used quite frequently within a comparatively short time of their purchase. It would not

69

be appropriate to judge the archival collections with these measures. In the appropriate circumstances, the measures indicate the effectiveness of the acquisition policy and of the book selection process. Figure 3 illustrates the process.

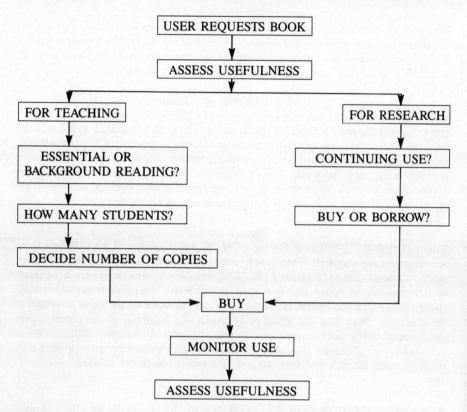

Fig. 3

Bibliography

Cline, H. F. and Sinnott, L. T., *Building library collections: politics and practices in academic libraries*, Lexington, Lexington Books, 1981.

Corrall, S. (ed.), *Collection development: options for effective management*, London, Taylor Graham, 1988.

Ford, S., *The acquisition of library materials*. Chicago, American Library Association, 1973.

Magrill, R. M. and Hickey, D. J., *Acquisitions management and collection development in libraries*. Chicago, American Library Association, 1984.

Spiller, D., *Book selection*. 3rd ed. London, Bingley, 1980.

Stueart, R. D. and Miller, G. B. (eds.), *Collection development in libraries: a treatise*. 2 vols. Greenwich, CT, Jai Press, 1980.

Whittaker, K., *Systematic evaluation: methods and sources for assessing books*, London, Bingley, 1982.

APPENDIX 1

SOUTHAMPTON UNIVERSITY LIBRARY

Form and Guidelines for Acquisition Policy Statements

COLLECTION PROFILE SHEET

Completed by:

Date	Subject	Collecting Level (use codes)			Qualifying Factors					
LC Class	Description	Existing Collection	Current Activity	Desirable Policy	Language Exclusions/Strengths	Chronological Exclusions/Strengths	Geographical Exclusions/Strengths	Form	Aspect

71

Collection profile sheet: guide to completion

A. *Collecting level*

Please use these codes when defining collecting level.

1 Comprehensive = collecting exhaustively in the subject field [very few subject areas are likely to be comprehensive]

2 Research = collecting materials required for dissertations and independent research

3 Teaching = collecting materials to support undergraduate and graduate course work

4 Basic = collecting materials to introduce and define a subject

5 Minimal = collecting marginally

Note that assessments are needed for:

(1) Existing collection

(2) Current activity − your current acquisitions policy

(3) Desirable policy − what is necessary to support present activities

B. *Qualifying factors*

Not all qualifying factors will be appropriate to all subject areas. Complete only those columns appropriate to your subject field.

(1) *Languages*

Please use codes as under:

No exclusions (i.e. all languages applicable)	A
All except English	E
Dutch	N
French	F
German	G
Italian	I
Portuguese	P
Russian and other Slavic	R
Scandinavian	V
Spanish	H
All non-Roman alphabets	B

(2) *Chronological*

Use dates where applicable

(3) *Geographical*

Please use codes where applicable

No exclusions (i.e. all areas applicable)	A
Africa	X
America	M
Asia	J
Australia	Y
Europe	E
France	F
Germany	G
Great Britain	B
Italy	I

Latin America	L
Netherlands	N
Portugal	P
Scandinavia	V
Spain	H
USA	U
USSR	R

(4) *Form*

Generally speaking we expect all subjects to be represented by books and serials. In some subjects additional forms of publication are acquired. Please use codes for these additional forms only:

Audio-visual material	A
Manuscripts	S
Maps	M
Newspapers	N

(5) *Aspect*

In some areas, the subject description and qualifying statements will not be sufficiently distinctive. Please use the final column to indicate the aspect you wish to emphasize.

APPENDIX 2

Flow Chart for Typical Manual Acquisition System

Ordering

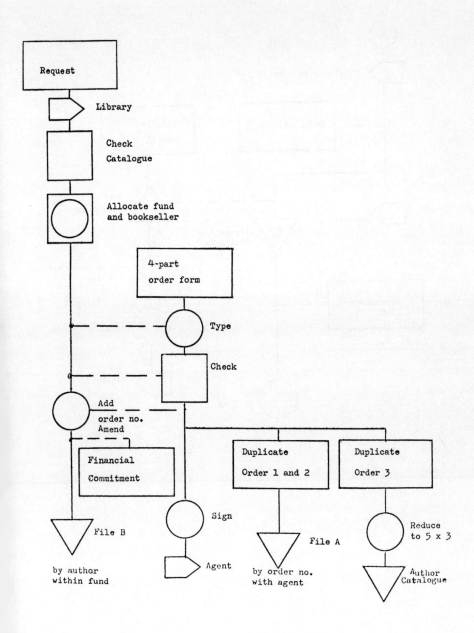

Receipt

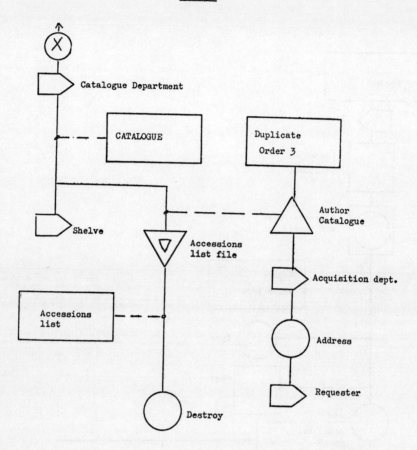

Catalogue Department

CATALOGUE

Duplicate
Order 3

Shelve

Author
Catalogue

Accessions
list file

Acquisition dept.

Accessions
list

Address

Requester

Destroy

76

Receipt

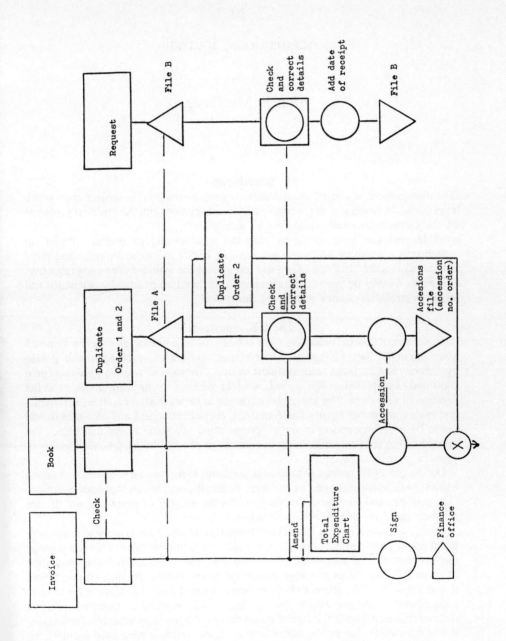

77

10

Acquisitions: journals

Alan F. MacDougall

Introduction

The management of journal acquisition may seem a comfortable subject upon which to expound. A reading of the literature and an association with the practical problems of the journals librarian rapidly dispel such a myth.

Miller and Guilfoyle succinctly state the problem and go further: 'Periodical selection is a complex subjective process that is difficult to accomplish and more difficult to explain'.[1] In that context, and recognizing the inability to be comprehensive, this paper focuses on particular key points. It is therefore practically orientated and explores strategies, rather than being theoretical.

The UK experience

The niceties of journal selection were not of vital importance or concern some 25 years ago in the United Kingdom. The 1960s are now known in retrospect as a 'golden age', money and horizons seemed almost endless. 'Expansion' was the word that could most aptly be applied to that period, whether within existing institutions, or in the creation of new ones. The atmosphere seemed to be somewhat carefree, if frenetic, and such concepts as rigorous self-analysis, cost-effectiveness and cost-benefit had yet to burn an impression on the corporate mind. To some extent that legacy has contributed to the present inability to come to grips with the hard-headed reality of resource management.

During the 1970s money became less plentiful, there was an economic recession and a very different atmosphere developed. Within the microcosm of journal provision, increased demand continued unabated, as did the number of new titles, yet finance for their purchase decreased in real terms.

While this state of affairs was acknowledged, little was done to come to terms with the problems, and certainly no radical solutions were implemented. This was perhaps due to the continued acceptance of the view that since journals were the foundation of research, their status and importance had to be revered. In such circumstances it would have been blasphemous to deny their continued future existence in the library; comprehensive and immediate physical access was regarded as essential. Without definite evidence, and in the face of the professional opinion of academic colleagues, it was difficult to dispute the assertion that all the journals were used regularly by staff and students and were therefore indispensable. Many librarians chose not to confront the problem of escalating costs, electing instead to opt for short term expedients in the hope that the problem would disappear. In such circumstances systematic collection management hardly existed.

Strategies that have been adopted by librarians as short term palliatives include:

- elimination or reduction of duplication
- reduction of foreign language titles
- moratorium on new titles
- acquisition of new title only on cancellation of an existing title;

and more commonly

- transfer of finance from other cost headings (most commonly monograph acquisitions) to journals.

These remedial actions could not be claimed as the universal panacea. Vickery's comments, arising out of his modelling work, should be noted:

'the continuing increase in the cost of journals, the growing bibliographical awareness of users (in the large part the result of technology) and the increasing cost of conventional interlending combine to make university libraries as presently constituted and managed, operationally non-visible. Unless there are policy changes the future looks very bleak indeed'.[2]

Policy changes have not been readily apparent − how then should the future be planned?

Factors and tools for decision making

Selection, or continued selection, is considered in this paper under three headings: present journal holdings; journals not in stock but already in existence; new journals. Selection is thus considered in its broadest terms. Since subscriptions are normally annual, all titles are capable of re-selection each year, and by implication therefore de-selection is examined.

What tools might then assist with decisions on selection? The following seven headings are suggested as a framework; the list is not comprehensive and there can be many sub-divisions:

- local usage
- reputation
- availability and accessibility elsewhere
- political dimensions
- citation analysis
- various cost factors
- consultation with academic staff.

It is worth stressing at this stage that selection involves evaluation.

Existing holdings
The following seven headings then can be considered first in terms of the present holdings:

Local usage

What role can local usage have in determining continued selection or de-selection? According to Line there is no doubt: 'No measure of journal use other than one derived from a local use study is of any significant practical value to libraries'.[3] This view was reinforced by recent research into optimization carried out at Loughborough University.[4]

The types and methods of local use studies that can be used have been discussed in detail by Christiansen[5] and are therefore not dwelt upon here; they include circulation records, use at the shelf, material left on tables, photocopying, etc. The dangers of adopting these approaches should not be overlooked. When considering methods it is important to bear in mind such questions as whether the information collected will be accurate or comprehensive enough, whether sampling will produce reliable data, and whether the information be too quantitative to the neglect of qualitative aspects. Again Christiansen[5] deals with these points.

Reputation

Under this heading attention would be focused more on information concerning the perceived quality of the publisher, editorial board, authors etc.

Availability and accessibility elsewhere

This is not always considered in the selection (or de-selection) process, but availability can be assured not only by local purchase but by other institutions. In the UK the existence of the British Library Document Supply Centre and its ability to supply material cannot be ignored. The relevant factors to be considered include the relative costs of local acquisitions and remote access.

Political dimension

This can be important, especially where cancellation and retention of items would have a direct effect on those who hold control of resources.

Citation analysis

It has often been suggested that the frequency with which journals are cited in the literature can be used as an indicator of journal usage. This subject could occupy a whole volume to itself; those interested in pursuing the subject are referred, in the first instance, to articles by Gross,[6] Pan,[8] and Line.[3,7] A reading of the literature suggests that while citation analysis may be useful in a teaching application, it has little practical relevance to libraries in their selection process. Research suggests that librarians' judgement could at least match the citation analysis approach.

Various cost factors

i)   one administratively easy practice is to axe expensive titles, but without information concerning usage this alone may not be cost-effective. Research at Loughborough University indicated that low cost journals can cost more per use than high cost journals.[4]

ii) 'free' titles may be protected or encouraged, but this can be expensive and not necessarily cost-effective. In a recent study[4] it was discovered that 91 so-called 'free' titles in economics cost in real terms £350 (processing, binding, accommodation etc.), and of those 91 only 24 were consulted, on 162 occasions.

It is clear that total costs need to be considered, not just subscription prices but also staff processding, binding, storage and other overheads.

Consultation with academic staff

This is one of the few qualitative ways of approaching continued selection, but it is inevitably subjective, being based on opinion rather than fact. There are several ways of collecting and analysing this information. For example, each title can be ranked on a scale; 100 points can be allocated to each academic to give to each title as he/she wishes (e.g. the academic could give 100 points to one title if thought appropriate); or all journals in a particular subject area can simply be ranked in order.

Journals not in stock

For titles not in stock already but that are candidates for purchase, the following methods *inter alia* could be employed to assist selection:

- interlibrary loan demand
- reputation
- consultation with academic staff
- cost.

New titles

For new titles, there needs to be a reliance on:

- reputation of editorial board etc.
- academic recommendation
- cost.

The use of some of the above criteria and techniques for selection purposes can result in a mass of facts and figures. Problems include a likely lack of qualitative information, and a neglect of the significance of browsing and serendipity. The scale of this was highlighted in recent work at Loughborough University,[9] which indicated that in the area of electrical engineering and electronics 62% of total journal use was browsing, in economics 57%, and in chemistry 43%.

More research is required on the value of browsing.

Future developments

Will future developments come to the assistance of library managers? At present the economics of electronic article provision and the existing pattern of demand are such as to suggest that this will not replace conventional hard copy subscription arrangements.[10] Full text online is still prohibitively expensive for regular use; group IV fax is still some years away from universal acceptance; and satellite transmission is possible but again very expensive. Overall in the short term there appear to be no immediate technological innovations which will help to solve the problems of serial provision.

The way ahead – approach and mechanism

The paper has briefly indicated some of the methods by which managers can help to arrive at a decision on journal selection. A number of questions are raised. Are all of the techniques required or indeed necessary? If not, what is required? How can the best or most relevant be established? It is suggested that their establishment can only take place effectively if the library has a clearly focused set of ground rules. Consequently it is emphasized that overall a *systematic approach* is required. How can this be achieved? The following is proposed:

- define library objectives
- develop collection plan (within library objectives)
- designate manager with specific responsibility for collection development/ management
- establish precisely the purpose of the journal collection and a precise journal collection policy.

In formulating and/or reviewing the precise collection policy some of the following questions will have to be addressed. What, if any, areas should be collected comprehensively? Should gaps be filled within serial runs? Should the present policy of selection be maintained? Should there be an examination of cost-effectiveness? What is the most efficient method of provision? What place has optimization? – and so on.

If collections are to be optimized, information on use will be required and that has to be related to information about total costs to provide cost per use figures. This means that all operations associated with journal acquisitions have to be costed while information on use is collected. The comprehensive collection of use data can be time-consuming and expensive, and sampling may be required.

Even this information may be insufficient, since other factors such as immediacy of need and the need to meet new and changing research interests also need to be taken into account, as must the value of browsing and serendipity.

How then can the collected information be utilized effectively? Theoretical models exist (for example, that of Kraft[10]), but these involve time and energy and may be considered over-complicated. For those who have the technology, spreadsheets can be used; and eventually expert systems will come into use.

A decision may be made (perhaps by default) not to use measurement or develop a collection plan; if it is, there is a very real possibility in the long term of chaos and perpetuation of a sub-optimal collection.

In these circumstances it is therefore advisable that the optimization of the journal collection be given high priority and be pursued with vigour.

References

1 Miller, R. H. and Guilfoyle, M. C., 'Computer assisted periodical selection: structuring and subjective', *Serials librarian*, **10**, (3), 1986, 9–22.

2 Vickery, B. C., *Information systems dynamics*. London: British Library, 1983. (BL Research and Development Report 5758).

3 Line, M. B., 'Rank lists based on citations and library users as indicators of journal usage in individual libraries', *Collection management*, **2**, (4), 1978, 313–16.

4 MacDougall, A. F. and Woodward, H. M., *Optimization of serials holdings: a study of the chemistry and economics serials holdings in a university library.* Report to the British Library Research and Development Department, 1988.

5 Christiansen, D. E. *et al.*, 'Guide to collection evaluation through use and user studies', *Library resources and technical services*, **27**, (4), 1983, 432–40.

6   Gross, P. L. K. and Gross, E. M., 'College libraries and chemical education', *Science,* **66,** (1713), 28 Oct. 1927, 338.
7   Line, M. B. and Sandison, A., 'Practical interpretation of citation and library use studies', *College and research libraries,* **36,** (5), 1975, 393−6.
8   Pan, E., 'Journal citation as predictor of journal usage in libraries', *Collection management,* **2,** (1), 1978, 29−38.
9   MacDougall, A. F. *et al., Modelling of journal versus article acquisition by libraries: an evaluation of the relative cost effectiveness of different kinds of journal provision by libraries in the light of the possibilities offered by the electronic transmission of journal articles*, London, British Library, BNB Research Fund, 1985.
10 Kraft, D. H., 'Journal selection models: past and present', *Collection management,* **3,** (2/3), 1979, 163−85.

11

Acquisitions: grey literature

David N Wood and John P Chillag

Introduction

Grey literature, sometimes referred to as non-conventional or unconventional literature, can most usefully be defined as literature which is rarely available through normal bookselling channels. In most cases this is because it is essentially non-commercial, i.e. there is little demand for it from either individuals or libraries. For this reason grey literature does not figure prominently in the collection development policy statements of most libraries. It is material rarely acquired except in response to individual requests, and heart-rending selection decisions are few and far between. However, although selection as such may present few problems the acquisition difficulties can be enormous. Locating the correct bibliographic details, discovering the price, identifying a potential source of supply, getting the source to respond, dealing with the often unconventional document that is sent etc., can create more than enough headaches for even the most experienced acquisition librarian.

Library materials which can be included under the heading of grey literature are research and development reports, discussion papers, technical notes, preprints, ad hoc translations, some official publications, theses, local government documents, some conference proceedings and so on. Together they constitute an enormous mass of literature. For instance, US Government agencies alone issue over 100,000 research reports per annum; the recently established and still growing System for Information on Grey Literature in Europe (SIGLE) covers around 30,000 items per year; and it was suggested some time ago that 50,000 items per year are issued by UK local government offices. Moreover the amount of such literature is growing as 'research' output increases, as conventional publication costs increase, as the market for conventional publications decreases with shrinking library budgets, as the academic rewards for publishing, in any format, increase, and as more and more organizations and even individuals have the capability of 'publishing' through in-house systems.

Although most of this paper will be concerned with the organized schemes and systems which have been put in place over the years to make grey literature more accessible either for collection building or, more usually, in response to demand from individual users, it should be realized that only a proportion of the world's output gets 'trapped' by these systems. For this reason it is necessary for acquisition librarians to develop a network of personal contacts to discover what has been produced and by whom and to obtain what they need before supplies run out. The expertise necessary to develop and maintain such a network is such that it is sensible to concentrate the acquisition of grey literature in the hands of one individual in the acquisition department or in larger libraries to create a special section to handle it.

The following sections deal in turn with different categories of grey literature. However, it should be pointed out that there is a significant amount of overlap between categories and also that some of the systems and publications referred to cover both grey and conventionally published material.

Reports

Reports probably constitute the largest single category of grey literature. Reports can be defined as documents which contain results of, or progress made with, research and/or development work, investigations and surveys. Typically, the report is issued by the funding or performing body, it is usually not commercially published, and its contents escape any formal refereeing. It may be only available in microform and it is usually identified by unique numeric or alpha-numeric codes.

Bibliographic control of report literature is better in the USA than elsewhere. There, the four main agencies concerned with its collection, abstracting and announcement are NTIS, NASA, DOE and ERIC.

The National Technical Information Service (NTIS) covers all subject fields and disseminates some 70,000 reports annually, emanating originally from 4,000 organizations. The vast majority is material of US origin, but there is now also a significant amount of 'foreign' input. Information about and abstracts of the documents are given in the fortnightly *Government reports, announcements and index* (GRA&I). Annual indexes and various cumulative indexes, including a 15-year NTIS Title Index (Keyword, author, report number) on microfiche (1964–1978, plus biennial supplements), make 'manual' searching easy. The NTIS database can, however, also be accessed on-line from 1964 onwards. Most documents listed can be obtained from NTIS singly or within subject profiles as Selective Research in Microfiche (SRIM). The microfiches are also available from the British Library Document Supply Centre (BLDSC) in the UK and more selectively from libraries elsewhere. Hard copies, usually blowback enlargements, may be available through NTIS commercial sales agents in a number of countries.

Scientific and technical aerospace reports (STAR) of the National Aeronautics and Space Administration (NASA), together with *International aerospace abstracts* (IAA) of the American Institute of Aeronautics and Astronautics (AIAA), covers aerospace grey literature world wide. STAR concentrates on report material, IAA covers mainly conference papers. Aerospace research embraces many disciplines, although even so one can be in for surprises as one browses through the subject indexes.

For energy related grey literature the main listing tool is *Energy research abstracts* (ERA) of the US Department of Energy (DOE).

Educational grey documents are listed in *Resources in education* (RIE).

The reports themselves are available from the agencies responsible and in most cases also from NTIS. DSC also holds virtually all documents listed, usually as microfiche.

The overwhelming majority of microfiches are of very good quality; alas, some with comments in the bibliographic entry stating 'document is part illegible' may not be available at all. More frustrating, however, are some DOE microfiches which look perfect, but contain only a single frame stating that the original document is illegible/irreproducible, and has not therefore been reproduced.

Institutional publications lists are also useful search tools. These include *Index of NACA technical publications 1915–1949* and updates, and *Publications of the National Bureau of Standards 1901–1947* and annual updates.

All the titles mentioned above, except for RIE, tend to indicate that the material covered by them is entirely scientific and technical. Whilst this may have been true many years ago, about one quarter of the current report literature covers social sciences and humanities – anything from linguistics and management to Zimbabwe area studies.

In the UK BLDSC and its predecessors have always paid particular attention to grey literature and have built up a report collection now numbering about three million documents. To improve bibliographic control of British grey literature and to help to promote its use, *British research and development reports* was launched by the British Library in 1969, later to become *British reports, translations and theses* (BRTT). One third of the entries in BRTT relate to social science and humanities documents. The reports listed in BRTT form part of the UK and Republic of Ireland input into the System for Information on Grey Literature in Europe (SIGLE), to be described later.

In the Federal Republic of Germany the Fachinformationszentrum Energie, Physik, Mathematik (FIZ) produces the monthly *Forschungsberichte aus der Technik und Naturwissenschaften* (Reports in the fields of science and technology), which is published commercially by VCH Verlagsgesellschaft.

International bodies producing and disseminating report literature include INIS at the International Atomic Energy Agency. It produces twice a month *INIS atomindex* and semi-annual, annual and longer span indexes. Copies of most of the reports listed can be obtained on microfiche from the INIS Clearinghouse in Vienna.

Results of research activities of the European Communities are detailed in *EuroAbstracts* and the *Catalogue of EUR documents*.

The Advisory Group for Aeronautical Research and Development, better known by its acronym AGARD, and its parent body, the North Atlantic Treaty Organization (NATO), are responsible for grey literature documents well beyond what one would expect from their names. They issue documents not only on defence matters, but also for instance in the fields of library management, multiple sclerosis, and in one instance on the decay protection of medieval stained glass in cathedrals.

Official publications are usually listed by and available from 'government printers' in most countries. However, an increasing proportion of output is now 'published' by individual government departments, making identification and access very difficult. To track down such documents in the UK, Chadwyck-Healey has produced since 1981 a *Catalogue of British official publications not published by HMSO*. Similar attempts have been made at listing in other countries, but most such bibliographies seem to have been short-lived.

Even worse is the coverage of local authority documentation. Here there may be a valid excuse, since most documents in this category are of very local or ephemeral interest. *BRTT* lists annually some 400 British local authority documents out of a reputed 50,000 produced.

The BLDSC is a main depository library of the European Communities. Although there are large numbers of European Documentation Centres and depository libraries, not only in Community member states but also in most other countries, the BLDSC has probably the most comprehensive collection of European Communities documentation outside the Commission. This collection, held partly in hard copy and partly on microfiche, is becoming increasingly important with the approach of 1992 and the single European market. *European Communities publications: a guide to British Library resources* gives details of over a thousand serial publications of the European Communities.

Also held at BLDSC is a microfiche set of FAO documents, though material from most other members of the UN family is obtained only on demand after identification in *UNDOC*, etc. With *UNDOC*, document identification is relatively easy, once the relevant bibliography is published after a very long delay.

Theses

Anyone who has tried to identify and locate dissertations and doctoral theses will know how apt the term grey literature is for this type of material.

In discussing theses and dissertations and their availability, it is convenient to divide them into American, British and others.

Theses presented at mainland European universities are generally available through the booktrade. They are listed in publications such as *Bibliographie de la France* (Sup D) , the *Jahresverzeichnis der Hochschulschriften . . .* etc.

The majority of American dissertations have for many years been abstracted in *Dissertations abstracts international* (DAI). Produced by the same publishers, University Microfilms International (UMI), are the retrospective searching aid *Comprehensive dissertations index 1861–1972* as well as *American doctoral dissertations* and *Masters abstracts*. Many, but not all, institutions whose dissertations are announced in DAI etc. make their dissertations available through UMI. Some – for example, the University of Chicago and Harvard University – have to be approached directly. In the UK many of the American dissertations are available through the BLDSC, which acquired from 1970 to 1978 the total output of current dissertations in the UMI programme. Most requests for US dissertations *now* are satisfied by the BLDSC either from its stock, by on-demand purchase or through interlibrary loans.

The BLDSC is the main source for most of the post-1970 British doctoral theses. In 1970 a scheme was started for the microfilming, announcement and supply of British doctoral theses. The scheme continues to expand, with most British universities participating (exceptions being London and Swansea), and by 1988 over 80,000 British theses had been filmed at Boston Spa. The filmed theses, all of which are available from BLDSC, are listed in BRTT, and more recently also in DAI. Select subject listings have also been issued by the *British theses service* (BRITS) operated in conjunction with BLDSC by Information Publications International.

Index to theses with abstracts accepted for higher degrees by the universities of Great Britain and Ireland and the Council for National Academic Awards, published by Aslib, should also be mentioned. It lists British doctoral and masters' theses. The theses themselves, however, are available only from the BLDSC, or in some cases from the university concerned.

In addition, universities throughout the world provide lists and information about their own theses and dissertations, and listings of particular subjects prepared by interested bodies may also be available.

Conferences – proceedings, papers, preprints etc.

It is a long and complicated journey from the first thought of holding a conference, through the organization of its venue and programme, inviting papers, chasing authors for their contributions to the climax of the conference itself and the subsequent publication of the proceedings.

The vast majority of conference 'proceedings', which are published as commercial monographs or as articles in conventional journals, fall outside the scope of this paper. However, about a quarter of them are disseminated somewhat haphazardly through non-commercial channels, in limited print runs, sometimes only as preprints and often only to conference delegates. Problems relating to their acquisition place this type of material well within the definition of grey literature.

In the United Kingdom, the BLDSC plays a major role in the identification, acquisition, bibliographic control, announcement and provision of conference material. At the end of 1988, the BLDSC's collection included material from over 260,000 conferences, with documents from some 17,000 conferences added annually. In addition to the announcement of these acquisitions in *Index to conference proceedings received*, the conference database is also accessible online through BLAISELINE.

Translations

Only about one half of the world's literature is published in English, and many scientists in the English-speaking world will on occasion face the problem of language barriers. It should be remembered that very large numbers of articles, reports and books have been translated, and that locating a translation is a very much cheaper task than commissioning a translation. Not all translations however fall into the category of grey literature. For example, there are many commercially translated and published books on the market. There are hundreds of (mainly Russian) journals which are regularly translated in their entirety or selectively. *Journals in translation*, published jointly by the British Library and the International Translations Centre, provides details of these.

However, there is a vast number of translations of individual journal articles, reports, etc. produced, often for internal purposes, by government agencies, universities, industrial companies and laboratories. Translations of this kind are rarely published. In the UK, the BLDSC has collected over the years over half a million such translations and maintains an internal card index for their retrieval. Current input of translations from British sources is also included in *British reports, translations and theses*.

Like many national centres BLDSC works closely with the International Translations Centre in Delft. It provides information which is incorporated into an international database, *World translations index*, made available by ITC in hard copy and online. Document supply sources are indicated on the database. Probably the largest centre for such ad hoc translations, the National Translations Center in Chicago, closed down at the end of 1988. Its collecting and document supply activities have been taken over by the Library of Congress.

System for Information on Grey Literature in Europe (SIGLE)

The problems of acquisition, bibliographic control and access to grey literature led the Commission of the European Communities to assist with the setting up of SIGLE in 1981. The main aim of SIGLE is to improve bibliographic coverage and accessibility of grey literature by combining the resources offered by important national information/document supply centres in a number of European Community countries. The main participants in the scheme are the British Library, FIZ Karlsruhe in West Germany and the Centre National de la Recherche Scientifique in France. Input is also provided by the Netherlands, Italy, Belgium, Luxembourg, the Commission itself, and by Ireland (through BLDSC). The SIGLE database now includes details of over 80,000 documents; it is accessible through BLAISELINE, STN and SUNIST.

Supplementary publications

For a variety of reasons publishers of conventional books and journals may decide not to print lengthy, often very specialized, texts in their entirety, and need to find ways of making these unpublished parts accessible. In the process another category of grey literature has been created. In the UK, in consultation with editors of learned journals, BLDSC operates a scheme for the storage and supply of the detailed material omitted from the articles in these journals. This collection of 'supplementary publications' now numbers some 13,000 documents. Similar schemes exist elsewhere. Reference to the availability of this material is usually given in the published work.

In conclusion it is worth reiterating what was said at the start of this brief paper, that although there are many and varied systems around the world to help provide access to lots of grey literature, much can still only be identified and acquired by making direct contact with the individuals and organizations which produce it. One way of obtaining this information is to consult research registers. These range from the highly specific such as *The role of women in society − a guide to European research*, to the very general such as *Current research in Britain*, published annually in four volumes and containing 70,000 projects in all subject fields.

12

Preservation and conservation

Peter Fox

Introduction

It is only comparatively recently that academic librarians have begun to take seriously their responsibilities towards the preservation of their collections. The great expansion of higher education in the years since the Second World War was accompanied by the development of a library management policy characterized by ever greater exploitation of the collections through open access storage, increased use, extensive photocopying, etc. The curatorial aspect of academic librarianship had, to say the least, become unfashionable.

Preservation − or, more accurately, conservation − was seen as the preserve of rare book or manuscript librarians and something remote from the high-technology information provision of the general academic library. Librarians in North America started to become aware of the error of this assumption in the late 1970s; those in the United Kingdom and other parts of Europe in the early 1980s. An American librarian commented that he attended a conference of the heads of British university libraries in 1983 and, although part of the conference was devoted to preservation, he noted that 'the apathy among the attendees was palpable'.[1] Fortunately progress in the last five years has been considerable.

In the United Kingdom the seminal document is the report of the Cambridge Conservation Project. This project had two objectives: 'to establish the facts about preservation policies and practices in libraries in the UK and to identify the educational and training facilities available to librarians and practitioners'.[2] In his preface Wilson comments that 'some readers might find the contents distressing: certainly its findings will come as a shock to many'.[3]

The report reveals that 'few libraries have a methodology for systematic screening of their collections and for conservation management. There is a vicious circle, whereby the practising element of the profession has neglected collection maintenance, the library schools have taken their cue in concentrating upon the use of new technology for library housekeeping and for information provision, squeezing out in the process that consideration of the physical book which has been regarded as redundant to the young professional librarian of these past 20 years. Consequently, middle and junior management in our libraries are often ignorant of the book as artefact and the vicious circle is completed by that lack of concern for the management of the collections to which one has referred'.[4]

The report was concerned with preservation policies in all types of library − public, academic and government. One of its principal findings was that preservation was − or rather should be − a matter of concern to all librarians, not just those in national or research libraries or those concerned with rare books or manuscripts. There are, it is true, a few libraries whose policy is to make their stock work as hard as possible over a relatively short period and then discard it. In those libraries which have adopted such a policy, preservation is, rightly, not a matter of concern. But libraries such as these are in a minority. The survey had responses from over 300 libraries, and only one university library proposed to retain none of its stock on a permanent basis. Only eight academic (university and polytechnic) libraries proposed to retain less than 10% of their stock, whilst over 50 academic libraries proposed to retain more than 80% of their stock.

Even in those libraries in, for example, technological universities, where much of the stock may be destined for eventual discarding, there may be collections of special significance − the books or papers of scientists or engineers, or other materials which will not be disposed of. If this is the case, then that library has a preservation problem and needs a preservation policy. The development of such a preservation policy is the topic of this paper.

Three essential elements for an effective preservation policy are:

1 an understanding of the factors which cause deterioration in library materials;
2 a knowledge of the options available to retard, reduce or repair this deterioration, including the use of surrogates;
3 an assessment of the value or importance of individual books or groups of items in the collection. This must be seen not just in the context of the individual library but in terms of the wider availability of library materials.

Some of the measures required demand a level of investment which is beyond the scope of a single library, however large, and must be approached at a national or international level.

The causes of damage to library materials are of four main types: environmental hazards, physical damage caused by inadequate storage conditions or improper handling, damage caused by chemical reactions in the materials themselves, and a disaster such as a fire or flood.

Environmental hazards

Temperature and relative humidity
If library materials are stored in unsuitable environmental conditions deterioration will inevitably result. It is important that the temperature and the relative humidity should remain constant and not fluctuate between extremes. A cool environment is preferable to one where high temperatures prevail as it helps to retard any chemical reactions resulting from other causes. Even a small reduction in temperature has the effect of greatly prolonging the life of a book or document. The IFLA *Principles for the preservation and conservation of library materials*, which provide very useful guidance, recommend a temperature range in storage areas of 16°−21°C.[5] There is an obvious conflict between the cool environment recommended for books and the demands of readers' comfort. Too great a divergence between the temperature

in storage areas and that in reading rooms should be avoided, as the movement of materials from one area to the other can cause the damaging fluctuations that have already been referred to. In modern, open plan libraries, where readers and books share the same environment, a temperature suitably low for books is not acceptable to readers and so it is necessary to reach a compromise. A range of 18°−20°C is acceptable, provided that the relative humidity is kept stable and fairly low. Too high a humidity can assist in the growth of micro-organisms. The IFLA *Principles* recommend a relative humidity of between 40% and 60%.

Many academic libraries are situated in the polluted atmosphere of large cities, where air-borne particles − dust and dirt − represent a further danger. Dust is abrasive and carries chemically harmful matter. Full air-conditioning, where it can be afforded and where continuous operation can be assured, provides the best protection, but in libraries without air conditioning every attempt should be made either to filter the air or to ensure that windows and doors are adequately sealed when closed.

The British Isles are fortunate in having a reasonably equable climate, which does not normally suffer from the great changes of temperature and humidity experienced elsewhere in the world. Clearly the above comments would have to be modified to suit local conditions. Where local factors, either of prevailing weather conditions or of inadequacies in the building, render it impossible to control the environment of the whole library, it may be necessary to restrict such controls to particularly valuable or vulnerable parts of the collection.

Light

Light is energy and it encourages the chemical decomposition of organic materials. Ultra-violet light, which is present in daylight and fluorescent light, is the most harmful part of the spectrum as it causes inks to fade and paper to become brittle. An ultra-violet filtering film can be fixed to the windows of areas where books are exposed to daylight and ultra-violet filters can be fitted to fluorescent tubes.

When books or papers are put on exhibition and the same page is held open for some considerable time, it is particularly important to eliminate ultra-violet light and reduce the overall light level. A level of 50 lux on the surface of the exhibits is regarded as the maximum safe light level. It is also important to limit the amount of time an item in an exhibition is exposed to light. In Trinity College Dublin, for example, we would never display the same page for more than six months at a time, and for particularly delicate material this period of time would be significantly reduced.

Physical damage

A great deal of unnecessary damage is done to library materials by staff and readers. Much of this is caused by carelessness and a lack of awareness. The development of a consciousness of and a commitment to preservation among all levels of staff, not just among conservators and binders, is a crucial element of any library's preservation policy. It is also an element that can be introduced with relatively little expense. A particularly constructive approach is to include instruction in matters such as book handling in one's general staff training programme. In this way a development of the awareness necessary to prevent damage to the library stock is not seen as something 'apart' but as an integral part of one's working life.

Behind such training would be the encouragement of a realization among staff that, in carrying out many of their daily routines, they may unwittingly be causing damage to the items in their care. There are several examples of guidelines which libraries have produced for their staff on matters such as how to handle books: when taking them from shelves or replacing them, when carrying them around, when loading trolleys, and in particular when using that infernal machine which has probably caused more damage to books than anything else over the past 20 years – the photocopier. The Public Archives of Canada has produced, for example, an attractive illustrated booklet intended for both readers and staff, with a series of do's and dont's.[6] Other libraries convey the same message by means of notes for the guidance of readers, placed in reading rooms, or by bookmarks with a simple message.[7]

Some examples of the type of measures which can be taken to reduce physical damage may seem so obvious as to be just basic common sense, but any librarian walking round his own library will see instances of potential or actual damage being done to books by either readers or staff.

Carefully planned use of shelving can help to reduce the risk of damage. Very large and small books should not be shelved together; pressure on the large books will be uneven and there is a risk that the small ones will slip down the back of the shelf. If books are shelved on their fore-edges because the shelves are too close together the bookblock will very quickly break away from the binding. If books are allowed to project beyond the side of a trolley they can easily be damaged by collision with a bookstack or doorway as the trolley is being moved. Library staff need to be taught to look and think critically with preservation in mind.

Repair and binding

There is a great temptation for untrained staff to carry out do-it-yourself repairs using, for example, adhesive tape. This should never be used on any library materials, as it begins to degrade almost as soon as it has been applied, and over a period of years it will separate from the paper leaving not only the original damage that it was used to repair, but also a brown stain which will chemically destroy the paper. There *are* simple techniques for the repair of books even by relatively untrained staff, but some training in the proper procedures is required.

There is also a need to exercise control over the activities of bindery staff, whether they be internal or external. One might assume that a commercial binder is aware of the correct techniques to be used; but while he may be aware of them, he may in fact use techniques which are positively destructive, in the interests of economy, which may transpire to be false economy. Each library should draw up clear binding specifications and should be aware that if a particular technique is selected purely because it is cheap it may render impossible any future rebinding.

Environmental control in the library and training in the proper handling of library materials will help to reduce or retard decay but they will not eliminate it.

Chemical hazards

A quotation from Rutherford Rogers, when he was Yale University Librarian, may help to place in context a discussion of the problem of 'brittle books': 'It has been said that the custodial staff at Yale sweeps up a book a day in the stacks of the Sterling Memorial Library. At that rate, it would take a long time to deplete the four million books shelved there. Unfortunately, however, the pieces added to the garbage cans each day are not from the same book'.[8]

Most librarians today are aware of the problem of the 'brittle book' or of 'brittle paper'. Unlike the other causes of decay in library materials which have already been considered and which are external to the book, the problem of brittle paper is inherent in the book itself. Until about the middle of the last century, paper was made mainly of rag. Much modern paper, however, is made of wood pulp, which contains chemicals − particularly lignin, alum, rosin, iron and copper − which render it chemically unstable and cause chemical reactions to take place within the paper itself. Control of the environmental conditions in which library materials are stored will, as has been indicated, help to retard these reactions, but it will not stop them completely. Furthermore, since the process is irreversible, it is clear that much damage must already have been done and that many libraries must have large numbers of books for which the only treatment is to confine them to Rutherford Rogers' garbage can.

Convincing documentation has been produced to demonstrate the scale of the problem. The British Library's collections in London have eleven million volumes published since 1850, and surveys show that about 15% have paper which is so brittle that it requires treatment. This represents over one and a half million books, for which conservation treatment would cost £80 million; or, if they were to be microfilmed, the microfilming would take 1,600 camera years. The Bibliothèque Nationale in Paris estimates that 800,000 of its books are in a similar condition. In the Library of Congress 77,000 volumes become 'brittle' *every year. All* books published in the Philippines between 1790 and 1900 are in poor condition. It is estimated that in the United States some $400 million is needed to address the brittle book problem.[9, 10]

Environmental control and the avoidance of physical damage are essentially preventative elements of a preservation policy. But it is inevitable that, however carefully the environment is controlled, however carefully staff and users handle the books, problems caused by chemical damage will still occur.

In drawing up a preservation policy, an obvious starting point is an analysis of the scale of the problem in one's own library. This is particularly important if additional funding for the programme is to be sought. A visual inspection of the shelves will indicate damaged bindings and loose pages. A survey is necessary to establish the extent of the brittle book problem, though the statistics quoted will indicate the probable extent for any particular library. An informal survey, carrying out a simple fold test, is a salutory exercise for any academic librarian sceptical about whether or not they have a brittle book problem. The fold test is a crude measure of paper strength and is in itself destructive but, for a more extensive survey, other, less damaging, methods have been devised, such as, for example, the use of a hand burst-tester to produce a small u-shaped cut, which then effectively closes again.

The result of such a survey will almost certainly indicate, in a library with a significant number of books published between 1850 and 1950, that the scale of the problem is such that traditional conservation treatment − the chemical processing and hand repair of each book and the rebinding of it to restore it, as far as possible, to its original condition − is out of the question. One must, therefore, assess the various options available, which range from this very expensive process to the opposite extreme of taking no action at all. This assessment must be carried out in conjunction with a review of the importance of the items involved.

Preservation options

Preservation treatment must be cost-effective. The measures taken must be appropriate to the value and use of the material.

A useful approach was given by Clements.[10] who developed a matrix setting out the broad types of preservation treatment and related them to the value and expected use of the item.

In very broad terms there are three principal courses of action in establishing a preservation policy:

to leave the item in its original format and carry out appropriate conservation
to produce a surrogate in a different format
to do nothing.

The first of these has been, and probably still is, the most common method of dealing with a preservation problem. An assessment of what is appropriate conservation is a task which should be carried out by the librarian or curator in conjunction with the conservator. The librarian can assess the importance of the item and the amount of use it is likely to receive. The conservator is then in a position to assess the appropriate treatment, based on his experience of the types of treatment possible, their comparative cost, and the condition of the item or collection in question. Generally the conservator will operate on the principle of minimum intervention.

There is a danger that the policy makers in those libraries which have conservation laboratories may have found themselves lulled into a false sense of security in taking the view that they were gradually catching up on the decay of the past and that eventually all of their collections would be restored to, if not pristine condition, then at least a usable condition. The awful truth is really only now sinking in that not only are they not catching up but that, even with additional resources at a level at present undreamed of, they will never be in the position of being able to ensure the preservation of all those items in their libraries which they wish to preserve. It is not so much a question of preserving an item now or later; it is a question of preserving it now or never. And it may have to be never.

It will be necessary for difficult decisions to be taken, in effect to select those items which will be allowed to deteriorate and will eventually be discarded. Until recently such deterioration has been taking place in a random fashion in libraries all over the world. A principal objective should be to ensure that the inevitable deterioration of large numbers of books is a planned deterioration. This involves not just devising a preservation policy for one's own library but ensuring that it conforms to a national or international policy. Put very crudely, there is little point in 20 libraries in different parts of the world conserving 20 copies of the same 'rare' book whilst in 100 libraries all the copies of certain titles published during the Second World War disintegrate to the point where the books, and the text inside them, are lost forever. Planning on an international scale is urgently needed, and the first moves in this direction are now taking place.

In determining appropriate treatment, one of the criteria must be that of value. Traditionally this has been held to be the bibliographical value of an item: perhaps an item which is important as an example of printing or binding technique, or significant in the context of the history of the book, or one in which the illustrations

95

are important. The fact that a book is old does not of course necessarily mean that it is valuable, and it is perhaps rather unfortunate that many libraries have hitherto concentrated their conservation work on their 'rare' — that is 'old' — books, even though they may be in fact more stable than parts of the modern collections.

Some libraries have a responsibility to maintain an archive or collection of national or local importance. This has meant until recently — certainly for the legal deposit libraries — that this collection should be maintained in its original format. It is clear, however, that the scale of the problem is such that this is no longer possible and that judgement will now have to be exercised as to whether some items should be transferred to other media, or whether they must be allowed to deteriorate. Value begins to take on a different meaning in this context and here co-operation between libraries becomes a part of preservation policy. The six libraries which receive United Kingdom publications under legal deposit legislation (the British Library, the National Libraries of Scotland and Wales, the Bodleian Library Oxford, Cambridge University Library and Trinity College Library Dublin) are at present discussing the formulation of a joint preservation policy for this type of material.

In a large collection an assessment of value is very difficult and time-consuming, but it is essential if a preservation policy is to be applied on a comprehensive basis. Individual items of value may be relatively easy to identify. In some areas there may be collections consisting of books which in themselves are of no great value but as a collection represent an important contribution to social or cultural history. Use of the conspectus methodology (see the paper in this volume by Heaney) may be a means of placing comparative values on the different parts of the collection.

Use, either perceived or expected, is the other major criterion to be considered. All use results in some wear and tear. On the whole library users prefer to have access to the originals rather than substitutes such as microfilm. In some cases the use to which an item is put, for example reference material in heavy demand, determines that the book is still the most appropriate format and that the item should be preserved in this format as long as possible. In other cases (newspapers are the most obvious example) microform is now so widely used as to have become accepted, even if it is not liked.

Conservation of the original

An item which is assessed to be in low use and which has, say, loose boards but a textblock which is chemically stable may need no further treatment than to be placed in an acid-free box. The phased box was developed in the 1970s at the Library of Congress and is so called because it forms a part of a phased programme of conservation. It is a simple box made of neutral board which can be quickly made up by staff with only a basic training. It costs only a pound or two. More elaborate drop-back boxes can be used for more valuable or more frequently used material; these can cost £40 or more.

Loose papers such as archives can be treated in the same way. Sometimes it is necessary to treat the paper to reduce the acidity before placing it in a box; with other materials the use of neutral interleaving is adequate, with deacidification essential only if the item is to be encapsulated. The principle of minimum intervention still pertains. One must stabilize the paper and then house it in a protective box to prevent further degradation.

Binding or rebinding is the traditional method of conservation for books and to some extent for manuscripts. But it is expensive, regardless of whether it is carried out in-house or commercially, and is coming to be used more and more only for items which are in heavy demand or which are of bibliographical importance. One must also ensure that the techniques used by the binders are not in themselves destructive to the material you are trying to preserve. The need to establish and insist upon acceptable binding specifications has already been referred to.

There are, however, methods of binding which are very much cheaper than those done to traditional commercial standards. The Conservation Laboratory in Trinity College Library Dublin has developed a method of strengthening modern paperbacks which is easily taught, costs almost nothing in materials and involves a unit time of about half an hour. Moreover the process is reversible, so that if a book turns out to be in heavier demand than expected, it can still be fully bound, as none of the original bookblock has been destroyed.

In locations where the visual appearance of the books on the shelves is important, for example in a library where they form an architectural feature, the use of boxes would be inappropriate. A possible solution here would be to use a so-called 'book shoe', which is a form of slip-case made from neutral board, creased to fit the individual book. It holds the text and boards together and provides the necessary protection without detracting from the appearance.[11]

The preservation of large numbers of books in their original format is possible at present only through the use of mass deacidification or similar techniques, and even these are beyond the reach of practically all libraries. It is to be hoped, however, that, through cooperative projects they will become more widely available. Mass deacidification involves the treatment of large quantities of books at a time with either a liquid or a gas which reduces the acidity of the paper and stabilizes it. It will not reverse the deterioration, but if the books are still in usable condition they will remain so. The Library of Congress has developed a process using the gas diethyl-zinc and the National Library of Canada a liquid-based process. There is also a mass deacidification facility in France, and West Germany is carrying out a feasibility study. Mass deacidification techniques can not only be used to prevent further deterioration of materials which are already partly degraded, but can also be used on new books. At the National Library of Canada, for example, all new books that are suited to this technique are treated as they are received in the library in order to prevent their becoming a problem in the future.

Surveys indicate that books published from about 1870 to 1920 tend to have become the most brittle, but as the years go by later books will of course reach the same state, and since the majority of modern books are printed on acidic paper the problem is simply being stored up for the future.

In order to try and reduce this, a number of bodies in several countries are trying to encourage the use of acid-free paper in book production, and a growing proportion of books are now being printed on such paper. In 1980 it was estimated that about 25% of the paper manufactured in the United States for book production was acid-free and, thanks to the efforts of bodies such as the Council on Library Resources, this percentage has now increased. In its report on book longevity the Council on Library Resources stated that 'acid-free paper need not be more expensive than acidic paper of the quality normally used in hardbound books'.[12]

The Ratcliffe report[2] suggested that many publishers did not use acid-free paper simply because they were not aware of its effect in prolonging the life of the book.

97

A campaign has also been undertaken in the United Kingdom under the auspices of the Library Association, the National Preservation Office and the Publishers' Association, and a leaflet called *Permanent paper* has been widely distributed.[13]

Surrogates

The second possible course of action is to produce a surrogate of the original in a different format. This course would be selected when the physical form of the original is of little importance compared to its content, and particularly when the original has reached a level of degradation that the sort of conservation work just discussed would be either impossible or too expensive for the value of the item concerned. Obviously format conversion means that all the physical elements of the original are lost and precludes any further study of typography, watermarks, binding or ink. But in many cases it may be the most appropriate course of action.

The most widely used medium at present is microfilm, and, although it is not generally liked by readers, the technology itself and the archival qualities of correctly prepared and stored silver-gelatin microfilm are now well established. The hardware needed both to produce it and make it available to readers is also well proven and easily acquired. The cost of microfilming a 300-page book would be about £20.

A great deal has been said about the text storage possibilities of newer media, such as digital optical disks, CD-ROMs, WORMs, etc. Their capacity for storing data is undoubtedly prodigious, but their archival properties are unproven and, with the rapid advance of new developments in this field, there is no guarantee that manufacturers will continue to support a particular medium. Care must be taken, therefore, in selecting a surrogate medium, as there is no point in choosing one which will have an even shorter life than the original.

Having transferred the text of an item to another format, one is then faced with the question of what to do with the original. In some cases, in the interests of economy, the microfilming programme for books of no intrinsic physical value is designed in such a way that the book is effectively destroyed in the process, and so it is simply discarded. Some libraries may decide to keep the original and restrict its use to those occasions when the microfilm is inadequate. Or they may simply keep the original without taking any further action, knowing that eventually they will have to discard it when it deteriorates, but in the knowledge that they have preserved the text in a surrogate form. Such an approach would of course also permit the subsequent deacidification of the original if cheap means of mass deacidification become available.

Although microfilming is usually cheaper than hand conservation, the cost of processing a large number of books is substantial. It is necessary, therefore, to ensure that the money is being spent wisely and is not being wasted by duplicating work carried out elsewhere. In an attempt to avoid this, registers of microform masters are being established, so that libraries can check if a particular book has been microfilmed before they embark on it themselves. The British Library has set up such a register for microforms held in libraries in the British Isles, and it is intended that this should be available via its online databases. The linking of this with a European register and with that already in existence in North America has also been proposed. The British Library has also recently received a grant of $1.5 million from the Andrew W. Mellon Foundation to assist with the microfilming of material in libraries in the British Isles for inclusion in this register.

Planned deterioration

The third possible course of action is to allow the item to deteriorate without taking any further action.. From the above, it should be clear that this is a course of action which will be forced upon most libraries in respect of some parts of their collections. But an objective of a library's preservation policy should be to ensure that this is planned rather than random deterioration. It should be the fate of the items which are of low value and in low use and, if possible, those which have been selected in coordination with libraries elsewhere so that at least one copy is being preserved either in the original or in surrogate form somewhere in the world and can be made available to the occasional scholar who may need it.

Disaster planning

The causes of degradation of library collections which have been considered so far are slow processes; a disaster is something which happens quickly but can be equally or more destructive, and a plan for dealing with a disaster should be a part of every library's preservation policy. One tends to think of a disaster in terms of a fire or a major flood. But small disasters are much more common than one might think and can be very damaging. Trinity College Library Dublin, for example, which has been revising its disaster plan during the last two years, has in that time suffered water damage to parts of the collection from two burst pipes and leakage into a basement during a severe storm. It has also been called in to assist two other libraries in Dublin with similar problems. Evidence from other libraries in the British Isles suggests that this experience is by no means unusual.

A number of sample disaster plans have been published, and it is unnecessary to repeat here the guidance given in them. That from the National Library of Scotland is an excellent example, which has been adopted as a model by libraries in several other countries.[14]

Conclusion

This paper has attempted to cover some of the management considerations in developing a library preservation policy. The preventative elements have been stressed as much as the curative ones not only because they *are* equally important but also because they represent an area where action costing relatively little can have an immediate impact. Perhaps the most important need of all is to develop a co-operative approach, at the local level, between the librarian and the conservator, whether he be a member of the library staff or a person hired on a contract basis. Only in this way can an accurate assessment of the appropriate treatment be arrived at in terms of the value and use of the item or collection concerned. This cooperative approach is also needed at the national or international level, through a shared programme between libraries with major research collections.

References

1   Stam, David, 'International programmes in preservation', *in Preserving the word: proceedings of the Library Association Conference, Harrogate 1986*, edited by R. E. Palmer, London, Library Association, 1987, 10.
2   Ratcliffe, F. W., *Preservation policies and conservation in British libraries: report of the Cambridge University Library Conservation Project*, London, British Library, 1984, iv. (Library and information research report, 25).

3   See ref.2, ix.
4   See ref.2, ix, x.
5   Dureau, J. M. and Clements, D. W. G., *Principles for the preservation and conservation of library materials*, The Hague, International Federation of Library Associations and Institutions, 1986, 7. (IFLA professional reports, 8).
6   Canada. Public Archives, *Fragile: handle with care; a guide to the preservation of archival materials*, [Ottawa], Public Archives Canada, 1981. Other guides are listed in the bibliography by G. M. Cunha and D. G. Cunha, *Library and archives conservation: 1980s and beyond*, Metuchen, N.J., and London, Scarecrow, 1983.
7   For example, a series of bookmarks depicting cheese, celery, bacon, bread and jam has been issued by the British Library's National Preservation Office.
8   Rogers, Rutherford D., 'Library preservation: its scope, history and importance', *in The Library preservation program: models, priorities, possibilities*, edited by R. E. Palmer, London, Library Association, 1987, 19.
9   See ref.1, 11.
10 Clements, David, 'Policy planning in the UK: from national to local', *in Preserving the word: proceedings of the Library Association Conference, Harrogate 1986*, edited by R. E. Palmer, London, Library Association, 1987, 19.
11 Examples of these and similar techniques are given in Cains, A. and Swift, K., *Preserving our printed heritage: the Long Room Project at Trinity College Dublin*, Dublin, Trinity College Library, 1988.
12 Council on Library Resources, *Book longevity: reports of the Committee on Production Guidelines for Book Longevity*, Washington, D. C., The Council, 1982.
13 *Permanent paper*, London, Library Association, 1986.
14 Anderson, H. and McIntyre, J. E., *Planning manual for disaster control in Scottish libraries and record offices*, Edinburgh, National Library of Scotland, 1985.

13

Cataloguing and subject access

Philip Bryant

Introduction

Just prior to his appointment as Librarian at Bath University, Maurice Line wrote with Michael Grose an article entitled 'On the construction and care of white elephants: some fundamental questions concerning the library catalogue'.[1] This has, over the years, provided a good deal of the motivation for the work of the Bath Centre. It argued that very little attempt had been made to consider cataloguing from first principles. They also said that 'the problems of mechanizing catalogues are such that it is essential that we know what exactly we are mechanizing and why'. At about the same time an authoritative voice, that of Donald Urquhart, questioned the need for individual libraries to have catalogues at all; in 1971 he wrote that the National Lending Library (now the Document Supply Centre) had asked itself the question 'What library records are really necessary?'[2] This question provides an excellent starting point for consideration of the management of cataloguing and classification.

Over the past 20 years there have been two quite distinct attitudes. One is a pragmatic approach which recognizes that money is limited. Economic pressures do not allow for the luxury of investing large amounts of costly staff time in the maintenance of elaborate and detailed descriptive cataloguing and classification practices which have often appeared to serve little purpose other than to create a mystique and a body of arcane knowledge. The second attitude is that of those dedicated librarians involved in activities like the IFLA programme for Universal Bibliographic Control (UBC) who believe strongly that the highest standards should be met by strict adherence to such protocols as AACR2, ISBDs, the MARC format, and by the inclusion of full bibliographic description in the catalogue records produced, and that such adherence is essential for the adequate sharing of records.

The first attitude has been adopted by an increasing number of librarians and has led to the downgrading, or abolition, of many cataloguing posts. Library schools have ceased to give the prominence to cataloguing and classification that these subjects once enjoyed in the curriculum. The assumption has been that either one joins a shared cataloguing service and acquires the majority of records from that source, or else that brief catalogue records are created in-house. But has this attitude been a well-founded one? I have definite views about the need to economize on cataloguing effort, both at the local and national levels; and about the need not to create unnecessary mystiques, and not to presume that we know what is best for our users. Nevertheless, I also believe that it is easy to over-simplify the situation.

Objectives

The idea of *service* is essential if we are to identify the right objectives. I have tried to sum these up in one sentence: 'Cataloguing and classification should be used for the *control* and *exploitation* of *library stocks* in a *cost-effective* manner.'

Control

This is surely at the core of the management of our libraries. We are not supervisors of chaotic warehouses, not knowing about, or caring for, what is in our charge — are we? I have to admit that some 'failure' surveys, and some of my own experiences, make me question sometimes how good the 'control' really is. The better we control our stocks the more likely we are to encourage their proper 'exploitation'.

Exploitation

One aspect to satisfactory 'exploitation' is the clear identification of what is in the collection to ensure that specifically requested items can be retrieved rapidly, and their whereabouts made known, in order that needless applications are not being made to other libraries for items already in the local library's own possession. A second aspect is the revelation of the content of the library's stock — especially subject content — in order that additional, or alternative, sources of information can be made available to users.

Library stocks

I said in a paper in 1982

> I am concerned about how well the catalogue can assist the user to exploit the stock for the 99%-plus of the loans made from it and for the countless uses of items within the library. I am particularly interested in how effective it can become in revealing material within the library's stock which would otherwise remain unexploited. Libraries' stocks represent a considerable capital investment. We all know about the poor return on that investment and how a relatively small proportion of the stock is responsible for the majority of recorded use. What is so worrying is that, although we put so much into the establishment of schemes of cooperation, we may well be making quite significant use of these schemes to satisfy demands which should be being met by the existing local stock.[3]

We know that we should have as our final objective 'cost-effectiveness'.

Cost-effective

The trouble with 'costs' is that they are so mercurial. Just when we think that we have contained them they have a habit of emerging elsewhere. Maybe we have joined a shared cataloguing cooperative, but are refusing to accept the records we receive as they stand. Perhaps we are saving costs for the library by simplifying our catalogue records and classification practices, but we may be transferring the costs to our users in terms of wasted time and missed items; maybe we are ignoring the costs that lie hidden in making schemes of resource sharing work.

Cataloguing may be being downgraded, and the term 'catalogue record' seems increasingly outdated, but interest in the 'bibliographical record' has never been greater. The great increase in the number of automated integrated library systems (ILS) with their associated acquisitions modules means that the bibliographic records needed in order for them to operate are required at a much earlier stage than previously. They also have to serve the whole range of library functions – selection, ordering, cataloguing, circulation and so on. The development of online public access catalogues (OPACs) and the networking facilities for linking them, not only to each other, but also to many other types of database, calls for a radical re-examination of the data to be included in the bibliographic records created and acquired. The whole of the bibliographic community – publishers, booksellers and commercial bibliographic data suppliers as well as librarians – are becoming increasingly interested in, and indeed concerned about, the content of the multi-functional bibliographic record.

Content

I first became involved in studying the content of catalogue records when I started in 1969 to develop the 'Bath Mini-Catalogue'.[4] This was a complete retrospective conversion of the Bath University library catalogue using a basic record format which was about one sixth the length of the then UK MARC record. The aim behind this exercise was to concentrate on providing flexibility of *access* rather than fullness of bibliographic *description*. As a result of developing the Bath Mini-Catalogue a grant was awarded in 1972 by the then Office for Scientific and Technical Information to undertake the Bath University Comparative Catalogue Study (BUCCS).[5] This compared the performance of four different physical forms (card, printed, COM roll-film and COM-fiche) and four different sequences of catalogue (name, title, keyword out of context, and UDC classified) using the same brief record format as that developed for the Bath Mini-Catalogue. In 1977, following an approach from the British Library, the Bath Centre commenced research into the relative merits of full and short entry catalogues. The aim was to find out how far the content of a bibliographic record should be influenced by users' requirements.[6]

A catalogue record consists of:

(a) bibiographic description
(b) access points
(c) main heading structure
(d) subject information
(e) local information (e.g. location and holdings data).

The Bath Mini-Catalogue, the BUCCS project and the full and short entry catalogues study were principally concerned with (a) and (b) and a little with (c), but (d) and (e) were excluded from the studies. During the last couple of years, however, (d) has been the focus of much discussion nationally and internationally. Recent developments in automation have led to a marked demand for more and improved subject information to be included. This requirement has been recognized as important by the bibliographic community as a whole and not only by librarians. The seminar *Bibliographic records in the book world*,[7] which brought together in Newbury executive representatives from all sectors of the book trade and library community in the UK, gave good evidence of this. Its aim was:

To identify the users' real requirements for bibliographic records, particularly as regards subject content and access, in this increasingly automated environment and to provide a forum in which the requirements of users could be aired in relation to the suppliers' capabilities to match those needs.

In his summing up at this seminar Smethurst stated the 'economic facts' and 'user facts as we know them' and concluded by saying:

Given the developing technologies of OPACs and CD-ROMs/optical discs capable of carrying much of the enhanced data, isn't it time that we got together and exploited our common resources by:
(a) developing an enriched database at the publisher's level;
(b) producing simpler, but well-constructed bibliographical records for OPACs to meet the immediate functions of integrated library systems in a timely way;
(c) utilising the enriched database ... as the bibliographical tool for reference/information retrieval.
What I have in mind is that the trade/commercial database is enhanced by the library bibliographic discipline, which may well result in a commercial database for permanent reference function, whilst the record service utility is designed to simplify, map across and fulfil the functional needs identified by Bath's short entry catalogue study.

Eighteen suggestions for further research into publishers' databases, record structure and content, and for further study of the economics and costs of record supply and use, were identified by the meeting. As a result the Centre for Bibliographic Management undertook in 1988 to examine how the various data elements present in bibliographic records were used for various functions by the bibliographic community as a whole.[8] This was intended to be a prelude to a major study by the Centre into the use and performance of bibliographic records with different levels of subject enhancement. My view is that, as with bibliographic description, care has to be taken not to overload the records with additional information which may only result in a loss in cost-effectiveness.

With regard to (c) − main heading structure − it should be noted that the 'authority file' is a very live issue within the context of discussions currently taking place in Europe on retrospective conversion and networking.

So what are the factors to be considered in relation to the content of a catalogue or bibliographic record? At Bath we distinguished three areas in our study of full and short entry catalogues. These were: user needs, usability and costs.

User needs
How often does omission of data mean that a user would fail to find a title which he otherwise would have found? How often would a user be put to some inconvenience by having to check a source other than the library catalogue for bibliographic details? ('Users' include both the public user and the librarian).

Usability
This relates to speed of use, accuracy of searching and preference. Usability interacts with both need and cost. It is possible to have a catalogue which can cater for any need for, say, 5% of users, but this might be achieved only by providing a catalogue

far more difficult to search by 95% of users.

System costs

The argument can be made that shorter records will save costs in record creation, processing, etc.

In order to examine these factors two experimental subsets of the UK MARC record were decided upon to use in a number of the constituent projects within the study. The first subset was based on the desire to eliminate as much 'description' as possible while retaining all access points. The second subset, in addition to leaving out the fields for bibliographic description, did not make use of added entries. The results relating to user needs indicated that more than 97% of reader and staff needs previously met by a full entry catalogue could be met by a catalogue entry consisting of the following MARC fields and subfields:

MARC tag	
001	ISBN or control number
100.00	Personal name entered under given name
100.10)	
100.20)	Other personal names
100.30)	
110	Corporate name
111	Conference, congress, meeting name
240	Uniform title
245$a,b	Title, subtitle
248$g,h	Volume number, volume title
250$a	Edition statement
260$c	Date of publication
503	Edition and history note
600 (as at 100)	Personal name as subject
610 (as at 110)	Corporate name as subject
611 (as at 111)	Meeting as subject
700 (as at 100)	Personal name added entry
710 (as at 110)	Corporate name added entry
711 (as at 111)	Meeting name added entry
745$a	Title added entry
9XX	References

The question of 'content' is of course relevant nationally as well as locally. Indeed the British Library Bibliographic Services 'Currency with coverage'[9] policy, which provides for a lower level of detail in the national bibliographic record for certain specified categories of material, brought much criticism from certain quarters. Nevertheless it seems certain that the object of the policy, which was to improve the currency of the BNB MARC record service by eliminating a massive backlog of uncatalogued material and also to keep pace with the ever-increasing quantity of published titles, is being achieved very largely as a result of its implementation.

Despite the apparent cost-effective performance of records containing less descriptive data, it must be noted that the need for details in bibliographic records varies; that of the export bookseller, for example, differs markedly from that of the end user of a library catalogue. However, whatever decision you make as an academic library manager concerning the level of content you regard as necessary for your users, you will also have to decide on the most appropriate 'source' for those records. How you create or acquire your records will have a significant bearing on your decision regarding 'content'.

Source

The question of how records should be acquired and/or created provided a major part of the stimulus for establishing the Centre at Bath in 1977. What are the relative benefits of acquiring records from an external supplier as compared with the creation of them in-house? We have never really tackled this question as fully as originally intended, but it is still one of considerable interest to many librarians in the UK, not least because of the installation of so many stand-alone ILS.

External supply

The main sources of externally supplied bibliographic records are:

- National bibliographic record service (in the UK the British Library Bibliographic Services)
- Shared cataloguing co-operatives (in the UK, BLCMP, OCLC Europe and SLS)
- Commercial bibliographic record suppliers (e.g. Blackwells North America, or library suppliers such as John Menzies. Library suppliers tend in the main to service the needs of public rather than academic libraries)

Other bibliographic agencies, for example Whitaker, maintain databases which are mainly used by libraries for acquisition purposes.

Libraries are now far more ready to accept records from a variety of sources in order to service their systems in a timely fashion. If the first record acquired is considered to be less than adequate, it can always be replaced later by a better quality record.

A new factor in record supply is the rapid development of wide area networks (WANs). In the UK, academic libraries are increasingly looking to the Joint Academic Network (JANET) to provide an additional facility for the acquisition and exchange of records. JANET is a network linking UK university and polytechnic computers for the purposes of research. But already, because of the tremendous potential for libraries, there is a lively JANET User Group for Libraries. JANET is an X.25, packet-switched network, with gateways to other academic networks, especially in Europe and North America.

In 1987 the Consortium of University Research Libraries (CURL), consisting of the libraries of Cambridge, Edinburgh, Glasgow, Leeds, London, Manchester and Oxford, received funding from the University Grants Committee to establish a pilot project for resource sharing using the facilities of the JANET network. This project aims to facilitate the exchange of information about library acquisitions and holdings and to arrange for the exchange of catalogue data between the member libraries. So far this database includes only the current MARC cataloguing of the seven libraries − nearly 2,000,000 records, but many fewer unique titles. There is at present considerable overlap and a process of elimination of duplicates will have to be set in hand in due course. At present the CURL database is available for reference only by the member libraries, but given the development of Open Systems Interconnection and improved file transfer mechanisms, together with significant retroconversion of the catalogues of these libraries, the database could become a very significant one. It would raise many questions regarding its relationship with the co-operatives.

Another area of recent activity relates to publishers' bibliographic data. At present there are only two or three publishers in the UK with their own established computerized databases, but in 1987 a new commercial venture − BookData − was established with the aim of assisting publishers with the creation and management of their bibliographic data. BookData's declared objective is

> to serve publishers, booksellers and institutional buyers − including libraries, with particular emphasis on the acquisitions function − by creating a database of very full descriptive ['descriptive' here refers especially to subject data] records about titles currently available or soon to be published, and by offering a range of services tailored to the needs of particular users.[10]

At the Newbury seminar the view was expressed that the 'continuum' of record supply should be harnessed to the needs of users, without the duplication at several stages of record generation. That continuum should extend from the time that a title is a scribbled note on a publishers' editor's desk to the time that details are consulted by an end user. It is agreed that more subject data is required in this age of interactive systems, so why continue to recreate data at so many different stages?

In-house creation and acquisition of records
However many records are obtained from an external source, there will always be a proportion of titles for which they will not be available and for which the records will have to be created in-house by the local library. There are three particular points to be made regarding the management of cataloguing:

(i)   If a decision is made to use an external source, especially a co-operative, then do *not* amend or add to the records unless an obvious mistake is spotted, or much of the cost savings will be lost. Indeed, it may be that you will find yourself spending even more money than if you had decided to create all your records in-house. Too many libraries have failed to make sensible use of schemes of shared cataloguing. If an external source cannot provide you with records which you are prepared to accept, do not use it.

(ii) Even if all your library records are created in-house, make sure that they are prepared in a MARC-compatible format. It is well worth considering UNIMARC and the use of a basic ISBD structure, but *not* the ISBD punctuation, which can be positively misleading to catalogue users.[11]

(iii) Whether one opts for a centralized cataloguing section for the library, or decides upon a decentralized approach where the responsibility for cataloguing and classification is dispersed among the various branches or departments of the library, is often largely dependent on perceptions about the 'geography' of the institution. (It can also be very dependent on whim or personal preference). Far more important than the centralization or decentralization of the work is the quality of its management.

Performance measurement and quality control

The Bath Centre has always maintained that the three essential elements of the 'quality' of a catalogue record, whether produced locally or externally, are *accuracy, consistency* and *timeliness* (i.e. availability of the record when it is required). Probably everyone agrees about the importance of *accuracy* and *consistency*, but not everyone agrees about *timeliness*. Following the publication of the British Library's consultative paper *Currency with coverage,*[9] a number of individuals and groups expressed the view that if waiting meant better quality (by which they meant 'fuller') records then they would prefer to wait. The problem with 'fulness' is how to define it: how far does one go? Certainly MARC records are considered by many to be far from satisfactory in their content; they contain a good deal of data which users rarely or never want, while lacking the subject information and other details which would provide far more terms for searching in OPACs and also enable better judgements to be made on relevance.

Fulness of bibliographic description may be important for 3% of catalogue users, but in order to satisfy the requirements of this 3% one becomes subject to the law of diminishing returns. How far can the necessary allocation of resources be justified for these users when a large proportion of the 97% are almost certainly going to find themselves disadvantaged as a result — especially in terms of ease of use? An examination of the economics demonstrated to us at Bath that it would be cheaper to purchase and give the required books to the 3% to keep — not a very realistic or practical suggestion, but one that gives some idea of the resourcing problems involved in detailed descriptive cataloguing. The ability of bibliographic records to indicate the intellectual level and subject relevance of titles to users is becoming much more important in discussions regarding quality, especially in the light of developing national and international networked databases of catalogue records.

While the Bath Centre has undertaken some research projects relevant to the 'accuracy' and 'consistency' of records I know of no ongoing performance measures in these areas. In relation to 'timeliness', however, we implemented a performance measure in 1980. This was the UKMARC Currency Survey,[12] which has for the past nine years monitored the currency and coverage of the UKMARC records at the time libraries have needed them for cataloguing their accessions promptly.

Access

Interactive catalogues are attracting new users with new expectations and requirements. I shall consider the topic of 'access' under three headings:

- data used
- techniques used
- why and for whom

Data used

I have already referred to the considerable interest currently being shown in the need for the additional subject data enhancement of bibliographic records and the recognition that the records we have at present are relatively poor in subject information. Until recently the two principal methods for providing data for subject access have been as follows:

(i)   Subject headings – Library of Congress Subject Headings (LCSH) or Sears Subject Headings, usually in a dictionary catalogue. This has been the main subject approach used in North America.

In the UK during the 1970s Austin developed the PRECIS (Preserved Context Indexing System)[13] for use in the *British national bibliography*. It was also hoped that it would be applied more generally, but its use by local libraries has been very rare because it was believed to be too labour-intensive. Nevertheless, the presence of PRECIS index strings within UKMARC records has provided some valuable annotation for those titles which are not indicative of content, and also a supply of additional terms for free-text searching in OPACs.

(ii)   Classification. This has been the main method used in the UK. Until the advent of OPACs over 80% of the subject catalogues provided in the UK were classified catalogues. This was not because of any careful logical reasoning, but because many librarians had decided to economize by simply producing extra copies of a unit entry for filing in a classified sequence – frequently, however, without providing a satisfactory subject index.

The public's understanding of classification and classified catalogues has in the past been very poor and, in the main, provision of the latter has been a waste of time. An article by Line and myself published in 1969 entitled 'How golden is your retriever?'[14] referred to the fact that libraries used classification to serve three functions simultaneously – stock arrangement, information retrieval in the catalogue, and provision of a link between the catalogue entry and the book on the shelf. The result was that none of these functions was really well served; e.g. the precision of definition required for information retrieval frequently led to notation being far too long and complex to serve as a satisfactory link between catalogue and book. Now, however, there are signs that with the development of OPACs, classification can have a major role to play.

Classification numbers can also be searched as 'free text' and can be used for the more precise definition of searches. Since the development of computer-held catalogues there has been a great deal of interest shown in the use of 'keyword' or 'free language' searching,[15] i.e. searching on words, or parts of words included in titles, subtitles, or other appropriate areas of the record. 'Appropriate areas', if they were not present, could include contents pages and abstracts, but until recently these have not been provided in catalogue records. Now BookData, in addition to traditional subject processing, is providing contents page data and brief and long abstracts in many records, and a good deal of current consideration is being given by librarians to the use of such data in OPACs.

It is no longer a question of which is the right approach to use. The old arguments about the merits of 'controlled' versus 'uncontrolled' methods are now largely out of date. The aim should be to provide users with the facilities for both approaches in order that they can select the one most appropriate for their particular requirement at the time of searching.[16]

With 'controlled' methods, whether subject headings or classification, a form of systematic control should be used. The lack of authority control in UK subject indexes, and in the relatively few dictionary catalogues which are provided, has not encouraged their effective use.

Techniques used

The main point to be made here is that improved retrieval techniques in OPACs can help a great deal to compensate for lack of data. This is important, as the enhancement of bibliographic records retrospectively is unlikely to occur except in a very few specific instances, and therefore any method which can exploit data which is present in the existing records is to be welcomed.

Over the past few years there has been a significant increase in the application of information retrieval techniques in the development of prototype OPACs but, with one or two exceptions, there is little evidence so far of the impact of this activity on the commercial systems sold to libraries. Two of the main IR techniques which have been applied to OPAC development recently (especially by Walker and the Okapi team[17] at the Polytechnic of Central London) are:

(i) *Fuzzy matching.* A method for retrieving relevant items despite users searching with only partial or inaccurate information, e.g. THOMSON instead of THOMPSON.

(ii) *Relevance feedback.* A method which allows the system to display an array of records in response to a user's search; if a relevant record appears in this array and the user selects it, the system will use some other element of data present in that record, for example the classification number, to look for other records with the same element. This presents the user with further alternatives from which to select. The system should be 'transparent' to the user.

More and more use is being made of external databases. Users can undertake subject searches using a range of databases on a host such as DIALOG and then check the catalogue in their library to see if the items they have traced are available in the local stock.

Why and for whom?

I still believe that it is the local use of our collections that should be the main focus of our attention, and that our cataloguing and classification efforts should primarily be geared to the exploitation of the local stock. We suffer from information overload. There are only so many citations that can be handled, so many articles and books that can be read. Nevertheless, in these days of networking and resource sharing, there is a mutual responsibility to see that access can be provided as flexibly and speedily as possible to users at a distance. The problem is in deciding how far one should be meeting the requirements of a shared system and how far one should be conscious of the resource implications for one's own users.[18]

The emphasis for today's librarians is on 'access' and not on their more traditional 'custodial' function. Resource sharing as related to the provision of 'access' is primarily concerned with three main areas: interlibrary loan, subject specialization and collection development. The interlibrary loan function requires no expansion, but my personal experience suggests that schemes of cooperative book purchase based on sharing of subject responsibilities are of very dubious value. Conspectus-like collection development policies, based on a sound knowledge of what other libraries are acquiring and discarding, seem to be a far more fruitful path to follow, and can only occur effectively given the provision of good 'access' to each other's databases.

Presentation

I cannot stress too strongly the importance within the management context of the need for good and effective 'presentation' of data. You can produce the fullest and most subject rich information in the world, but unless people can use with ease the equipment provided, and comprehend with speed and clarity the visual presentation of the data, a great deal of time and effort will have been wasted.

Physical form

Whether you are providing a traditional form of catalogue such as card or book, a more modern form such as COM (Computer Output Microfilm) rollfilm or fiche, or a present-day OPAC, the quality of the equipment and its ergonomics are all important. Do not provide catalogue cabinets two metres tall with the bottom drawer near to the floor; make sure that there is space for a notebook or a sheet of paper for writing down details; if you have COM readers do ensure that they are robust and that on/off switches and focus controls are clearly marked; make sure that any equipment with a screen, whether microfilm reader or VDU (Visual Display Unit) is not placed facing bright daylight.

The OPAC is of course one of the most talked about and written about features of the modern library scene. There have been many silly statements made about OPACs. Nevertheless, they are popular with users and I suggest that there are three main reasons for this:

(i)   they provide 'availability' data, e.g. details of whether an item is on loan or on order.
(ii) the majority offer a 'keyword' or 'free language' searching facility.
(iii) they provide for 'distributed access', e.g. across all departments or branches of the library, from offices or even from the home.

Latterly we have witnessed the emergence of CD-ROM systems. There appear to be two main services which they can best provide within cataloguing:

(i)   they can hold databases that are invaluable for downloading records in retrospective conversion projects.
(ii) they can be used for 'archival'-type collections which are not dynamic and subject to change.

Visual presentation

In whatever physical form the catalogue is presented, the visual clarity and ease with which the data can be comprehended is dependent on the:

(i)   nature of the data;
(ii) quality of the graphics;
(iii) its spacing and layout.

It is important that jargon be avoided, whether this be about the data, e.g. 'uniform title', 'holdings'; and, in the case of OPACs, that used in the system itself, e.g. 'TYPE PS and RETURN'.

Excessive abbreviation should be avoided at all costs. If a full form of words can

111

be used then do so, but if space does not allow for this then at least use meaningful abbreviations − vol. *not* v., illus. *not* ill. Punctuation can also cause a great deal of confusion to users.

The quality of the graphics used for presenting alpha-numeric characters and other symbols is also of importance. As a general rule italics should be avoided, but judicious use of 'bold' can be very effective.

If you do not have access to facilities that provide the graphics quality ideally desired, then sensible use of spacing and layout of the data on the card, page, frame, or screen can greatly aid its legibility. Some of the best work in legibility studies was undertaken at the Royal College of Art in London.[19]

The presentation of data on OPAC screens has been the subject of much comment but relatively little experimental study. The conventional 80-character 24-line screen is very constraining, but the new work-station screens with their high resolution graphics and the availability of software packages for facilities such as 'windowing' offer the prospect of better things to come. The Centre for Bibliographic Management has undertaken some experiments using a conventional screen.[20, 21] One area where further work is required is in what I call 'screen dynamics', i.e. the ease with which one can not only move backwards and forwards within an array of entries, but also 'slip' entries, or move from brief to full entry and back again.

If funds are limited then care with the presentation of data is, in my opinion, far more important than the amount of information which is included.

Conclusion

(i)   Research the requirements of your users
(ii)   Do not confuse brevity with over-simplification
(iii)   Meet the three criteria of quality
(iv)   Introduce performance measurement.

Finally, do not forget the inherent nature of a library. I recommend Jesse Shera's article 'The quiet stir of thought or, what the computer cannot do'.[22]

References

1   Grose, Michael W. and Line, Maurice B., 'On the construction and care of white elephants: some fundamental questions concerning the catalogue', *Library Association record*, **70**, (1), 1968, 2−5.

2   Urquhart, Donald J., 'On catalogues', *NLL review*, **1**, 1971, 80−4.

3   Bryant, Philip, 'The library catalogue: key or combination lock?', *Catalogue & index*, **67**, 1982, 1−7.

4   Bryant, Philip et al., *The Bath mini-catalogue: a progress report*, Bath, Bath University Library, 1972.

5   *Bath University Comparative Catalogue Study. Final report, 10 pts. in 9 vols.*, Bath, Bath University Library, 1975. (BLRD Reports 5240-48).

6   Seal, Alan et al., *Full and short entry catalogues: library needs and uses*, Aldershot, Gower Publishing Co., 1982.

7   Greenwood, Derek (comp.), *Bibliographic records in the book world: needs and capabilities. Proceedings of a seminar held on 27−28 November 1987, at Newbury*, London, BNB Research Fund, 1988. (BNB Research Fund Report 33).

8 Dempsey, Lorcan, *Bibliographic records: use of data elements in the book world*, Bath, Bath University Library, 1989.

9 British Library, Bibliographic Services, *Currency with coverage: consultative paper*, London, British Library, 1987.

10 Martin, David, 'BookData: a progress report', *Vine*, **73**, 1988, 24–6.

11 Bryant, Philip, 'Bibliographic access to serials: a study for the British Library', *Serials*, **1**, (3), 1988, 41–6.

12 Seal, Alan, 'The hit-rate for UKMARC', *Vine*, **42**, 1982, 31–5.

13 Austin, D., *PRECIS: a manual of concept analysis and subject indexing. 2nd ed.*, London, British Library, 1984.

14 Line, Maurice B. and Bryant, Philip., 'How golden is your retriever? Thoughts on library classification', *Library Association record*, **71**, (5), 1969, 135–8.

15 Bryant, Philip (ed.), *Keyword catalogues and the free language approach. Papers based on a seminar, 19th October 1983*. Bath, Bath University Library, 1985.

16 Hildreth, Charles R., 'To Boolean or not Boolean?', *Information technology and libraries*, **2**, (3), 1983, 235–7.

17 Mitev, Nathalie N., et al., *Designing an online public access catalogue: Okapi, a catalogue on a local area network*. London, British Library, 1985. (Library and Information Research Report 39).

18 Bryant, Philip, 'Cooperation, resource allocation and the 'win/win' situation', *Outlook on research libraries*, **10**, (5), 1988, 1-4.

19 Reynolds, Linda, 'Legibility studies: their relevance to present-day documentation studies', *Journal of documentation*, **35**, (4), 1979, 307–40.

20 Kinsella, Janet, 'Prospects for browsing: experimental approaches to the presentation of brief entries and the design of 'browse' screens.' *In* A. H. Helal and J. W. Weiss (eds.), *Future of online catalogues. Essen Symposium 1985*, Gesamthuschulbibliothek, Essen, 1986, 227–41.

21 Prowse, Steven G., 'Use of BRS/Search in OPAC experiments', *Program*, **20**, (2), 1986, 178–95.

22 Shera, Jesse H., 'The quiet stir of thought or, what the computer cannot do', *Library Association record*, **72**, (2), 1970, 37–42.

14

Reference and information services

John Fletcher

What do we mean by reference and information services? I shall adopt a very broad definition: 'all those library services not directly concerned with the acquisition, stocking and lending of the library's own stock'. This definition includes the passive services, such as having the right stock available in the right place, through to the provision of equipment to view film or videotape; and the more positive, active services such as answering readers' enquiries and assisting in the selection of bookstock. The latter are probably the most important group of services offered by an academic library. As a group they certainly take the largest percentage of our professional staff time, and the quality and level of the service is rising.

There are four factors in the provision of reference and information services, and this chapter will examine each in some detail. They interrelate very closely, so sometimes the definitions will not be clear-cut. The headings are:

1 the readers, and the service demands they make;
2 the materials used to answer enquiries, including the impact of new technology;
3 the library staff providing the services: their characteristics, training and organization; and
4 the services themselves, and the way in which they have changed and are likely to develop in the future.

To begin with the readers: there are three groups, first of all the teaching staff, research assistants, research students, and postgraduate students. These are the most experienced. They may have been working and teaching in their subject for many years. They should, and often do, know a great deal about the literature and the sources of information, but usually in a very narrow subject area, and, as the years pass, these subjects seem to become even more narrow and specialized. This makes the information librarians' task much more difficult, since they cannot possibly match the subject expertise of these readers, and there is a danger of their role as information providers being diminished to that of suppliers of known, requested items. On the other hand, the quantity of published and semi-published material now flooding the world each year from commercial publishers, research groups and international and national organizations, is such that even in their ever-narrowing specialist fields lecturers and researchers are unable to keep abreast of new developments, and come to rely more and more on their librarian colleagues to help them out.

Where academic staff and researchers are working together as a team, it is not uncommon for one of them to act as 'gate-keeper': a person whose task is to keep an eye on the new literature, bringing to the attention of members of the research team any item relevant to their project. The gatekeeper may be a librarian, but more frequently is a junior research assistant, who may rely heavily on the subject librarians' expertise. The librarians' strength is in their breadth of knowledge. They know that information peripheral to the subject, but nevertheless important, may be found in sources outside the specialist's increasingly narrow experience.

The second group of readers comprises the students: undergraduate and sub-degree. In Britain this group has until recently been almost exclusively the 18-year-olds, straight from school. Increasingly now, and even more so in the 1990s, a larger proportion of this group will be mature people, most of them with considerable practical experience of work and, possibly more importantly, of life. Mature students may not have any greater knowledge of, or expertise in information sources, but they are much more aware of the value and importance of information, and thus willing to learn from those librarians who are prepared to help them. They are often more motivated.

A great change is taking place in the methods used for undergraduate teaching in polytechnics in Britain, possibly more quickly and more positively than in universities, though university librarians may disagree about this. The traditional picture of higher education is of a large class being lectured to by a member of the teaching staff, with the students scribbling notes, frantically trying to keep up with the lecturer, who only rarely hands out useful summaries of his lecture. These 'mass transfers' of the accepted wisdom are then followed up by small seminar or tutorial groups in which semi-structured discussion between students and a tutor takes place. These are often built around a set piece of written work completed by one member of the group, whilst the other members have only a sketchy background knowledge of the topic.

Tutorial and seminar groups are becoming more important, and the large lecture less so. Increasingly now, however, students are given projects, individually or in groups of up to six or seven, or even the whole class, sometimes with a specific, carefully prescribed, title, but often more open-ended, with the students themselves deciding on the specific topic within broad guidelines laid down.

This apparent digression into educational practice is not irrelevant, because these changes have a great impact on library information services. There are now very large numbers of students carrying out library-based projects, for which they need a great deal of assistance. And the wide range of topics covered presents librarians with enormous problems of stock selection and purchase.

The third group of readers is a relatively new category: external readers. Most, but not all, British academic librarians have allowed use of their collections by individual people not employed by or registered as staff or students at their institutions. With greater pressure being placed upon them to earn income, universities and polytechnics are looking to companies, industrial and commercial, to local and national services, such as the health service, and to law practices, to use their libraries, and to pay for the services they receive. The demands made by such external bodies are usually very different in nature from those of the traditional academic clientele. Enquiries are detailed, specific, and often highly technical, made by people with a wealth of experience and expertise in the subject. Above all, these readers have business acumen: they know that time is valuable, so enquiries must have answers quickly. But information too is seen as valuable, and good information has a price which they are willing to pay. This category of information services is one which the traditionally non-commercial academic community, and this includes libraries, must now provide.

Next, the materials required to support a good reference and information service. The bookstock, and above all the periodical stock, is still, and will always remain, the mainstay of a library's reference service. Increasingly new technology is being used to disseminate information, and academic reference services must come to terms with it. Film and videotape are being used as teaching media, and can provide literally a new dimension, the visual image, to the answers given to enquirers. Let me give two examples. A student of sculpture wants to examine in detail Rodin's 'The Thinker'. He cannot afford to go and visit the statue, and still photographs only allow him to see it from those angles which the photographer thought were important. A film or videotape, lasting several minutes, can however give him a lengthy tour of the statue, seeing it from all angles, including some which it would be impossible to achieve in person. Students of physiotherapy and occupational therapy need to understand the way in which limbs move in order for the human body to perform certain actions; these are easily and cheaply shown on film or videotape, and in slow motion which makes it easier to see and analyse the movement.

Computerized databases are now an everyday tool of the reference librarian. The majority are still bibliographic, lists of books or periodical articles, now with greater flexibility and sophistication in the means of access. Full-text databases, which produce on the screen the complete newspaper article, or legal judgement, are becoming more common. These online, off-campus services are a major new information source, an important weapon in the reference librarians' armoury, which they must learn to use both efficiently and effectively.

To these off-campus databases must be added the facility to download databases from outside the institution, to create new specialist databases in-house and make them available on computers on campus. More and more academic campuses are being wired up as local area networks allowing access to a family of computers from anywhere on campus. Once installed, this is a cheap alternative to online use of off-campus databases.

One important extension of the local area network is its link to other such networks. In Britain, the Joint Academic Network, JANET, links most higher education institutions' computing services, thus allowing cheap access to databases held in other institutions. Knowledge of what institutions hold which databases, and how to access them, is another new skill essential for the reference librarian.

Finally, the most recent newcomer to the scene is CD-ROM: databases on compact disc, with built-in information retrieval packages, allowing quite substantial databases to be made available in the library, on a microcomputer linked to a CD-ROM player. Once the capital outlay has been made, and, where required, funding has been found for the necessary updates, access for library users can be freely available. Thus students can gain practical hands-on experience of online searching without incurring the high cost of off-campus access.

One final comment on materials. The impact of the expanding output of information, combined with the increasing specialization of readers, and thus the more specific nature of their enquiries, creates a series of problems for academic librarians. In the past it might have been possible for them to feel reasonably confident that they could supply, from their library's stock, the vast majority of the items needed by their readers. This has not been true for many years, and interlibrary co-operation and the low-cost interlibrary lending of books and periodicals are now central to the operations of all our library information services.

This has had an interesting, and to some chief librarians unexpected, increase in the importance of the interlibrary loans department. Hitherto this was often regarded as a rather lowly section of the library. Once the accuracy of the bibliographic record of the item sought had been verified, all other operations were seen as clerical. Most chief academic librarians now appreciate more keenly the expertise brought to the job by a good interlibrary loans librarian. Expertise in bibliographic searching, in identifying the correct item from inadequate information, is only the beginning of this service. Even in Britain, with the centralization of interlibrary lending as a result of the existence of the British Library Document Supply Centre, the expertise and experience of a good interlibrary loans librarian is invaluable in ensuring the speedy delivery of wanted items. In other countries, without a centralized system of interlending, their knowledge of the most likely sources of wanted items is crucial to the efficiency of this service.

Finally on materials, there is the question of the organization and location of reference stock. Most academic libraries are now open access, so the stock is used by readers directly, as well as by librarians helping readers. The reference stock must be located in a convenient place, and well sign-posted. Whether the reference stock for all subjects is in one place, or in several places in the library, rather depends on the location and organization of the reference librarians. Placing reference tools, which cannot be borrowed, close to loanable books or periodical stock on the same subject would seem to be the most efficient solution. Often reference librarians use items in the loan stock to answer an enquiry; they are providing information, and information comes in many forms.

The second, but perhaps more important, resource in reference and information work is the library staff. The discussions which raged 20 years ago in our profession about centralization of reference services, about subject specialist librarians, about the separation within one library of teams of reference and information librarians, all of these seem to have been resolved. The increasing subject specialization of readers, their inability to cope with the tide of new literature, and in some cases with the new technology, made it inevitable that librarians should become subject specialists to some degree or other. It became impossible for even the most widely experienced librarian to cope adequately with enquiries on such a wide range of subjects as semi-conductors, Marcel Proust, the national accounts of Norway, the social impact of imbalances between population growth and food production, and the stresses in suspension bridges.

Inevitably librarians specialized, and became more expert in their narrower subject areas. The sensible concomitant of this was to locate their enquiry desks close to the library's stock on their subject, and to keep the reference tools specific to that subject near the enquiry desk. This is now the general pattern in British higher education libraries, though clearly there are variations where the layout of the library building precludes it, or where departmental libraries dominate (though departmental libraries are of course usually subject specialist libraries, with subject specialist librarians).

What this has meant in practice is teams of reference librarians, each looking after the needs of one or more subjects, manning enquiry desks close to the reference and lending stock for their subjects. By working as a team they can provide backup, mutual support, for each other, and also cover the inevitable interlinking of subjects. The librarian responsible for computing, for example, will often need to seek help from his electronic engineering colleague. Cooperation between members of different subject teams is also important, and this is made more difficult in institutions with several separate subject libraries. For example: probably the second heaviest users of computing literature, after the computer scientists, are the business studies students. Cooperation and mutual support between the business and computing librarians are easy when they are in the same building, but much more difficult when they are some distance apart.

The penultimate section of this chapter concerns the skills required by a good reference librarian. First, there has to be a deep interest in the subject(s) handled, and from this will grow a detailed knowledge of the structure of its literature, which forms are important, and which peripheral. Knowledge of the sources of information, in all forms, is clearly essential, as is expertise in their limitations and their use. Second, a good memory is needed, to retain information about the contents of the bookstock, and the sources used to answer previous enquiries, for few questions are completely unique. A degree of tenacity is an advantage, since it drives the librarian on to search wider and deeper in the literature for the elusive answer.

The reference librarian needs patience and diplomacy in dealing with an enquirer, so that both the reader and the librarian are absolutely certain what the question is before beginning to search for the answer. All good reference librarians are extroverts, not merely because they need to be able to talk easily with enquirers, but also because they should be involved with professional colleagues. They should be active professionally, attending meetings and conferences, meeting other reference staff in their subject area, because knowledge of other librarians' expertise is an essential part of their expertise. They should also be active in the university or polytechnic. And finally, they should have good communication and teaching skills.

Must subject librarians have a degree in their subject as well as a qualification in librarianship? Most chief academic librarians would now agree that whilst it is desirable, it is not essential. Relevant subject qualification is desirable for many reasons: to have a basic understanding of the subject, its philosophy, structure and terminology, to make it easier to understand the questions asked by readers, and to relate better to, and be more accepted as equals by, the teaching staff. But there are very few qualified engineers, lawyers, or computer scientists in librarianship: they can command much better salaries in their chosen professions. There are many excellent subject librarians with degrees in subjects far removed from that which they serve in their libraries. Often this expertise comes as a result of experience. The personality of the individual subject librarian is perhaps more important than the level of his subject qualification. Given the will, most graduate librarians can absorb from experience sufficient background in their subject to cope with the normal level of enquiries they receive.

This absorption process can be speeded up if subject librarians are responsible for classifying the book stock in their subject. If they assist the teaching staff to select new books to add to stock, and, when the books arrive, are responsible for classifying them, they gain a good working knowledge of the stock, and its contents, and this is the mainstay of reference librarians' expertise. The act of classifying a book necessitates looking through it in detail, examining its chapter headings and contents to identify its subject matter. This same exercise also highlights any special sections which are valuable, but perhaps outside the main subject matter of the book. A book on financial management, for example, may contain a case study of a specific industry which could be of value to someone studying that industry.

Finally, what are the services which a good reference librarian will offer? Some of these are evident from what is written above, but the scene is changing in British higher education. More is being demanded of teaching staff, and of libraries. The methods of teaching are changing, and these are having an enormous impact which is not always recognized outside the library.

To begin with the most obvious service: answering readers' enquiries. The ideal, and perhaps even the norm now, is for teams of qualified graduate librarians to staff enquiry desks on a rota basis. There will be several teams, staffing several desks, each specializing in a group of allied subjects, with each subject specialist librarian calling on the assistance of more appropriate colleagues when asked questions which fall outside his or her own expertise. The enquiry desks should be located out on the open floor of the library, clearly visible and accessible to all library users. Subject teams may well have offices in which they work when not engaged on their enquiry desk session, but these should be close to the enquiry desk so that subject specialists can be called out when required. Above all, subject librarians should not be hidden away in inaccessible offices.

This might be seen as the passive side of information work − sitting at an enquiry desk waiting for someone to ask a question. It is not really passive, for not all subject enquiries are answered from books or other printed sources. A good reference librarian has a wealth of knowledge in his or her head, information gleaned from answering previous enquiries, information which is not written down anywhere.

In addition to enquiry desk work, subject teams should be providing more active services. Examples of these are information sheets or display boards on, for example, 'What's new in engineering?' culled from current journals and newspapers; the production of printed guides to the literature − short descriptions of the structure of the literature of their subjects, the relative importance of different forms of publication, such as patents, or research reports and drawing users' attention to important bibliographies, abstracting services and online databases.

In some subjects librarians will be scanning newspapers and journals for articles on topics known to be of interest to researchers, or useful for student projects. These may be passed on to individuals, staff or students, or gathered together into cuttings, or information files. These current awareness activities are useful too in enabling the information librarians to keep abreast of developments in their subject and know of new publications. These are just a few examples of the services in which an active information librarian will engage. They will enhance the librarian's standing with his academic colleagues, and will have a great impact on the library service.

Higher education is changing, and with it, the role of the information librarian. As education methods change, from teaching to student self-learning, subject librarians are becoming a part, and an increasingly important part, of the education team. They are often members of course teams, playing a full part in deciding the content of courses, advising on the availability of books and periodicals to support the proposed course, and the feasibility of project work as part of it.

Beyond this, they are teaching students, and sometimes researchers, and even academic staff. They are teaching students the skills which they will need, not just for the few years they are in the university or polytechnic, but for all their lives. For the most part they are not teaching facts, they are teaching a methodology: the collection of data or information, the selection of what is useful, its evaluation, and its presentation. This implies that librarians have a skill, an expertise, which should be passed on to the students in just the same way as the teachers' subject knowledge.

Library staff in higher education are now increasingly involved with teaching staff in designing courses. Their expertise is accepted, and their willingness to pass it on to students is taken for granted. Nowadays in most universities and polytechnics new students are given an introduction to the library: an exercise in orientation, finding their way around the building, and the services the library offers.

After that, later in their courses, further instruction is given by library staff. Post-induction courses, given by subject librarians, are now an integral part of a wide range of courses in most universities and polytechnics. Typically these courses will include some or all of the following:

- the structure of the literature of the subject;
- the relative importance of different forms of literature, such as books, periodicals, theses, research reports, company information, patents, standard specifications and statistics;
- how to use the range of tools and services available; and this will now include online searching and the use of CD-ROMs in addition to traditionally published abstracting and indexing services;
- the selection and evaluation of the information and data found;
- and the presentation of the resulting distillation of information in report form.

Clearly, this cannot be carried out separately from the mainstream course teaching. Close liaison between the subject librarians and the course teaching staff is essential. The librarians must be accepted as full members of the course team, and be regarded as members of the teaching department as much as of the library. It is essential that their library input is integrated fully and logically into the course. The quality and value of the librarians' involvement in the teaching of students will depend partly on their ability to teach, but equally on the willingness of teaching staff to accept the librarians' input as a valuable part of the course. This is where the personal relationship between librarian and teaching staff is crucial. Not all subject librarians would feel confident in giving talks on some of the topics listed above, report writing, for example, so it is important that they should tackle only those subjects in which they are confident.

The librarians' part of such a course of literature awareness and use may be as a structured series of talks and practical sessions, and these must be timed to fit into the mainstream course teaching. Or the same information may be transmitted through carefully planned project work, assessed essays, or even library 'trails', a series of questions devised by the subject librarian which the students are asked to answer. The questions are designed to lead the students through the various services which the library offers, and ensure that they are able to make the most efficient use of those services. These library and information inputs to courses are now commonly assessed as part of the qualification awarded at the end of the course.

Student project work can create problems if the library staff are not made fully aware of the subject matter and been given the opportunity of checking it through in advance of the students. Ideally teaching and library staff should discuss project topics, and be clear about what information or skill the students are expected to acquire as a result of doing the project, how much assistance the tutor wants the librarians to give to the students, and whether this can be given in groups or must be on a one-to-one basis.

Ensuring this integration of the library service into the educational activity of the institution is the most challenging problem facing academic librarians today. Despite universal problems of inadequate resourcing it must be accepted that such changes in teaching and learning methods require the shift of staff resources from teaching to academic support services. Progress and success in this change vary greatly between different institutions. Success is often the result of the personality of the librarians and their academic colleagues, and of good working relations between them. Some academic staff accept readily the concept of librarians as teachers, others are less willing to do so.

All in all, it seems that the gloom and despondency which was not uncommon among reference librarians some ten years ago were unfounded. They were worried that with end-users able to carry out their own online searching, with books and periodical articles possibly accessible in full text online, librarians would be reduced to carrying out clerical tasks of cataloguing and reshelving what few books were left in libraries. Librarians have found a new role in higher education. Their expertise is being appreciated, and it is accepted that students need to have that expertise imparted to them before they graduate.

15

Lending services

Geoffrey Ford

This section covers three main topics: lending policy, the design of procedures for lending systems, and finally the measurement of performance in these areas. In another paper, Ian Winkworth discusses the overall aspects of a stock management policy: lending policy is one component of that overall scene.

Lending policy

One of the most basic questions which a librarian must address is that of providing access to the stock of the library. Should it be on open access or on closed access? And should it be kept in the library where everybody can use it? Or should it be made available for loan so that readers can take the books away to use them at times and places which are more convenient than those constrained by the library's location and opening times? Most lending policies adopted by libraries are compromises in some way or another.

If we start with the individual users of the library, we find that each user wants to have immediate access to all the books he wants at any time. Having borrowed the books he wants he wants to keep them as long as possible. However, if one borrower has books on loan for a long time then it may be extremely discouraging for another potential user of the library who wants the same book. If we assume that each book in the library has more than one potential user, then if one of them keeps the book for a long time the less chance another potential borrower has of finding that book when wanting to use it. So if books are allowed out of the library only for short periods at a time they will return more frequently and be on the shelves longer for people to find them when they want them.

Demand level

However, not all books are the same. Some books are needed by many users, others by comparatively few. For books which are needed by many borrowers it is reasonable to suggest that borrowers should return books as quickly as possible after they have used them, but for books which are needed by very few people a longer period of loan can be allowed so long as other users are not thereby inconvenienced. There will always be special cases, for example a book which is needed by three people more or less at the same time. It would not be just for the first person to get the book to be allowed to keep it for a long time. It is of course possible for libraries to satisfy the demand for books by buying additional copies. The extent to which this is possible at all depends on the library's budget. But it is not necessarily the best choice: a library might be better served if two different books were purchased rather than two copies of the same book. On the other hand, if demand for a book is very high then a single copy will be insufficient.

Retention time

What do users do with the books when they do get hold of them? Perhaps that is not the librarian's concern so long as they bring them back in one piece, but how long they keep the books is important. I think it is generally accepted that users will keep books as long as they can − either until they are due back from loan, or until they are recalled from loan for any reason. Buckland[1] has published some graphs illustrating this tendency, showing that the most popular day for returning books from loan is the day they are due back. A cumulative frequency graph shows that this picture may be modified by the imposition of fines. The *effective* loan period may differ from the *official* loan period if there is a 'period of grace' allowed. Figure 1 shows that, while the official due date is the most popular day for returning books, a much more informative figure is the percentage of books returned from loan before fines are imposed: in the two libraries (A and C) which charge fines as soon as the books are overdue, 70−75% are returned by the due date, while in the third library (B), only 51% are returned by the official due date. In this third library there is a period of grace and fines are charged on average after 13 days, which is the effective loan period during which 82% of the books are returned.

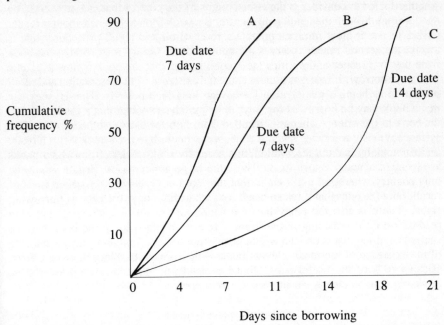

Days since borrowing

Fig. 1: Official and effective loan periods

123

Borrowing limits

The necessity for limiting the number of items which may be borrowed by an individual is dependent on the stock levels. In most mature libraries, it is probably unnecessary to enforce limits, since few users will go to the trouble of removing large quantities of books for their personal use. Where books are in short supply, clearly different considerations apply.

Serials

In the scientific field in particular, users depend on speedy access to the most recent publications, in order to keep up to date, and to past serial volumes in which methods are described. For this reason many libraries retain serials for reference only. The corollary of this policy is that the library needs a good photocopying service – and to many people, a working photocopier is the sign of an efficient library!

Teaching patterns

An academic library must take into consideration the teaching patterns and traditions of the institution it serves. If there are large classes of students who need to use a limited number of books, then it is appropriate to buy duplicate copies and to organize a *short loan collection*, with loan periods of 3 up to 24 or 48 hours, in order to maximize the students' borrowing opportunities. For more extended pieces of work longer loan periods will be necessary. The need for close liaison with the faculty hardly needs emphasis.

Control procedures

Another factor to consider is the effectiveness of the control that can be exerted by the librarian through the lending procedure. If a book is on loan when another reader wishes to use it most libraries operate a reservation and recall procedure: that is to say, the second reader reserves the book and the library then recalls that book from the first reader and notifies the second reader that the book is now available for him to borrow. Librarians usually quote the existence of the reservation and recall procedure as being a justification for having long loan periods. That is, they say that a book may be borrowed for, say, three months provided that a reader returns the book to the library when it is recalled from him for use by someone else. This system obviously works very well if all readers who wish to use a book that is already on loan actually make a reservation, and secondly if all readers from whom books are recalled actually return them. These are large assumptions; Britain is not the only country where the users claim that they 'did not receive' the earlier notes of recall, only the ones that threaten penalties such as fines or suspension of borrowing rights. There is also the point that reservation and recall procedures do not help readers who are browsing in the library. If they are looking at the books on the shelves anything that is on loan will obviously not be seen, and they may be unaware of the existence of the most relevant book to their interests. Since anywhere from 10% to 80% of the useful books found in academic libraries are discovered by browsing, this is clearly an important consideration.

Administrative aspects

It is also important to consider the administration of the lending procedure. Different lending policies have different implications for the design of the lending procedure,

124

and if a library already has one particular lending procedure then a new loan policy may require an alteration to that procedure.

Political aspects and categories of borrower

Finally, it is important to consider political aspects. Most academic institutions operate in a strictly hierarchical fashion. Professors are more important than assistant professors, assistant professors are more important than research fellows, research fellows are more important than research assistants, postgraduate students are more important than undergraduate students. At one time in Britain it was quite common for the members of the faculty to be allowed to keep books on loan much longer than postgraduate students, and they in turn could keep books much longer than undergraduate students. This structure can be justified in two ways. One way is to say that professors are more important than undergraduate students and so they should be allowed to keep books much longer. This argument may be put in cash terms by saying that the time of a professor is more valuable than a student so it is best for him to have the books he wants conveniently in his office for as much time as possible. The second way of justifying the structure is to say that professors use different books from undergraduates and so there is no conflict of interest. This argument is partly true but only partly.

As I have shown, there are a number of factors that can affect decisions about loan policy, and it is not surprising that the loan policies adopted by different libraries can be very different one from another. It is the duty of the librarian to consider these factors within his own institution in order to determine a rational loan policy for his own circumstances. The policy must obviously relate to the library objectives and to performance measures relating those objectives.

Lending procedures

The lending procedures of a library should be determined by the loan policy. It is possible sometimes for the structure of the lending procedure to determine the loan policy, and this may affect the library's ability to meet its objectives. I can give an example of this. About 20 years ago it was quite common for university libraries in this country to have a loan period of only one week for all undergraduate students. Since many students did not return the books after one week the libraries incurred labour costs in sending letters of recall to students saying that the books were overdue. In order to save this labour the libraries extended the loan period from one week to one term; this saved much labour but it was achieved at the expense of decreasing the availability of the book stock and there was thus a loss of benefit to the users.

What are the technical requirements of the lending procedure? I believe there are five:

- access to named items of stock
- positive identification of borrowers
- a means of identifying overdue items
- a method for reserving and recalling items in demand
- feedback on the use of the stock.

Access to named items

The lending procedures are part of the library's general stock control system and must be integrated with it in some manner. The record of a loan must contain sufficient information to identify the item borrowed uniquely. For most purposes a simple book number is sufficient, but this number must be linked to author and title details on occasions. It must also be possible to link the loan record with the catalogue record for the same book so that queries arising from the catalogue can be answered satisfactorily. To be effective the file or records of books on loan must be up to date; this is clearly a problem with some manual systems.

Identity of borrowers

For many loans it is not actually necessary to know the identity of a given borrower. Provided a borrower has authorization to borrow a book and returns it before another reader requires it then there is no need to keep a record of the borrower. It becomes essential when a book has to be recalled for any reason: since we cannot predict which books these will be, the loan record has at all times to include a unique identification of the borrower.

Identifying overdue items

If a library specifies loan periods this means that it is interested in getting the books back. If borrowers do not return books on time there are a variety of sanctions which can be operated. Many libraries fine users who return books late. Some libraries find it difficult to actually collect money from senior members of the faculty. Some libraries send out letters to borrowers indicating that their books are overdue; some libraries send second letters for overdue books and even third ones. Although it is not absolutely necessary to send reminders to ensure the return of most books it is necessary to be able to identify items which are excessively overdue. In many systems this may be labour-intensive.

Reservation and recall

Reservation of books is necessary because for certain items the demand outstrips the supply. The reservation procedure can provide useful feedback on the use of items which might lead to a change of availability of particular books – either by duplication or by shortening the loan period. As well as providing a means of recalling desired items, the reservation procedure must include a method of flagging so that returned books are caught effortlessly at the point of discharge.

Feedback on the use of library stock

I believe that there is still comparatively little use made of information about the use of library stock, even though automated systems are capable of providing much information about the use of books. In libraries where the loan period of a book is determined by the demand for that book feedback is absolutely necessary. A book which is not used sufficiently to justify a short loan period must be allocated to a longer loan period section of the stock, and vice versa.

Administrative characteristics

There are four considerations about the administration of lending procedures. They should be simple for the public to use; simple for the library staff to operate; economical; and integrated with the rest of the library's operations.

The library-user interface

If the users can borrow books easily, quickly and without effort, this is obviously preferable to a system which is complex, slow and labour-intensive. Some manual systems are very efficient in these respects, others inefficient, and the same can be said of automated systems. Similarly there should be a simple procedure for returning books; there is very little incentive to return books if this involves queuing for any length of time. With some systems queuing is inevitable. Some libraries operate systems in which boxes to which books can be returned are located at various points outside the library. This makes it very easy for books to be returned, but they need to be secure to prevent theft and readers must be discouraged from leaving books on top of a box which happens to be full.

Operational simplicity

A procedure which is simple for the user is likely to be simple for the library staff to operate, and the simpler the system the less chance there is of error. One particular manual procedure which is prone to error is what I call the 'two-slip self-charge'. In this system a borrower fills out a two-part form for each book that he borrows. Forgery could be a problem but there are three principal causes of error: slips completed incorrectly, slips completed illegibly, and misfiling. Other manual systems are more error-proof but are still prone to errors of filing.

Economics

The costing of library procedures is a complex problem, but I think it is often overlooked that the users' time should be considered when examining the costs. In one manual system I examined, the inputed cost of the users' time accounted for 30% of the total cost of the system.

Integration with other systems

The file of books on loan to readers is conceptionally a sub-file of the library's stock control master file; in an ideal system one file would contain all records of location and use of all materials ever suggested for, purchased by, or borrowed from elsewhere by the library. This file would naturally include records of books on loan, being bound and so on. Such an ideal file can actually be achieved in a library making full use of automation. Of course, automation is not necessarily the answer to everyone's problems. A thorough systems analysis is needed in every local situation. It is not enough to buy an automated system just for prestige: the cost of equipment maintenance, and the need to consider replacement in due course, have to be taken into account. Where the costs are justified, there can be savings, but in my experience the justification for automation lies with the improved stock control and feedback on stock use that become available.

Measuring performance

There are three aspects of performance which can be measured in relation to lending services. They are the effectiveness of the lending policy in meeting library objectives; the technical efficiency of the system; and the administrative effectiveness of the procedures. I will deal with these in reverse order, and save the most interesting until last.

Administrative effectiveness

One of the requirements of the lending system is that it should be quick, easy and simple to use. The borrowing procedure should be quick, and one measure of performance is the length of queues of people waiting to borrow books. Queues do not always measure this aspect of the system, however; in some libraries there is always a queue waiting at the time when otherwise restricted books are allowed out for the weekend — these are usually the so-called 'short loan' books, for which the normal loan period is a few hours. At a general loans desk the length of queues is an indication of the performance of the system itself. Queues are not limited to libraries and they occur in many institutions — post offices, banks, government offices, bus stops. The length of the queue is dependent on the amount of time taken to serve each customer and the rate at which customers arrive wanting service. Figure 2 shows the relationship between the number in the queue and the percentage of time a service point is occupied serving users. It shows that when the service point is occupied serving customers for half of the time, the average number of people in the queue will be two; when the service point is occupied 80% of the time, the average number in the queue doubles.

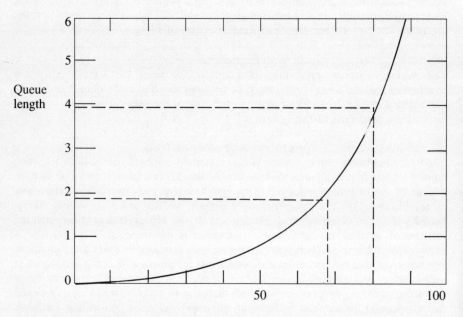

Fig. 2 Queue length and service occupation rate

The most efficient system is one in which each service point deals with only one kind of transaction — that is, if the people requiring to borrow books go to one desk and those wishing to ask questions go to another. This specialization of function is probably necessary in large libraries, if users are not to suffer excessive delays. If the librarian observes that users are queuing for an excessive length of time then he may be able to take action to reduce the size of the problem. The simplest is to open an additional issuing point adjacent to the first, and this is quite commonly done, especially at times of peak traffic. It is a matter of observation when these hours occur. Alternatively, changes may be possible to the procedures in use which speed up the amount of time required to service each borrower and thus reduce the length of time waiting in the queue. It is a matter of judgement on the part of the librarian to say whether a queue is excessively long or not. My own rule of thumb is that a queue of six people is too long, and if queues of this length occur frequently action should be taken.

Another measure of the administrative efficiency of the system lies in the number of errors which are detected. For how many books which return from loan is there no record of the loan having occurred? How many borrowers from whom books are recalled claimed that they have return the book and that the loan record must therefore not have been discharged? If a book has been reserved is it always detected when it returns from loan? If a book which has been reserved is detected when it is returned, can the library staff then find out who reserved the book? The increasingly efficient use of automation has cut down the number of errors which used to occur through misfiling, but they can still occur, and in any case not all libraries can afford to have automated systems. What can be done to prevent misfiling? Filing of manual records usually depends on the ability of staff to work with the alphabet and to know that the letter 'g' always comes after 'f' and before 'h', for example, or that gamma comes after beta and before delta. In situations where filing alphabetically is an important part of the procedure then the staff selected should be tested on their abilities before being appointed. Literacy is not enough. Many literate persons have difficulty with spelling and with alphabetization, just as many mathematicians have difficulties with adding up.

Feedback on the use of stock

In systems where the loan period depends on the demand for a book it is clearly important to measure the use attracted by each book. This information can be tedious to collect in manual systems, and libraries may flinch from the effort involved. Sample surveys may be carried out, but these are necessarily inadequate for the effective operation of a variable loan policy although they may be useful in other contexts. In the library which operates a variable loan policy it is necessary to know for each time period how many loans a book has achieved. Libraries usually work on annual cycles and this is particularly the case in academic libraries. For this reason loan statistics are usually accumulated over a period of one year. The decisions as to which loan period shall be applicable to each book are then determined by reference to the number of loans per year. For example, it might be decided that if a book attracts less than four loans in a year then it shall be classified as a long loan book. If the number of loans is more than the four it will be treated as a short or medium loan book. I would define a short loan period as anything less than 48 hours and a medium loan period as anything from 48 hours to two weeks. A long loan period would then be greater than two weeks. The decision as to what books should be placed in the short loan category will vary. In most libraries these books are those which have been specially recommended by the teaching staff, which they expect most students to use, and of which there are insufficient copies for all students to borrow for lengthy periods of time.

A further use of data on the use of books is as a check on the effectiveness of the acquisitions policy. If it is found that the use made of books purchased in one subject area is consistently high, then that is a measure of success, whereas if the use of books is conspicuously low then that is a measure of comparative failure if the objective of the library is to obtain books which are to be of use. Of course this does not apply to libraries which have an archival function, where the responsibility of the library may be to maintain copies of books for future use and the fact that they are not used by the present clientele is of little relevance. It may however be relevant to the actual location of books, and books which are not used much can be relegated to closed access or compact storage where they will be available but not in prime sites.

Policy effectiveness

We have to choose measures of performance which relate to the policy objectives of the library. These will differ between libraries and over time, but for present purposes I will suggest that the two objectives to be considered are to maximize the benefits derived by users from the library service, and to maximize the proportion of users who obtain access to the books they require. Both of these measures require some kind of survey of users. The first objective, that relating to the benefit derived by the users, is not confined to the effects of the lending policy and procedures. Similar techniques may be used to measure the benefit derived from any library service. There are two possible approaches which I will describe to measuring the benefits specifically derived from the lending service.

Document exposure

It can be argued that the time spent by a user reading a book is a measure of the benefit derived by the user from that book. It is possible to ask readers when they return books from loan how long they have spent actually reading the book, but this is an unreliable method since it is common for people to over-estimate the time they have spent actually doing things. This would be particularly the case in the instance of library books, where users might think they ought to say that they have spent some significant amount of time on the book when they might not in fact have read it at all. It is best to use the kind of anonymous survey in which readers are asked when they borrow a book if they will keep a note of the time spent reading on a card which they are given at the point of borrowing. This card can act as a bookmark and can be returned anonymously with the book at the end of the loan period. I have used this method myself and I believe that it is reasonably reliable for long periods of up to about two weeks. Beyond that time the number of cards returned declines and one can place less reliance on the results. It does however seem as if the document exposure may be a reasonably valid measure of benefit gained from reading books by undergraduates. Figure 3 is a graph showing the relationship between document exposure against retention time.

Availability

Another measure of performance of a lending policy is that of availability. This can be defined in a number of ways, but it is usually taken to be the proportion of books that are found by the users when they require them. A number of libraries have measured this in the last 25 years, using a variety of methods, but they are all based on the same concept: users are asked to make notes of the books they are looking

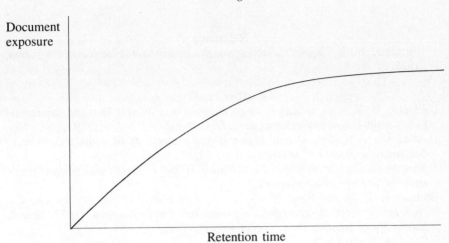

Fig. 3   **Document exposure and retention time**

for and whether they found them or not. A more sophisticated approach requires that library staff try to identify why the books were unavailable when the users were looking for them. There can be of course as many as ten or more reasons: the books may be on loan, lost, being used in the library by somebody else, being repaired or bound, not owned by the library, owned by the library but not yet catalogued, and so on. Depending on the results of the survey, the librarian may take action to improve the performance. He might allocate more resources to cataloguing so that fewer books are unavailable for this reason. If he identifies particular books which are in heavy demand he may buy additional copies or alter the loan period of the items in question.

Libraries in which availability is measured regularly have observed a curious phenomenon. Immediate availability of books is nearly always in the range of 60−70%, that is to say two thirds of the users find the books they want when they want them. It is possible to change this figure by making some change in policy; by changing the loan periods, for example, to reflect differences in demand. However, the improvement achieved by changing policy is soon reduced in proportion owing to an increase in demand. This is because, if the service improves, the users start making more use of the service, and it is natural that the performance of the system declines again. The proportion of the users then who get the books they want stays roughly constant, but if the service is improved more people will use the service. That then is the measure of performance, the level of demand.

We can summarize this section by listing the data which we might collect for purposes of measuring the system performance.

The *cost per loan* and the *average queuing time* are measures of the administrative efficiency of the system. The distribution of *loans per book*, the average *loans per user*, the *stock turnover rate* (number of loans divided by the total number of loanable items), the *percentage of stock on loan* and the *percentage of items overdue* all provide feedback on the use of stock and are thus measures of the technical efficiency of the system.

Availability and *document exposure* are measures of policy effectiveness.

131

Reference

1 Buckland, M. K., *Book availability and the library user*, New York, Pergamon, 1975.

Further reading

Buckland, M. K., 'An operations research study of a variable loan and duplication policy at the University of Lancaster', *Library quarterly*, **42**, (1), 1972, 97 – 106.

Hindle, A., 'A theoretical note concerning the adaptivity of demand for library documents', *Journal of documentation*, **33**, (4), 1977, 305 – 8.
This suggests a way in which the economic theory of supply and demand might apply in library book provision.

Hudson, R. F. B. and Ford, M. G., *South West University Library Systems Co-operation Project: A report for the period July 1969 – December 1972*, Bristol, University of Bristol, 1973. (OSTI Report 5151)
See Appendices Q – V for details of the kind of systematic data collection and analysis necessary for the design of circulation procedures, whether automated or manual.

Morse, P., *Library effectiveness: a systems approach*, Cambridge, Mass., M.I.T. Press, 1968.
Covers some of the same ground as Buckland, and other topics, but has a more mathematical bias.

16

Services to external users

Lynne Brindley

Introduction

The environment of higher education in the UK is one of constrained resources, a three- to five-year planning horizon of continuing downward pressure on budgets; increasing competition for the most able students, as we go sharply into the demographic dip; the widening of access to higher education for groups with non-traditional qualifications; and constant pressure from Government for greater efficiency and accountability. In this context universities and polytechnics are increasingly looking to generate income to support their activities, supplement their central budget allocation, and become more independent of their traditional funding sources. Examples include the endowment of chairs, exclusive contracts for research work, often in exchange for equipment donation or buildings, and fund raising from alumni. All this activity is being encouraged by the Government. In addition to wanting to generate income, institutions are also concerned to improve their image with the public at large by reaching out into the community and looking beyond the 'ivory tower', which is the public perception of universities, towards serving the needs of a wider clientele.

Academic libraries operate as part of that environment and the consideration of services to external users, including income generating activities and joint ventures with the private sector, gradually becoming part of library thinking, although still at a fairly low level of overall activity.

Motivation

Libraries may have a wide variety of reasons for providing external services and very different scope for the provision of these services, both in terms of their potential external clientele, and the richness of resources to draw on, through collections, services, and staff expertise. What is important to establish, for any external service is the reason(s) for providing it all. Reasons may include the following: improvement of the image of the library, possibly by the provision of wider information services; response to a particular local need, for example, if there is a cluster of professionals working nearby, maybe in a hospital or law courts; desire to heighten the library's profile, to look more outgoing and dynamic; or to earn money, not least as a response to the Finance Officer, who probably regards the library as a 'bottomless pit'. There

133

may be spin-off benefits, such as favourable treatment in the allocation of equipment, or the gaining of useful expertise that can be fed back to the primary user groups. Contacts made through services might also help to foster wider contracts to the university, for example, research or placement opportunities for students. None of these reasons is mutually exclusive. However, it is unlikely that income generation *per se* is the primary motivation for most external services, and even in examples of the more successful external services large sums of money are not being made, either in turnover or profit.

So the first lesson is to establish a rationale for service provision, beyond the primary clientele of the academic library. In doing this it is important to consider any service from the library in the wider context of the institutional purpose and objectives, and try to build on areas of strength or particular concern of the university. Insofar as the university is itself reaching out, say to industry or the local community, so then is the climate right for academic libraries to act similarly, either directly or as part of a wider institutional effort or package of services.

Examples of this follow. Aston University relates to industry in a variety of ways, but in particular, it has a Science Park, here on campus and is the home of the West Midlands Technology Transfer Centre. The Library and Information Service focuses its external information service provision on meeting the needs of the Science Park and works through the WMTTC as an agent, if local firms have particular information requirements or consultancy needs. Hatfield Polytechnic has a long tradition of links with local industry and commerce, and has the associated successful business information service in HERTIS. The London Business School is a centre of excellence for business education, likewise the library runs an outstanding business information service, with a wide clientele on its metropolitan doorstep.

Balance between primary and external services

Before we get carried away by the opportunities it is important to consider another underlying concern, that is the difficulty of maintaining a proper balance between primary service provision and revenue-earning or other external activities, without distortion of the primary purpose of an academic library, namely to serve the teaching and research needs of the institution. There can be little or no justification to permit external activities to detract from the quality of that primary service, and indeed even if librarians were willing, academics would certainly not be. This is a very important point and has to be watched on a continuing basis if you are involved in external service provision. There is a certain paradox inherent in this position. It has already been suggested that external service provision is most likely to be successful if you build on the various institutional strengths, including those of academic departments. This has been done, for example, in the Warwick University Statistical Service, and through the Barnes Medical Library Service to National Health Service staff in Birmingham. Yet it is in these very areas of strength that we have high demand from our own internal users, leading to potential conflict of interest over access to stock and services, unless very sensitively managed. The problem is compounded if the service is commercially offered, when external clients can reasonably expect fast and professional service provision and usually want the information yesterday. This is intended not as a negative point, but one for careful thought before launching into external service provision.

It might also lead to consideration of some form of joint venture with the private sector, whereby there can be a sharing of effort, in a variety of ways, between the library and the commercial body, to mutual benefit. This might, for example, take the form of a joint publishing venture, using the library's collection resources and the publisher's marketing expertise; it might involve the employment of an information broker, where the library has rich primary resources, but cannot afford or chooses not to exploit these resources directly for wider service provision. This is not yet a common pattern in the UK, but is well established in the USA. The effort and skill needed to bring off a joint venture should, however, not be underestimated, and in some cases, may simply not be worth the time taken to bring it to fruition.

Service options

With the above provisos it is now possible to turn to a consideration of the range of service options open to the library, and the pros and cons of their supply, either free or on a charged basis. This paper will not go into depth on the free versus fee debate, and the implications of cost recovery policies, as that is dealt with elsewhere in more detail.

At a fairly basic level academic libraries generally offer access to the stock of the library, for reference and lending purposes. In a survey carried out in 1986 by Birmingham Polytechnic Library.[1] of the 62 libraries involved, over 80% lend material to personal callers, although less than one third lend by post. Most of these external users are individuals, not corporate borrowers, with 13 libraries registering over 250, many of whom are likely to be alumni. More than half of the libraries charge an annual subscription for this kind of external service, charges ranging widely, but no individuals are charged more than £50 a year. Few libraries make specific charges for loan of material from their own stock, rather this is part of a basic subscription service.

A second common provision is the supply of photocopies from library stock. From the same survey, 90% of libraries supply photocopies to personal callers, and slightly over half will supply by post. The most common rate for self-service photocopies was 5p a page; serviced photocopying attracted a range of charges from 6p to 12p a page, plus postage if necessary, with some libraries charging a minimum charge of £2.

The third area of general provision is supplying interlibrary loan requests. 45% of libraries surveyed will obtain material for external users through the interlending system, charging between £5 and £6 an item.

The provision of information is also cited as a general service. Information is provided to personal callers by over 90% of the libraries, while two thirds supply by post, and nearly one third by phone. 92% provide answers to quick enquiries; 58% will answer longer enquiries; 73% will carry out online searches; 27% prepare reading lists and bibliographies. Charging policies for online searching vary from library to library, but some notion of direct cost recovery plus a surcharge for staff time is a common approach.

This group of services has been considered in some detail as by and large most academic libraries could be involved in external service provision at this level, without undue detriment to their internal clientele, and with the possibility of some, but not substantial, income generation. Although this kind of service is fairly low key, it is a useful entry into the external market, and will serve to build up a clientele, to whom, at a later date, more advanced, value-added services might be offered. In addition, such a group might well form the core of a Friends of the Library initiative, if fund raising became of relevance. Some care needs to be exercised in the use of staff time, which in these services, tends not to be fully costed. It is important to monitor external usage, particularly where staff time might become intensively used, for example, in answering a very involved query, and reserve the option of negotiating a price for the job where longer pieces of research are requested, assuming that the library is willing, and able, to undertake the task.

We can now move on to a second level of services which are more focused on particular groups and meeting their service needs, and which offer a greater depth of service than previously mentioned. The most common area in which such added value services are provided by academic libraries is in business information, for which there appears, at least superficially, to be a large and growing market in the business and industrial community. Detailed case studies of major providers in this area are available in Brenda White's report, which covers this whole area.[2] Major UK service suppliers are HERTIS, London Business School, and Warwick Business Information Service. Public libraries and other agencies, such as chambers of commerce, are also actively involved in service provision, so care needs to be taken when planning services not to unwittingly target or go into unnecessary competition for the same groups. In particular instances the case for provision of service may be stimulated by the presence of a business park, an industrial estate, or a science park nearby.

But we should heed Brenda White's warning, that 'despite these obvious attractions and advantages, provision of information services to local firms is fraught with difficulties, and poses more questions than can be answered by the average academic library from its own experience'. She points to such problems as the ill-defined nature of 'need', the fact that business firms frequently seek answers to problems elsewhere, using their own informal grape-vines, and the question as to whether they are prepared to pay for information in any case. In addition, most librarians are not familiar with the concerns and culture of business, especially small business, and may not be well geared to provide a service to this kind of clientele.

Successful service models of this kind are largely subscription based, around the £350–£500 a year mark, with additional charges as appropriate, for a bundled package of documents, information and consultancy time to call on. Some services have a casual user basis charge, on an hourly rate. Policy issues that are raised include the question of whether the income generated can be kept by the library, and ploughed back directly into the service. There is little incentive if this is not the case, at least in some measure. There is also the dilemma faced by successful services of how far to expand and maintain the balance between primary and secondary service objectives. In some cases this can lead to decisions to split off the commercial service from normal service provision and have dedicated staff for the external users. There are pros and cons of operating either way. If the service remains integrated there is the advantage of sharpening up the whole approach to timely service provision, with the difficulties of split loyalties, to a mix of duties. If split off, it can be perceived as an elitist group of staff, and it still has to rely on the core collections of the parent library. There might also be the detrimental effect on the image of the library if such a service becomes disassociated from it. On the other hand, a separated service might provide the flexibility of paying the market rates for the right kind of staff, who may be employed on an information brokerage basis, and probably gives more freedom for growth.

At Aston we are taking our first steps in the provision of an information service to the Science Park and its tenant companies. This is an obvious group for the LIS to serve, as already there are close links with the university, and the site is virtually on the library's doorstep. The Park now supports well over 45 small high-tech companies in the small units, and some expanded companies in larger units. The LIS has dedicated half a person to serve these companies, largely with a mixture of technical, standards, marketing and business information. This is over and above access, in a more passive way, to the general collection, services and facilities of the university library. The information specialist concentrates on stimulating awareness of relevant information, providing tailored online information searches, and packaging of information to meet particular company needs. Common requests are related to competitor information, mailing lists, and financial results.

What are the key issues to consider with such an emerging service?

- how to promote the service, both initially and on a continuing basis. Techniques such as open evenings, promotional brochures, sample searches, open house lunches, have all been tried.
- how to persuade small, very busy companies to even find time to listen to what you have to offer. They frequently do not see external information as relevant.
- how far and for how long to subsidize such a service. Especially difficult points come when the workload being generated is larger than the allotted staff time but the revenue has not yet reached a stage which allows the taking on of more staff on anything other than an *ad hoc* basis.
- how far gaps in the collection should be filled to provide an improved service for external customers, although the material is not priority for the academic areas.

These are a few of the questions that have emerged so far in a fledgling service. We have a research grant from the British Library to study some of the special information needs of Science Park companies, and feeding the results back into the service, as a potential model to be made available to other libraries.

Moving on from business information services, there are numerous other opportunities for academic libraries. Maurice Line mentions some of these.[3] He suggests cooperation with academic departments, combining information resources with personal expertise. He points to a good market for facsimile reproduction of rare and beautiful books, and for copies of manuscript illuminations, providing opportunities for major research libraries to exploit their collections, possibly in conjunction with the private sector. In this connection it is worth referring to the LISC publication on joint enterprise,[4] and a related commentary.[5]

Skills and attitudes

A major consideration when planning services to external users will be the attitudes and skills of existing staff, for above questions of whether they can handle the anticipated volume of activity, there is the more serious point of whether their skills are suited, or can be developed, to do so. Brenda White's report is hard hitting in its criticisms of the profession and its lack of a range of managerial skills, and certainly it is true that many people in mid-profession and higher management did not come in to librarianship because of opportunities to be entrepreneurial or to sell their skills.

Even where they recognize the need to change, the process is slow.

Marketing skills are crucial to the success of any external venture, from the market analysis, through product and service design, to launching and promoting the offerings. However, these skills would seem to be equally important whether the service is for profit or not.

Financial acumen is also not highly developed in many librarians, nor has it until recently been a required skill, as it is now that accountability moves from mere stewardship to value for money accounting and performance assessment. However, before venturing near the provision of commercial services it is imperative that full costings are done, market pricing is considered, and so on. The number of librarians who still confuse income with profit is rather worrying.

Further skills – in communication, presentation and use of information technology – are all increasingly required for survival in a commercial environment.

All of these skills, to a greater or lesser degree, are required as part of running a modern academic library: the key problem is the time it takes to develop these skills in existing staff. The opportunity afforded by joint venture involvement for a mixing of cultures to mutual benefit might well accelerate the learning process and supply quickly complementary skills, to enable new initiatives to be progressed.

Conclusions

It is clear that academic libraries are increasingly in an environment of opportunity for the provision of services to a wider range of clientele. There are plenty of possibilities and care is needed before moving ahead in appropriate ways. Some analysis of the market is necessary and clear planning through the potential problems and policy issues that will inevitably arise. Consideration needs to be given to the professional acceptability of some options and the match of skills required for the successful provision of service, which might range from an extension of the use of basic facilities to external users, to the value-added, tailored information service.

The choice is ours – it all depends on individual circumstances and local opportunities, but with some determination and imagination, the academic library can serve the wider community in new ways.

References

1 Beardwood, Jennifer, *Academic library services to the industrial and business community*, Birmingham Polytechnic Library, 1986.

2 White, Brenda, *Striking a balance: external services in academic libraries*, London, British Library, 1987 (British Library Research Paper 30).

3 Line, Maurice B. *The research library in the enterprise society*, London, University of London, Library Resources Coordination Committee, 1988 (LRCC Occasional Publication 8), *reprinted in LSE quarterly*, **2**, (4), 1988, 361–78, *and in Australian library journal*, **38**, (3), 1989, 197–209.

4 *Joint enterprise: roles and relationships of the public and private sectors in the provision of library and information services*, London, HM Stationery Office, 1987 (Library Information Series no.16).

5 Brindley, Lynne, 'Joint enterprise: its importance for academic library services', *New library world*, **88**, (1049), 1987, 205–6.

17

Interlibrary access, national and international

Maurice B. Line

Introduction

Academic libraries have become far more dependent upon external resources since World War 2. The reasons for this are obvious. There has been a great growth in scientific and other research (though this growth is now far slower than it was in the 1950s and 1960s), and this has led to a greatly increased volume of publication. Moreover, the cost of publications has risen much faster than general inflation in most countries. If libraries were to keep up with the increased growth and cost of scholarly and scientific literature, they would need an annual average increase in their budgets of around 15%. Academic institutions have also expanded greatly, leading to greatly increased demand for services. At the same time, acquisition funds have at best kept up with inflation, and in real terms have fallen far behind desirable provision. Whereas before World War 2 most libraries seemed to consider it a disgrace if they could not supply everything from their own resources, and regarded interlibrary loan as something very special, access to external resources is now accepted as an essential fact of life.

Academic libraries are typically much the largest category of user of interlibrary access systems. In Britain, they account for about 50% of interlibrary demand. Their demands also spread over all subjects and all forms of material. Other characteristics of academic library demand are that between half and three-quarters is in science and technology − a reflection of the proportion of research accounted for by these subjects, which affects both the volume of publication and the volume of demand. About two-thirds of demand is for journals. If these two characteristics are combined, between a third and a half of total academic demand is typically for scientific and technical journals.

The development of interlibrary access schemes

The history of interlibrary access schemes shows a gradual − at times fast − progress from the Stone Age to the modern Automated Age. Stone Age systems are in fact not systems at all: libraries contact other libraries they hope or believe will have the items they want, and if this fails try other libraries. This is very much a hit-and-miss operation, which is not appropriate even when interlibrary loan demand is very small; if demand attains any scale it is totally inadequate. In fact, demand under such a system is unlikely to attain any scale, since the probability of satisfaction is so low and the delays in supply so great that few demands are made.

Iron Age schemes are based on manual union catalogues on cards. These are maintained in centres, and cooperating libraries submit cards for their acquisitions to them. Requests have to be made to the centre, which then re-directs them to libraries listed as holding the materials, or sends the requesting library a note of such libraries so that it can send requests to them direct. These systems were just about adequate before World War 2, but they have numerous disadvantages. In the first place, they are entirely reliant upon efficient notification of new acquisitions by cooperating libraries. They may send them in batches at infrequent intervals, or forget to send them at all. At best, they are not up to date. Moreover, libraries often forget to notify the union catalogue centre when items are lost or disposed of, with the result that a high percentage of locations are no longer valid. Iron Age systems are not very effective, they are slow, and they are cumbersome and costly to use.

A refinement of Iron Age systems is the production of printed union catalogues, which libraries can acquire and use to locate materials themselves; these can obviate use of the centre for many requests, but are out of date when printed and grow progressively more out of date unless and until they are revised. They are of much more use for journals than for books.

A breakthrough occurred with the creation in the United Kingdom in 1961 of the National Lending Library for Science and Technology, a library that has now become the Document Supply Centre of the British Library. The NLLST as originally envisaged worked with Iron Age technology but cut out many of the processes involved in Iron Age systems; the concept was, and still is, that a large central collection dedicated to document supply can achieve a higher fill rate and a faster speed of supply than systems involving cooperation between libraries. Union catalogues are largely bypassed. The BLDSC now handles about three-quarters of all British demand. Smaller and less radical but effective systems, mainly concerned with journals and with science and technology, are the Centre de Documentation Scientifique et Technologique (CDST) in Paris and the Canada Institute for Scientific and Technical Information (CISTI) in Ottawa. If the volume of demand is high enough such systems can be more cost-effective as well as faster than cooperative systems. They have not been superseded by technological and other developments; rather, they have been in the forefront in using them. They are not realistic possibilities for countries with a small demand, because the unit costs would be too high, but such countries might consider a core collection of scientific journals, which would be able to deal with a quite high percentage of total demand.

The Bronze Age arrived with the advent of cheap and efficient electrostatic copying machines, which made it possible to supply journal articles without the necessity of lending the actual issue or volume. This did not help the supply of books, but these are a minority (though a large one) of interlibrary requests.

The contribution of automation and telefacsimile

That it has been possible to move out of the Bronze Age has been largely due to automation. In the Automated Age, manual union catalogues have given way to union catalogues held on the computer. Submission of new entries may be in manual form, in which case they have to be key-punched into the catalogue, or, much better, they are notified in electronic form, in which case they can be incorporated directly if the catalogue records are sufficiently standard as to be interfilable. In this case the union catalogues are much more up-to-date; how up-to-date depends on the speed of cataloguing in the cooperating libraries. Notification of losses and disposals is still unreliable.

Automated union catalogues can be used to print out union lists, though unless this is done frequently they soon get out of date, or, better, they are accessible online and they can be searched direct by requesting libraries. It should also be possible to submit requests electronically directly to libraries listed as holding items; and a further refinement is the ability to switch requests from libraries that do not have an item to those that do. The processes of location and requesting are thus greatly speeded up. However, supply is still in the hands of the holding library; the only effect automated systems have on the speed of supply is a psychological one, in that libraries may feel under more pressure to supply items quickly when they have been requested electronically than when requests may have taken some time to arrive by mail.

A further electronic refinement is the use of telefacsimile to send copies of journal articles (though it can also be used to send requests). Here it is necessary to emphasize the distinction between journal articles and papers in conference proceedings — 'copiable' items — and 'non-copiable' items such as books. The latter are of course not amenable to transmission by telefacsimile. There are several reports in the American library press of telefacsimile supply systems that purport to be cost-effective. However, Group 3 machines — the commonest in current use — nearly all require articles to be photocopied first because they will accept only sheets of paper, not original journal volumes or issues. Allowing for photocopying, logging on and slow transmission times, it can easily take 20 minutes or more to transmit a 10-page article. This means that a maximum of 30 or at the most 40 articles can be transmitted in a day. In order to justify the capital costs of the machine, it is necessary to send at least 20 or 30 items a day (although it may of course be used to transmit matter other than journals). While it may be suitable for urgent items, therefore, it is hardly possible to use it as a general means of transmission. The cost to the British Library Document Supply Centre of supplying an article by telefacsimile is incidentally about two or three times as much as of supplying an article in the ordinary way by photocopying and mail.

The situation will be changed by the advent of Group 4 machines, which are much faster, produce copies of better quality, and much cheaper to use: the unit cost of transmitting an article may be only a tenth of that by Group 3 machines. Group 4 machines are however a good deal more expensive, and require digital telecommunications links rather than the normal analogue links; they thus need either ISDN (Integrated Services Digital Network), which is coming but slowly, or a dedicated digital link. If they are to come into general use, many libraries would need to have them, and this is very far from the case at the moment. In due course however they could compete for cost with conventional photocopying and mail systems.

Interlibrary access and its impact on local acquisition and retention policies

As noted above, efficient interlibrary access systems are of the greatest importance to academic libraries. Where there is a reliable system to which they can turn, they can optimize their acquisition and retention policies in a way that would be impossible otherwise. For example, they need not buy the journal wanted by one professor very occasionally if they know it is available elsewhere in the system, and they may be able to discard a back run of a little-used journal. With cooperative systems, there is of course a danger that the same items will be disposed of by several libraries at the same time, leaving no copy nationally available; a national repository plan is needed to provide for this.

Where there is an effective access system, libraries should compare the cost of acquisition and retention with the cost of interlibrary access. If an average journal is wanted more than eight or nine times in a year it is more economic to buy than to borrow it, but few journals are average, and the balance depends on the cost of the journal (the total cost, including processing, binding and storage, which together can add very significantly to the cost). There should always be a bias in favour of acquisition, because of the importance of current scanning and browsing; when a journal is chosen solely or mainly for this reason, it should not be necessary to retain it more than two or three years, and it is pointless to bind it.

The foregoing applies to journals. It is much harder to optimize book acquisitions; current books are often very hard to obtain on interlibrary access, since they have been acquired by libraries for their own users and they are rarely willing to lend them in the first six or twelve months after purchase. (This problem can be dealt with to some extent by central supply systems, though if the demand is heavy waiting-lists will build up; over 25% of requests to the British Library Document Supply Centre for books, mainly recent ones, have to go on waiting lists). There is no ideal system for book supply, though the American OCLC system probably comes fairly near to it. The USA has a large number of libraries, many of them with rich resources, and it is generally possible to locate at least one copy of a wanted book. Similar conditions apply in no other country in the world.

National acquisition schemes: cooperative versus decentralized
Improved access systems on their own can only make available material that has actually been acquired by libraries. Various attempts have been made to deal with this problem by cooperative acquisition schemes, and nearly all of them have failed. The reason is fairly obvious. Unless additional resources are made available, libraries are in effect required to sacrifice items they wish to acquire for their own users in order to acquire materials that may be of some use nationally some time in the future. Such a degree of altruism is hardly to be expected, particularly at times of diminishing budgets. It can of course be argued that such cooperation is to the national good, and if they make some sacrifices they reap still greater benefits by having better total national access because the total national resource is larger; in practice, pressures to maintain local acquisitions are generally so great that this argument does not carry a great deal of weight.

If, on the other hand, extra resources are put into the system they have to be allocated among libraries; this requires agreement among libraries, and some kind of identification of the items acquired with the extra money as part of the national resource so they are not disposed of in future. The only good example of such a scheme is the one in the Federal Republic of Germany. Here the scheme works well, but in most countries the question would need to be asked why, if extra resources are to be made available, they should be scattered among many libraries rather than concentrated on one which can give a national service much more effectively. The British Library Document Supply Centre has a fairly comprehensive acquisition policy; it would in theory be possible to spread its acquisitions among many libraries, but the resulting system would be far less cost-effective.

In some countries, such as the Netherlands, there is a *de facto* national system, in that particular libraries accept a national role in, for example, agriculture and technology. The scheme is not comprehensive, and not all subjects are covered, but it is better than no plan at all.

The possible impact of electronic storage and transmission

Hopes have been expressed that we are about to move into the Electronic Age — that the electronic revolution will be carried one step further and prove the salvation of interlibrary access. This does not in my view seem a reasonable expectation. First of all, few publications are in electronic form, contrary to the forecasts in the mid-1970s that the economic cross-over point between conventional journal publication and electronic journals would occur in the mid-1980s. The ADONIS project, by which 219 mainly biomedical, mainly high-use, journals are issued on CD-ROM, is still an experiment, and its future direction is not yet clear. One of the next steps is to transmit directly from the electronic version, rather than doing what the British Library does at present, namely, scan and print articles and send them by mail — a system which produces no benefits whatever for the user, except that the quality of copy is higher, particularly where illustrations are concerned (one main reason why biomedical journals were chosen is that they posed a severe test of the scanning system and storage medium).

In theory, it might be possible to sell or lease CD-ROMs of journal text direct to libraries, thereby greatly increasing their local self-sufficiency; the effect this would have on interlibrary loan demand could be profound. However, the market would have to be large to bring the price of CD-ROMs down to an attractive level, and the price would in any case be set by the publishers. Moreover, the libraries would not have the freedom to use the CD-ROMs in the same way as they do printed text; for example, every copy made for a user would probably have to be paid for, and if the discs had, as is not unlikely, to be leased rather than bought outright, there would be no assurance of continuing availability. There is a further problem: if the journals on CD-ROM are not in heavy use, the market will not be big enough. On the other hand, if they are in heavy use, not only will multi-user access be required — this is now coming in — but several copies of discs will be required, since simultaneous access will be required to some of the many journal issues stored on the disc. There would have to be numerous work-stations; the total cost would be high, and quite probably cancel out any economic benefits.

Moreover, CD-ROMs are not an acceptable form for scanning and browsing of current journal issues; even if articles are specially redesigned for easy online viewing, the process is still slower than flipping over the pages of a journal issue to see whether there is anything of interest and then scanning a likely article. This still leaves open the possible use of CD-ROMs for storage of back issues, but in this case libraries would be either buying material they did not need or substituting CD-ROMs for journals they already held, in which case they would be paying twice.

For the above reasons, the sale or lease of CD-ROMs to individual libraries does not seem a very likely proposition. It is more likely that they will be used in centres, whether these are libraries in the public sector or centres operated by the publishers themselves. In that case, it will be up to libraries to choose between purchasing journals in printed form and obtaining articles directly from remotely stored CD-ROMs. How the costs will compare with present interlibrary access is anyone's guess. The choice will almost certainly exist, since most journals in high or medium use are making substantial profits, and publishers will not want to risk losing those by substituting them entirely by CD-ROM or by pricing access to CD-ROMs too low.

As will be apparent, I am sceptical about the Electronic Age of document supply. There is no doubt that some text will be available in electronic form, but much or most of this will also be available in conventional printed form, and print will remain the basic medium for most journals and nearly all books for the foreseeable future.

Improving interlibrary access

It is clearly in the interest of academic libraries to consider how interlibrary access could be improved in their countries. They can do this by cooperating among themselves, or with other types of libraries; it has always been a source of surprise to me that in many countries academic libraries have quite different cooperative systems from public libraries and special libraries. If a system is to be a cooperative one, it needs to be very carefully planned so as to be as cost-effective as possible. In general, the more that resources are concentrated on relatively few libraries, the better the system is likely to be, since these libraries can gear themselves specially to give a good supply. It is rarely satisfactory to let the system grow up gradually by a process of evolution, since the end result is likely to be highly sub-optimal. What should be aimed at is a total national system.

National systems of acquisition and document supply need to be very closely linked. Acquisition is of little use if the items acquired cannot be accessed, and document supply is impossible unless the items have been acquired. Systems can be basically centralized, as in the UK, concentrated on select major sources, as in the Federal Republic of Germany, or decentralized. As indicated earlier in this paper, the more centralization the more cost-effective the system is likely to be, and the better service academic libraries will have. The pros and cons of various systems are indicated in the table.

Summary of features of different systems

	Centralization	Concentration on 3 or 4 Libraries	Planned Decentralization	Unplanned Decentralization
Satisfaction Rate	Very high	High	High	Low
Supply Time	Very good	Good	Fairly good	Poor
Cost:				
Basic Provision	Very high	Moderate	Moderate	Very low
Operating	Low	Fairly low	Moderate	High
Ease of Use	Very easy	Easy	Fairly easy	Difficult
Ease of Monitoring	Very easy	Easy	Fairly easy	Impossible

144

Charging for access

Traditionally, supplying libraries have paid for interlibrary lending on the supposed principle that outgoing and incoming transactions balance, and that the cost of recovering money is too high. The first is rarely true; academic libraries usually supply far more than they receive, since they have the greatest and most varied resources. As for charging systems, the cost of recovering money can indeed be high if each individual item is invoiced and claimed separately, but this is totally unnecessary. Efficient charging systems can easily be operated, with standardized forms, standard charges, without differentials for the number of pages or the cost of postage (inequalities even out), and the purchase of forms in batches rather than as single units. Such a system has been used for 25 years in the UK, where a single form is used for all kinds of material and for transactions between libraries as well as for requests to the British Library.

Since interlibrary access costs money, it seems extraordinary that the supplier rather than the requester should be expected to pay; it is as if booksellers were required to pay for the books libraries acquire from them. Interlibrary access should be part of the same budget head as acquisition, since it is a temporary form of acquisition. Payment of full direct costs by requesting libraries is not only a matter of fairness, it has other advantages. In particular, it forces (or should force) requesting libraries to make a cost comparison between purchase and interlibrary access; there is no incentive to make this comparison if interlibrary access is 'free'. Imbalances between demand and supply cease to matter because the supplier recovers its costs; ideally it should be able to convert the money into staff.

International access

I have left international access until last. International demand has risen a good deal faster even than national demand; certainly foreign demand on the British Library Document Supply Centre has increased at an enormous rate, from 130,000 in 1973 when the British Library started to 770,000 in 1987/88. This represents over 3,000 requests every working day. National access systems should be planned in the context of international access. For example, in the case of a small country, it may be deemed more efficient beyond a certain point to rely on international access, even though it may be quite costly, than to build up a national system. Scandinavian countries tend to use the British Library in this way, because it has a fairly comprehensive journal collection (55,000 current titles and about 150,000 dead ones), and one of the best collections of conference proceedings, report literature and English-language books in the world. Even those that have good national systems will need to supplement them by international access; the British Library sends over 20,000 requests abroad every year, twice as many as 20 years ago.

International access is becoming easier, as more and more catalogues are automated and become accessible online. Preferably these should be union catalogues, but even the catalogues of individual large libraries can be of assistance. Within Europe, most of the more developed countries should have access to one another's union catalogues in a few years' time, and this should greatly improve interlibrary access, particularly to books. This could incidentally have a substantial impact on national acquisition planning; if, for example, it is possible to rely on rapid access to Germany for any German book, the need for Britain to have very extensive collections of German books is reduced. Just as individual libraries should make a cost comparison between purchase and interlibrary access, so libraries, and indeed countries, should make this comparison for international access. For these reasons, one would expect international access to continue to grow faster than national interlibrary access, except in countries where national systems are rapidly developing from a low basis.

Conclusion

To summarize. Interlibrary access is of great importance to academic libraries, both to supplement their own resources and to enable them to optimize them. It is entirely in the interest of academic libraries that they should encourage and support the development of efficient planned national interlibrary access systems. International access will become a more important supplementation of national schemes.

Relevant reading

Line, Maurice B., 'National interlending systems: existing systems and possible models', *Interlending review*, 7, (2), 1979, 42–6.

Line, Maurice B., 'Resource sharing: the present situation and the likely effect of electronic technology', *in* Fjallbrant, Nancy (ed.), *The future of serials*, Gothenburg, IATUL, 1984, 1–11.

Line, Maurice B., 'Universal availability of publications in an electronic age', *IATUL quarterly*, 3, (4), 1989, 214–23.

Line, Maurice B., 'Interlending and document supply in a changing world', *in* Cornish, Graham and Gallico, Alison (eds.), *Interlending and document supply: proceedings of the first International Conference ... London ... 1988*, [Boston Spa], IFLA International Office for International Lending, 1989, 1–4.

18

Cooperation in collections

Henry J. Heaney

Introduction

A few days after taking up my first library post in Belfast in 1957, I was given an 'NCL list' to check in our catalogue. I had used that same university library as an undergraduate and almost always it had met my needs. Now I was faced with a nine- or ten-page list of books which the National Central Library circulated among university libraries in Britain. These were titles which had been requested on interlibrary loan by readers at home and abroad and which the NCL could not trace in its own catalogues. I was amazed that my library had only a few of them. Some were rather esoteric, I thought, but surely the library was better stocked than our performance against the wants list would suggest. The following week brought another NCL list, and the next yet more, but week by week our success was negligible. Even when seeking books about Ireland we often failed, though we thought our Irish collections were extremely strong. How humbling it all was for a beginner to discover!

Thirty years later, there are no more NCL lists to check. I work in a much larger library now but I know that my ability to supply would not be significantly better. In 1977–78, Glasgow University lent 7,134 items to other libraries and borrowed 9,420. Last year, we lent 2,856 and borrowed 17,287. Part of the explanation is that the National Central Library has long been incorporated into the British Library Document Supply Centre which, because interlending is its specialism, is able to satisfy a very high proportion of requests from its own stock. Through its union catalogue records it is also able to direct requests for items it lacks less speculatively than in the past.[1]

There are other factors. Publishing output has increased; our sophisticated search services of bibliographic databases draw our readers' attention to titles of which they would otherwise be unaware. Just as important is the fact that though in 1977–78 we added 80,000 items of all kinds to our stock and last year we added 118,000, our budgets have not kept pace with publishing output nor with our readers' declared needs.

Networks

Cooperation comes naturally to librarians. We have been cooperating for much longer than any of our colleagues in universities. Even in the days before we recognized that no library could ever be totally self-sufficient, we knew from experience that most of us were not. Today, cooperation is being aided through automated systems in individual libraries and by opportunities for networking between them. Almost every British university library has computerized its catalogues in some form or other and most either have or aspire to on-line public access catalogues. The really advanced are considering CD-ROM output. Networks are being established with the encouragement of the University Grants Committee (now sponsored by the Universities Funding Council) to link libraries more closely together, not only in cooperatives, but also in the Joint Academic Network (JANET) which links all our universities, polytechnics and research institutions; and that includes the British Library and the National Libraries of Scotland and Wales.[2] Libraries are not yet as active in using the network as they might be but this, too, is being tackled through Project Jupiter. A two-year programme, based in Glasgow University Library, is being funded by the University Grants Committee and managed under the auspices of the JANET Library Users Group. It began in February 1989 and is intended to promote greater and more imaginative use of JANET by libraries.

CURL

CURL, the Consortium of University Research Libraries, is engaged on a different two-year project also funded by the UGC. CURL comprises the seven major British university research libraries — Cambridge, Edinburgh, Glasgow, Leeds, London, Manchester and Oxford. They are mounting those portions of their catalogues that are so far in machine-readable format on a national computer facility at Manchester. Through a central joint index, the records will be available for interrogation over JANET from the beginning of 1990. We foresee benefits in tracing locations and in promoting retrospective conversion of catalogue records, not only among the seven participants but throughout the JANET membership. Eventually the CURL database should have implications for interlending but in its first phase it will not be end-user friendly and the prime users will be librarians.[3]

SALBIN

Making networked access to online public access catalogues more user-friendly is a problem which we in Scotland are addressing in our Working Group on Library Cooperation. This body reports to the Trustees of the National Library and comprises also the eight Scottish university libraries and the two major public reference libraries in Edinburgh and Glasgow. The part of its work which concerns us here is the SALBIN project, based in Edinburgh University Library and supported by a British Library Research and Development grant. The acronym stands for the Scottish Academic Libraries Bibliographic Information Network. It aims to provide a front end menu from which library users at a dedicated terminal will be able to gain access over JANET to a range of online catalogues of other libraries in the same way that a local reader would. In its first stage SALBIN will offer 11 choices on its menu, but the system will be portable and can be adapted to local variations. We are already considering the possibility of further development to integrate the menu as an option on a library's internal OPAC system. The ultimate refinement, if anything to do with library automation is ever ultimate, would be that users should be able to construct searches of their own catalogues and carry them across, without having to re-key the basic elements, into searches of other libraries' databases. There are as yet no plans to embark upon such developments.

These two initiatives illustrate how automation will spur cooperation. Uncertainties, of course, remain. For example, the University Grants Committee has now been succeeded by the Universities Funding Council and we must hope that it will be at least as keen as its predecessor to encourage better links between libraries, if only to optimize the use of declining resources.

Assuming that the technology can be made to work and keep on working and can be upgraded as need and opportunity arise, the beauty of the ventures that I have been describing is that they rely more upon JANET than upon continued commitment at every stage from the active participants. All that needs to be agreed and maintained is each library's link to its own institution's JANET access point; two years ago the UGC made funds generally available to promote such network access where it had not been already established. It will by now be readily apparent that the UGC has been very active in promoting interlibrary networking, both technically and functionally. Librarians have a corresponding responsibility to make good use of the facilities now coming into place.

Obstacles

We know from past experience that the factors which most bedevil cooperation are lack of will or ability in participants to carry their local share of the burden. Enthusiasm for the original objectives can wane and funding cutbacks can cause library managers to reassess priorities. The gain that each manager considers his or her library gets from its involvement is crucial. There also needs to be commonality of interest.[4]

The Farmington Plan in the United States is often quoted as an example of cooperation becoming out-of-date. On a smaller scale, we in Britain can cite another. Over 30 years ago, academics and librarians alike were worried that there was no concerted national policy to ensure that seventeenth century British publications which came on the open market were being kept in this country. At that time, the risk of their being bought up by United States institutions seemed very great. So university libraries carved up the seventeenth century into decades and half-decades. Each took a period and undertook to acquire, from booksellers' catalogues or at auction, the volumes published within their allocated five- or ten-year span. Existing strengths and subject interests in the participating libraries were taken into account in allocating the periods, but when funds became tighter libraries were less and less willing to collect works in the national interest which were irrelevant to local needs. Gradually the plan was ignored; eventually it was abandoned. Libraries become unwilling to cooperate in acquisitions when they lack resources to meet immediate current demands; but other deterrents can also arise.

Corporate commitment can suffer when the original team who negotiated the cooperation changes, and the spirit which motivated them is lost. Personality clashes or even antipathies can hurt cooperation, but this is true of more than librarians; it is a human factor, universally recognized. Another version of it is institutional, rather than individual, disaffection. In its modern guise this emerges as the conflict arising where pressures to generate income introduce competition between universities and, by implication, between their libraries. Even more damaging is when the competitive element shows up adversely in comparisons between institutions. One feels threatened by another, usually because of their relative sizes, subject strengths or reputations. Suspicions of domination militate against cooperation with a presumed rival. A library seems to need to be able to maintain its self-respect. If it can no longer be proud of its performance based on its own resources it will be less happy to continue with cooperation which might reveal its weakness or loss of stature. The weakness may merely be a loss of self-confidence; others who wish to cooperate with that library may not share its own perception of its decline or may not be influenced by it, but self-perception is the crucial element.

In the present fluid state of British higher education the financial future looks bleak. The subjects taught in each university are being reviewed and there is anxiety about the profile that each institution will have at the end of the process of departmental rationalization. In these circumstances, some disinclination away from cooperation is understandable. A further uncertainty concerns the long-term future for universities as a whole. Emphasis on scholarship seems to be ideologically at odds with a government which views public sector investment with disfavour unless it can be shown to contribute directly to the national economic well-being. Government bias favours privatization and private sector involvement. This is not a good time for fostering mental attitudes to enable interlibrary cooperation to flourish along traditional lines, yet technically there has never been a better time to develop mechanisms to promote it. Demoralization has set in; it may be easily summed up in the adage that if there is one thing worse than being poor it is having been rich. But against the fall in purchasing power of our bookfunds we must recognize that funds are still available for information technology developments in universities and that these can be fruitfully deployed to pursue shared objectives.

Continuum

I propose to explore cooperation in the area of library collections by following the continuum which operates within a single library for stock collection, from selection and purchasing through cataloguing and lending to relegation or preservation. All of these procedures have cooperative aspects.

Ideally, every country should have national acquisition, catalogue access, interlending, conservation and retention/preservation plans. None has established the whole continuum. Where fragments exist they have happened through leadership initiatives by the few which others subsequently followed. Government inducements help but leadership within the library world is essential for permanent progress.

Selection

A national acquisitions plan must be based on policies determined within individual institutions for stock development, catering firstly for its own perceived needs. Few libraries have written selection policies, hence the problem of elaborating a national plan. The Federal Republic of Germany, by determining centres of excellence for broad subject groups, has come closer to this than any other country. Dutch libraries operate a similar scheme. Later in this paper we shall see how Conspectus provides another basis for countries to plan their acquisition programmes strategically.

Hitherto, among academic libraries, there have been few examples of joint acquisition on a subject basis; some attempts have been made to share the purchase of expensive series. The difficulties are obvious. How are costs to be apportioned? Which library among the contributors will hold the items? Will they be available only to readers from the subscribing libraries or to others as well? Will the items be catalogued only by the holding library? How will the others, and their readers, remain aware that they have bought a share in the material? An added complication is that such series are often catalogued only under a uniform heading as a publisher's compendium. The individual titles within them are too numerous to record individually, so that use is limited by how well the contents are remembered.

Even under a Conspectus-type arrangement, sharing purchasing responsibilities by subject faces the difficulty of matching them with the current profiles of individual universities. These are unlikely in older institutions to reflect past inheritance, and in times of uncertainty cannot reliably be expected to remain firm for the future. Fringe subjects of peripheral but enduring interest and specialism within major subjects could be identified as candidates. Some such might well be found among Special Collections where it is important to anticipate competition at book auctions and consult other possible interested parties. This already often happens informally, with beneficial results.[5] If more libraries had and were able to exchange statements of their book selection policies broader coordination should be possible. Evidence emerging so far from the few overlap studies that have been undertaken encourages this view. Common experience is that even between similar institutions like Edinburgh and Glasgow, or within aggregate groups such as London University's colleges and institutes, the number of duplicated titles is low, representing, in the main, undergraduate level or core materials not amenable to sharing.

Acquisition

Selection is only the beginning of the process. Would cooperation be fruitful at the ordering stage? Yes, but not very. One or two publishers have taken initiatives, offering groups of universities reduced rates for multi-copy orders of certain publications, but only as a way of attracting more customers, not merely among existing subscribers. Such approaches need to be carefully evaluated but are welcome in principle. An unpublished investigation a few years ago among SCONUL libraries compared the rates which they paid different subscription agents for the same journal titles. The hope was that a 'best buy' could be identified and that even better rates could be negotiated if several orders were concentrated through one supplier. Rather surprisingly, no clear pattern emerged. No one agent showed up as the outstanding performer, especially when delivery times were also taken into account, and there was the strong suspicion that, as in any monopoly situation, performance would worsen when the opposition dwindled. It was, of course, helpful to explore the possibility, even without a positive outcome, as evidence to our financial controllers, should they ask, that there is no mileage in it.

Even in the absence of formal book selection policy statements automation will improve information at the ordering stage, using the kind of networks already described. Few fully integrated library automation systems are yet operational. When they are and the bibliographic record appears at the ordering stage, rather than as a catalogue record, networked on-line access will give librarians better information about each other's buying intentions and help to influence individual decisions. There might even be room to announce that an expensive item was being considered for purchase by one or two libraries in a cooperative group and become the subject of an electronic mail exchange of views. The danger is, of course, that the initiators will suffer if the rest of the group sit back hoping to benefit from their enterprise. 'The early bird catches the worm'; but the rest of the aviary might be happy to survive on a different diet until the worm can be regurgitated for them later. That is only to repeat my warnings at the outset about the conditions necessary for any cooperative venture to be successful.

Cataloguing

With cataloguing also a national programme, were such to exist, would bring benefits. Through cooperatives and from central services such as the British Library Bibliographic Services such a framework has emerged. Plans now being formulated for involvement of the other legal deposit libraries with the British Library in sharing catalogue record creation to improve the scope and currency of the national bibliographic record. The cooperation between the BL and the Bibliothèque Nationale in their joint CD-ROM publication could also be a factor, but for routine catalogue input for new acquisitions we need more machine-readable records at the order stage. These should be created on behalf of publishers and booksellers, and though beginnings have been made in this field, and librarians are being consulted, we cannot yet foresee the outcome.[6]

For retrospective conversion of catalogue records, a national plan would help but will probably take a long time to emerge, derived from uncoordinated initiatives. The CURL database and the conversion of the British Library's printed catalogue into machine-readable form in a few years' time could add significant impetus. A sharing of responsibilities, particularly for non-English language material, through some Conspectus-type scheme would then be timely.

Interlending

The interlibrary loan system developed in the United Kingdom is powerful evidence of the advantages of planning and coordination. Further automation, at the British Library, in the regional library bureaux and over the JANET network give opportunities for greater refinement. Among universities, CURL, for example, should aid foreign monograph supply when its database access has been developed to make a contribution.[7] The lending arm of the British Library maintains close and attentive relationships with the academic sector; we, in turn, are interested in its involvement with the ADONIS project though what we hear leads us to expect little impact from ADONIS on existing structures.

Deselection

Next in the continuum of cooperative possibilities in collection management is the selection of stock for storing or discarding. University libraries cannot look forward to unlimited growth enabling retention of every item that we have acquired, any more than the British Library can. The wisdom of such a policy, were it possible, is questionable. Again, we need a plan to ensure that the national interest is served, that older stock is retained or transferred to where it will be most useful, and that long back runs of little used journals are not needlessly duplicated. Conspectus-type data would form a helpful framework for such planning; some coordination is certainly necessary.

Few libraries, over the past decade, have avoided the need to prune their journal collections in face of the exceptionally large price rises which periodicals have incurred and the many new journals being published each year without signs of abatement or adequate allowance in budget allocations. It is tempting to cancel titles in collaboration with libraries nearby, but as Mermin points out[8] fewer subscribers will lead to yet higher prices and all that will be achieved is less intake at greater cost.

I heartily endorse his solution to the problem: cooperation among and between academics and libraries to make certain journals redundant.

Preservation

Allied to retention and discard policies is preservation policy, whether by physical conservation, mass-deacidification, microphotography or electronic conversion. In the United States, the Research Libraries Group have shown in their RLIN database what can be done cooperatively.[9] Even in the absence of a national plan, duplication of preservation effort and expense can be reduced. This is an area where international cooperation would be even more beneficial. The task facing individual libraries is so enormous and so identical that what little funding there is must be used to best effect. IFLA has, I believe, a role to play in promoting such work but, meanwhile, perhaps the Western European countries could begin to tackle the problem on their own behalf. In matters of preservation, the large research libraries have special responsibilities that should draw them together, urgently. Cooperation is needed in technical expertise, in determining policy for applying the different options available and in identifying and recording action being contemplated, undertaken and accomplished with individual titles.

Subject library and information plans

We have come to the end of the continuum which I delineated early in this paper, but two further aspects of cooperation should be touched upon. The first is the recent move to devise LIPs, Library and Information Plans, on a sub-regional basis in this country, encouraged by the Library and Information Services Council (England). University libraries have been involved in most of the plans which are now coming forward. It is only proper that they should be, since they have a part to play in information provision in their own locality. My impression is that their contribution will be limited in many instances because of local circumstances and that a different kind of Information Plan might show them to better advantage. Alongside local plans, there is, I believe, room to investigate the utility of subject plans of broader territorial scope, covering particularly the sciences. Coming from Scotland, a large area physically, with a new Scottish Science Library (based on the National Library) and eight universities all with science specialisms, such an idea naturally appeals to me. Scotland's LISC, however, lacks the statutory authority, and the funding, of the English LISC. We are at present seeking a way around this problem but it will take time.

Conspectus

Scotland is particularly well placed to undertake a subject-orientated Library and Information Plan because of our involvement in the Conspectus exercise. Its transatlantic origins and application are already well described in the literature.[10, 11] The British Library's and the Scottish experience have also been written up.[12, 13, 14] The National Library of Wales is also applying the technique, but other United Kingdom libraries have been slow to follow. While its protagonists freely admit Conspectus to be a far from perfect instrument upon which to base collaborative activity,[15] its imperfections are marginal judged against the joint action which it can prompt. A database of coded records of inherited and current stock in our libraries can be useful along the entire continuum followed in this paper. A group of libraries which collectively have assessed their subject strengths and can share the information among them have already achieved from the exercise an identity of interest. This can be built upon in refining individual selection policies, planning the retrospective conversion of their catalogues, coordinating weeding and storage practices and collaborating in preservation of what they retain. The staff costs incurred in applying Conspectus, particularly if the Scottish 'fast track' approach is followed, can be quickly repaid in the savings to be achieved in other ways.

The main obstacles to cooperation in Britain at present are at root psychological: the fear of dominance, the supposed conflict between cooperation and competition, the insecurity that permeates institutions undergoing 'rationalization'. We must rid ourselves of our insecurity. If the speed of the convoy is the speed of the slowest ship and proper engine maintenance is beyond our resources, it is only sensible to pool spare parts, before we find ourselves having to share the life-rafts.

References

1 British Library, Ad hoc working party on union catalogues. *Report*, Boston Spa, British Library, 1983.
2 Wells, M., 'JANET: the United Kingdom Joint Academic Network', *Serials*, **1**, (3), 1988, 28–36.
3 Heaney, H., 'UK University Research Library Initiative', *Outlook on research libraries*, **10**, (4), 1988, 13–14.
4 Gregory, V. L., 'Library cooperative programs and coordinating agencies of higher education', *Library and information science research*, **10**, (3), 1988, 305–29 esp. 317.
5 Corrall, S. (ed.), *Collection development: options for effective management*, London, Taylor Graham, 1988.
6 Greenwood, D. (ed.), *Bibliographic records in the book world*, London, British Library, 1988.
7 Heaney, H., 'Interlending implications for British academic libraries of current networking developments', *Interlending and document supply*, **17**, (2), 1989, 46–8.
8 Mermin, N. D., 'What's wrong with this library?', *Physics today*, **41**, (8:1), 1988, 9–11.
9 Kruger, B., 'Automating preservation information in RLIN', *Library resources and technical services*, **32**, (2), 1988, 116–26.
10 Gwinn, N. E. and Mosher, P. H., 'Coordinating collection development: the RLG Conspectus', *College & research libraries*, **44**, (2), 1983, 128–40.
11 Reed-Scott, J., *Manual for the North-American inventory of research library collections*, (Washington, D.C.), Association of Research Libraries, 1985.
12 British Library, *Conspectus in the British Library*, London, British Library, 1986. This includes microfiche version of the library's completed worksheets.
13 Hanger, S., 'Collection development in the British Library: the role of the RLG Conspectus', *Journal of librarianship*, **19**, (2), 1987, 89–107.
14 Matheson, A., 'The planning and implementation of Conspectus in Scotland', *Journal of librarianship*, **19**, (3), 1987, 141–51. *See also* Matheson, A., 'Cooperative approaches in Scotland', in Corrall, S., (ref.5).
15 Pringle, R. V., 'Conspectus in Scotland: report to SCONUL', *LIBER news sheet*, **23**, 1988, 5–17.

19

Other forms of cooperation

Alan F MacDougall

Introduction

This paper reviews aspects of cooperation other than those that are dealt with in other papers. It examines some types of cooperative endeavour available to academic libraries, explores advantages and disadvantages and future possibilities, and suggests various ways forward. In doing so it uses a framework for examining cooperation which was originally developed by Wilson and Marsterston[1] and developed by Edmonds.[2]

'Cooperation is the reciprocally beneficial sharing of resources, developed or pre-existing, by two or more bodies'.[2] It is a way of exploring the possibilities of maximizing resources; more recently it has been extended to include the creation of additional income if a wider interpretation of the definition is accepted.

This paper studies cooperation in three aspects:

- exchange — what forms are there that involve exchange/reciprocity?
- coalition — working together
- one-way marketing and entrepreneurial activity.

Cooperative exchange

Examples of exchange include:

materials exchange (interlibrary loan and donation are dealt with elsewhere).

user exchange — access to each other's library facilities. This type of activity can be limited to 'reference only' or it can be extended to the borrowing of material for individual users. These arrangements may appear obviously acceptable but there can be drawbacks; for example, overuse by readers from one of the participant libraries can put pressure on the host library, and excellent resources elsewhere might encourage management to avoid its basic responsibility to provide adequate resources for its own users. Such matters can be a legitimate source of concern, and some libraries have been cautious in offering access to specific groups — for example, academic and research staff only may be allowed borrowing rights, as in the case of the major academic libraries of the East Midlands of England; the major libraries in the Birmingham area permit access to each other's libraries but with severely limited borrowing rights.

information exchange is an activity which need not necessarily involve large expenditure or commitment. It could be confined to the exchange of working papers, minutes etc. between participating libraries. It can be more formalized by publishing working papers. Exchange of information and hence ideas can be a valuable contribution in a time of stagnation.

user information exchange − the exchange of user enquiries − could entail agreement between libraries to telephone one another to check facts and information on behalf of readers. This can be a relatively unstructured activity, and although there might be imbalance of use, unless this was particularly pronounced it should not cause undue problems.

bibliographical exchange, excluding automation and networking; examples could include exchange of holdings of serials lists (in whatever format) or exchange of microfiche catalogues.

exchange of staff can provide insight and help to broaden horizons. This would contribute to the provision of better service for readers. The types of exchange could involve

- simultaneous staff exchange
- part exchange i.e. visiting each other in turn
- home and abroad exchanges.

The duration of staff exchanges can be as short as half a day or long as one year. Experience in the UK has not been particularly encouraging; the problem of domestic upheaval is one of the main obstacles.

Cooperation coalition

The second type of cooperation can be defined as coalition, where 'services are carried out in conjunction to provide common services or mutual development of resources in service'.[2] Examples of this approach are as follows:

Development of service tools

Under this heading institutions might work together to produce

- printed service tools, for example, index/abstract bulletins, directories of cooperative services
- microfiche. A UK example is microfiche of ISBN locations produced by the East Midlands Regional Library System; this is used as a locating device particularly for interlibrary loan purposes.
- software; for example, to assist with ease of access to each other's library catalogues. Such access is being developed in the UK by the Scottish Academic Libraries Bibliographic Information Network (SALBIN).
- networking (it should be noted that even with improved communications technology, problems of actual line access and queuing can be a major practical limitation.)

Development of resources

Under this heading could be included:

- acquisition (and disposal) of material, this could include use of the Conspectus.

- joint staff appointments and finance; for example, health service and cathedral libraries in conjunction with academic libraries.
- joint use of buildings; for example, learned societies sharing facilities with academic libraries.
- joint purchase of equipment.

Training

Training and staff development can be a lonely and isolated activity for a library training officer. There are many common problems in training which could be resolved by sharing and cooperative training can have an important role to play. To discuss matters together can offer a better standard of training provision and in doing so could reduce unit cost per trainee and offer a better bargaining position when buying in external expertise.

The types of structures which can be adopted for cooperative training, and the various types of training activity which have been carried out, have been discussed at length elsewhere.[3] Experience suggests that there is no definitive model for the establishment and management of a cooperative training group. Groups in the UK consists of as few as two institutions and as many as approaching 200. They can be drawn from one type of library or differing types of libraries, and can be formally constituted with paid secretarial support or informally on a self-help basis. The most appropriate constitution depends on the requirements of the constituent group.

Cooperative research

Under this heading the following examples can be considered:

- libraries combining to undertake cooperative research, as has been done recently by the major academic libraries of the East Midlands of England.[4]
- libraries working in conjunction with companies to improve software or equipment; for example, British Library involvement in the development of a photocopier for rare or archival material

Cooperative publishing

Examples include:

- publication, in conjunction with a commercial publisher, of the contents of a particular library or its catalogue.
- publication of scholarly works by individuals including library staff, which appear under a joint institutional and commercial imprint, for example, Gower Press and Leicester Polytechnic.

One-way entrepreneurial activity and marketing

The third type of cooperation could be classified as one-way entrepreneurial activity and marketing. This is somewhat controversial as a subject of cooperation, since it can be regarded as service undertaken in return for payment, but it can be argued that it is a two-way process — unless cooperation is apparent the market will disappear. Examples under this heading could include the services of the British Library Document Supply Centre, information services via subscription, provision of automated services, and the business community, which offers library services to information brokers.

Advantages and disadvantages of the cooperative approach

A whole range of cooperative ventures have been suggested. Are they meritorious? Are they cost-effective? Are there drawbacks? Can they work? These are a few of the questions which could be posed. The answers must depend on individual, local, and national circumstances, but whatever they might be, any contemplation of cooperative endeavour must be approached in a careful analytical manner, conscious of the need to look for cost-effectiveness and cost-benefit. In doing so evaluation must not be ignored.

Consequently, the following questions *inter alia* should be asked:

- What return will there be?
- What outgoings will there be?
- What are the resource implications?
- How will the proposals fit in with existing or proposed priorities?
- Can staff be persuaded to comply with the envisaged cooperation?
- What is the 'quid pro quo'?

If the cooperation looks promising then some form of structure has to be implemented which will signal a clear understanding and undertaking from all the participating members.

Even with these clear understandings cooperation relies on motivation, goodwill and the attitude of the chief.

The future

The future of cooperation is difficult to predict, especially when academic institutions are having to compete with each other for resources and students, while paradoxically at national level their libraries are being encouraged to cooperate for maximum utilization of their existing resources. It may well be tht there is an increase in the amalgamation of institutions, and consequent rationalization, rather than cooperation. Notwithstanding, there is likely to be an increased use and development of networking especially as decreasing costs make it more economical to contemplate. Libraries will look to set up cooperative groups while the inadequate published information about cost-effectiveness and cost-benefit of cooperation will be improved through research.

How should managers of libraries react to these scenarios? They need

- increasingly careful thought about their own library resources
- needs, wants and demands
- identification of strengths and weaknesses − what is there to offer and what is required to complement the service?
- identification of extra-mural resources in the locality, regionally and nationally − would such resources complement their own existing resource?
- identification and establishment of mechanisms to consider feasibility, development, and review of cooperative proposals
- evaluation to ensure balance between priorities.

No library can fulfil all of its requirements. There is a need to plan and look ahead with confidence and maturity but within a context of realism. Sensibly managed cooperation offers exciting possibilities, but without proper economic analysis of its effect it may remain 'a good thing' in theory but in practice a poor solution.

References

1 Wilson, T. D. and Marsterston, W. A. J., *Local library cooperation: final report on a project funded by the Department of Education and Science.* Sheffield, University of Sheffield Postgraduate School of Librarianship and Information Science, 1974.

2 Edmonds, D. J., *Current library cooperation and coordination: an investigation*, London, HMSO, 1986. (Library Information Sries, 15).

3 MacDougall, A. F. and Prytherch, R. (eds.), *Library cooperative training*, London, Gower, 1989.

4 MacDougall, A. F., Wheelhouse, H. and Wilson, J. M., *A study of various aspects of cooperation between the East Midlands university and polytechnic libraries.* British Library Research & Development Department Research Report, 1989.

20

Management styles and systems

Ian Rogerson

The word *style* requires some definition. A commonly used compact English dictionary provides a number, of which the following have some relevance: 'A manner of doing, especially as contrasted with the thing done, as for example, different styles of writing, swimming, etc', and 'Noticeably superior quality or manner, e.g. she has style *or* let us do the thing in style if we do it at all'. Conversely, a phrase not uncommon amongst those who dislike, or profess a dislike for material things, will express disapproval of a neighbour's new car, for instance, by stating 'it's not my style'.

Whilst the former definition would appear to be that which is applicable to management, clearly identifiable by, e.g. Likert's familiar classification into authoritative and participative styles,[1] the second is by no means insignificant in British management for, particularly in England, personal style is admired or envied and many of those who possess noticeably superior qualities or manners also possess qualities of leadership, for they are usually positive, assured and secure. In this sense, style is often found in partnership with taste, this being defined as 'the faculty of discerning beauty or other excellences'. It is commonly believed that one is born with a sense of style or taste, or indeed both. However, both qualities are important factors in British class structure and are likely to be the products of formative influences such as home and school. Nevertheless, such qualities, plus the essential requirements of standard pronunciation and correct grammatical usage of the English language, can be acquired in later life, as today's leading political figures daily demonstrate.

In my readings in the literature of management I have been perplexed by the relatively scarce use of the word 'leadership'. Perhaps there is a common assumption that authoritarian management is management through leadership, although this is not necessarily the case. Authoritarian management without clear leadership exists in a number of well-recognized styles, such as management by fear, or management through bureaucracy, both of which result in rapid demotivation of personnel with consequential deterioration in performance.

Academic libraries in the United Kingdom are now moving into a cost-led rather than a service-led environment where styles of autocratic management are becoming increasingly identifiable. The terms 'Rambo management' and 'macho management' are frequently encountered in newspapers and television. As resources are continually squeezed in the United Kingdom as a matter of political dogma, so some managers are becoming increasingly reluctant to take risks, either for fear of the consequences or because of the rules and traditions which encumber most hierarchies and make managers hide behind precedents. As Peter and Hull say in *The Peter principle*, 'such employers lead only in the sense that the carved wooden figurehead leads the ship'.[2]

Robert Townsend, a former President of Avis, retired in 1965 from attempting to manage unmanageable situations in order to write upon the subject. In *Further up the organization*, he identified the two parts a leader must play: 'First the open door, always available decision-maker, the problem-solver and advice-giver: in this part he is ready to run the Xerox or answer the telephone if that is what needs doing. His other role may be that of chief business-getter, and in this capacity he needs service — he should be treated like an emperor — all his people should run to supply his needs. All involved in the enterprise should understand that these two opposite roles exist'.[3]

The importance of leadership in library management is stressed by Jones and Jordan in their now standard work on personnel management in libraries. Indeed, after explaining lucidly the theories of management of Marlow, McGregor, Likert, Blake and Mouton and others, they invite readers to identify their own leadership styles in terms of the Blake/Mouton analysis by answering a number of multiple choice questions.[4] Unfortunately, in taking part in exercises of this type, candidates rarely possess a totally objective view of themselves. Some years ago, one sphere of activity in the author's institution came to an abrupt halt whenever its director was absent. This was because of a constant refusal to delegate power during such absences. Now the person in charge of this activity was extremely sensitive to criticism and had to be handled carefully. In an attempt to rectify matters, it was suggested to him that 'it is only possible for a large institution to function efficiently when there is effective delegation'. His immediate and honest response was, 'it is a good job then that I do'.

Let us for a moment examine Likert's view of management styles. On the Authoritative side, this varies between the exploitative style and the benevolent style, and on the Participative side, between consultative and fully participative. The exploitative mode can be simply explained that 'buying a man's time gives the employer control over the employee's behaviour'. In this mode, what communication exists is almost inevitably downward and there is a concentration upon output without much regard for human relations. If any criteria exist to establish levels of job satisfaction then these will almost certainly have been determined by the autocrat. Any attempt to relieve tedium will be restricted to job rotation with the objective of increased productivity rather than increased job satisfaction. This style directly conflicts with what Stewart claims is the most effective, namely that a wide range of studies has proved that 'best performance is obtained by leadership that is employee-centred'.[5] Although Jones and Jordan claim that the exploitative ethos is rare in libraries 'perhaps because it is not common for libraries to measure their outputs and to improve clearcut standards or levels of productivity on their staff', nevertheless at least one large academic library's technical services division was run on draconian lines during the 1970s.[6]

Probably the most chilling presentation of the resource view of human management is by Stafford Beer in describing a typical industrial incentive scheme:

A work-study investigation of the process is carried out, and this results in . . . a model of the dynamic system. That is, proper times are measured for each element of the work done, and suitable allowances are made for incidental factors. An assessment is made of the rate at which the operatives work, so that the answers can be adjusted against standard human effort. Fatigue should also be assessed, and a factor which allows for this incorporated. In this way the model is completed, and its predictions compared with actual results on the job. This finishes the work study. Management then uses this study to devise an incentive scheme in which bonus payments are set out which are calculated to induce operatives progressively to raise their present performance, until the optimum output assessed from the work study is achieved at a wage level that the management regards as of maximum attractiveness to the operatives and of economic benefit to the company. The system exactly resembles Porter's open-sequence control for a steam-turbine driving a generator, in which the value, (i.e. payment) is adjusted by a calibration depending on the speed required, (i.e. output) of the generator . . . [7]

Such inhuman planning was much in vogue 30 years ago and is today again becoming fashionable, but this time in educational circles using less direct language.

The other face of Likert's authoritative style is that of benevolence. This is a curious word for management style, for it implies 'well-wishing' or 'doing good' and is no more descriptive of the general understanding of Likert's notion than its antithesis 'malevolent' would be of exploitative authoritarianism. According to Jones and Jordan, benevolent authoritarianism is common in libraries, 'marked by some show of staff views', while retaining all the decision-making at the top of the hierarchy'.[8] In writing on this, the authors should have given greater acknowledgement of the experience and competence of senior professionals of proven worth in resource acquisition and distribution and in forward planning. The additional difficulty of working in an increasingly hostile environment, often trying to implement politically inspired policies which in some cases are mutually contradictory, tends to shift decision-making upwards. With benevolent management, the structure will be 'tall and narrow, favouring centralised decision-making'. Manchester Polytechnic's cash crisis of 1980 was marked by a decline in enthusiasm for participative management through decision-making committees and a reliance upon top management to 'solve the problems of the institution'. In looking at management hierarchies, one should note that, according to Townsend, each level of management lowers communication effectiveness by about 25%.[9]

Let us now consider Likert's two stages of participative management. The first, Consultative, can be real or just an exercise in stage management. Staff are consulted upon their views although, even when based upon their direct experience at the librarian-user interface or in senior-junior relationships, these are usually ignored when decisions are taken. Similarly, personnel may be consulted upon wider issues where a trade-union view may also impinge. Regular meetings which have definite objectives can be helpful in this scenario, even if they are only advisory rather than decision-making bodies.

The fourth mode, which can be regarded as genuinely participative, concentrates upon the necessity for communication and influence to be built into the organization, the leadership of which, in addition to possessing the normal management and leadership skills, should hold the philosophy required to build and operate an interaction-influence system within an overlapping group structure. This structure, incidentally, is pyramidical, arranged in overlapping groups, as for example, 1, 3, 9, where the group size is 4. Likert affirmed that such a structure should be outstanding in its performance if it has competent personnel and leadership which develops highly effective groups, structured to achieve effective communication influence with decentralized and coordinated decision making. Such an organization should set high performance goals and have high motivation.

I wish to digress at this point to look at a few well-recognized styles of management which exist largely outside the manuals of management theory. No doubt they will be familiar to you all, because I believe that they manifest themselves across national frontiers. In describing these in a written paper, one has to exercise some care, because one does not wish to offend former colleagues, or insult the dead, or for that matter transgress the laws of libel. However, I have known an institution where the top manager believed in *leading from behind*. The proclaimed style was fully democratic, participative through a network of committees each reporting directly to the main decision-making board. Over a period of time, a few strong heads of department and trade-union nominees began to dominate certain of these committees and some of these committees began to usurp the more important areas of control in the institution. Political and trade union nominees on the governing body worked hand-in-hand with staff trade union and student union activists to oppose management or to attempt to introduce radical or inflammatory policies. Not infrequently, the outcome of such a scenario was student unrest. The lack of direction or leadership at the top resulted in massive damage and disruption to the institution, often for periods of weeks rather than days. Inevitably, written instructions to administrators on how to deal with the situation arrived after the troubles had finished.

A more obvious style of management is that of *sitting on the fence*. If the continental label for the British workman's laziness was the 'British disease', then the British manager's deliberate indecision is surely also pathological. Of the chief librarians or principals of institutions of higher education I have met who fall into this category, few lack self-esteem. They are not concerned with achieving the objectives of the institution. They are not interested in winning. These people, above all, have one objective and that is not to lose. A common example in British academic institutions is to agree to the release of 'frozen' posts, i.e. posts which have become vacant and not advertised in order to save money. In a desperate situation, the agreement to advertise is given, but administrative obstructions are introduced in order to delay the appointment for as long as possible and thus save money but prolong the misery. A third style which can be found with both strong and weak top managers is that of *divide and rule*. A typical example of this is to establish two lines of communication leading down to the front-line workers. The first can be explained in an academic context. A channel from principal through faculty heads to departmental heads is used to deliver instructions or information which would be generally welcomed by academic staff and the staffs of the educational support services. More unwelcome news, and bureaucratic annoyances thought up by minor administrators trying to acquire power by, e.g. centralizing control over departmental secretaries and technicians, are delivered through the registrar's office. In one instance of this style of management, it became obvious that academics grew so resentful over the latter channel, i.e. registrar's notices, that few cooperated, and indeed one head of a large academic department took great care to do exactly the opposite of what was instructed.

Lastly, the mode I have called *picking up the bits*. Here, the top administrator employs a fully participative style and is prepared to wait patiently to pick up the bits. He or she is frequently the winner in this situation, for if the participants work intelligently and together towards the objectives of the institution, then the top job is easy, for the greater part of the job is done for the incumbent. However, if, as is frequently the case, sensible agreements or results do not emanate from boards or committees, then the manager can use his freedom to make the decisions which others have shirked. Examples I have encountered include an invitation from the director to an academic board to merge two small departments subsequent to the resignation of one of the heads, in order to divide one very large department into two, thus creating a new head of department within fixed financial parameters. There was an immediate demand for a new head of department without sacrificing the unnecessary post, and the inevitable management decision came about some months later. Similarly, in a departmental board where there was a motion demanding an increase in the number of periodicals taken in a given subject by the library, figures were presented by library staff giving breakdowns of periodical and monograph expenditure and inviting the Board to reallocate the resource according to their wishes. The Board voted to maintain expenditure on monographs at the existing level and vastly increase the number of periodicals taken, although the library materials fund was at that time in decline. Such naive behaviour, largely due to inexperience, bedevils participative management and is extremely costly in wasted time. It delays achievement. I believe that the present trend towards authoritarianism in all aspects of public sector administration in the United Kingdom is due to the misuse of power by participants in the 1960s and 1970s. Golden opportunities were ignored, and participation was ruined by posturing.

Even Likert and other writers on theory of management acknowledge the gap between theory and practice. Let us for a moment consider what difficulties lie between the starting gate and the finishing post in our journey towards organizational perfection. The first high obstacle in our path is that of economic constraint. Consequent upon local government reorganization in England and Wales in 1974, many local authorities took the opportunity to adopt corporate styles of management. Librarians were often in the forefront of these changes, with more participative structures and styles, only to see successive cutbacks in expenditure coupled with the necessity to adopt political postures bring about the impossibility of achieving perfection, or indeed anything approaching it. In some instances, public libraries are now much poorer instruments for information, education and recreation than they were in the 1960s.

Academic libraries too, have had severe cutbacks in resourcing. Alongside this, governmental interference and ministerial indifference to quality have been echoed by polytechnic and university administrators, producing low morale and demotivation among library staff. The increase in autocratic management outside and above the library is partly, I believe, because the freedom to make decisions without taking a view from below makes it easier for principals, directors, or vice-chancellors to balance the books. In Manchester Polytechnic Library, the result of this has been to lose, or have frozen, each post as it becomes vacant. Consequently, each team, or group, in the Technical Services division of the library has been effectively destroyed within a period of 18 months. Library plans, such as the overall development plan and the five-year library automation plan, are, at a moment's notice, no longer valid.

What has this to do with style? The point here, of course, is that style is to a large extent determined by the mores, the customs and conventions of the institution, and the library is a microcosm of that institution. The day has gone when the chief librarian can be 'a character'. Style is now largely set by the institutional style, and in the framework of the organization. The librarian is likely to be just another grey flannel suit. No polytechnic director, at this point in time when massive changes in funding are taking place, is interested in what librarians feel about their contribution to the well-being of the institution through particular management systems.

A most significant obstacle on the race to perfection is that survival is now more important than directing one's attention to the original goals of the higher education institution. John Henry Newman's idea of a university and Matthew Arnold's views upon the continuance of culture are absent from the agenda. The enterprise culture dominates and there is now a number of academic libraries who adopt the enterprise style, proud of how much money they can raise by selling services.

The ultimate deterrent to good management is one admirably stated by Stafford Beer, whose views on the relationship between man and management seem to have changed radically in the 20 years between the publication of *Cybernetics and management* and *Platform for change*, the latter a book overlaid with profound cynicism.[10] In this, he presents a universal truth:

> Theory is the only reality countenanced by our culture. This means that the accepted account of our affairs becomes more real to those concerned than the truth on the ground. And the facts have to fit this theory, rather than that the theory should at all be changed.

I have spent much of my life in higher education fighting this ethos, and if that is my style, then I am not ashamed of it.

References

1 Likert, R., *New patterns of management*, New York, McGraw-Hill, 1961, 223.
2 Peter, L. J. and Hull, R., *The Peter principle*, New York, Morrow, 1969, 68.
3 Townsend, R., *Further up the organisation*, London, Hodder Coronet, 1985, 122.
4 Jones, N. and Jordan, P., *Staff management in library and information work*, London, Gower Press, 1987, 283.
5 Stewart, R., *The role of organisations, new & rev. ed.*, London, Macmillan, 1985, 88.
6 See ref. 4, 50.
7 Beer, S., *Cybernetics and management. 2nd ed.*, London, EUP, 1967, 167.
8 See ref. 4, 50.
9 See ref. 3, 14.
10 Beer, S., *Platform for change*, New York, Wiley, 1975, 14.

21

Staff structures

Christopher J. Hunt

Introduction

People are the primary resource of libraries. Whatever the quality of the collections, the access to databases, and the efficiency of the building, effective organization and motivation of library staff are the most crucial factors in success or failure. They are also the most expensive element in library service. Faculty members, although prepared to pay tribute to one or other member of the library staff, as a wonderful librarian without whose help their research would not prosper, are generally not keen on what they see as excessive sums of money going on librarians rather than to buy books. Library staff are also the most permanent feature of the library budget, with a monthly salary being paid indefinitely and the skills (and deficiencies) of each individual member of staff making themselves obvious for years or even decades. There are many ways in which a library can be organized. No one way is right, with all others being wrong. There must, however, be internal logic and reasonable consistency over time whatever structure is in place.

An academic library performs many functions, carries out very varied activities, services its public directly at a number of service points, and operates for 12 or more hours out of every 24. A considerable amount of organization goes into so complex a service, with, compared with other public services operating over long hours, relatively few staff. There is a constant tension between the desirability of specialization and the necessity for flexibility. I am referring here to the need for professionals (trained at considerable expense in information skills, languages or subject special-isms) to have, at times, to help barely literate undergraduates, or to shelve books or to handle problems in areas foreign to their expertise and training. There is also the need for non-professional and clerical staff, principally employed to type orders or receive periodical parts, occasionally to staff an issue desk, or vice versa. Professionals fairly regularly have to do non-professional tasks; non-professionals occasionally may have to do professional. If they frequently have to do the same tasks which more senior people are being paid more to do, there is something badly wrong with the library structure.

The front-desk tasks, directly serving the customers, have to be carried out during all hours when the library is open. They must have priority in staffing including those when the whole library is overstretched and staff are in short supply because of illness, or a rash of resignations, and all the other occurrences which make the job of drawing up the roster the least popular in the library. The immediacy of the demands and continuing physical presence of customers must dominate service. Because of these pressures no structure can usually produce anything approaching self-sufficiency for each departmental unit, however organized. The necessary degree of redundancy in the staffing of the unit to bring about a situation where it never needs to draw on other units would cost too much even for the best funded institution. Students and faculty cannot be served without the backroom jobs being carried out but the front desk services always take day-to-day priority.

Functional structure

A structure dominated by administrative function is still probably the most common. In its simplest form the library is bifurcated, with a reader or public services division for the back-room tasks. Further sub-division can take place according to size of operation. The advantages of such a structure are clear cut. The first is that it is the obvious way to organize an academic library to those who work within it. The goal of the entire library is to serve the teaching and research needs of the university community. The aims of the cataloguing department are to catalogue books, of the issue desk to lend them, and so on. Objectives are equally clear. The librarian is a cataloguer, or a serials specialist. Considerable expertise will be built up by such specialism, by non-professionals as well as professionals. Departmental spirit can focus on an obvious range of tasks, within a limited physical area of the library which hopefully feels like home, working with a limited number of immediate colleagues. There is a direct resemblance to 'the assembly line structure of manufacturing industries' which has been the dominant industrial organizational pattern of our century.[1]

The disadvantages, however, are equally obvious, particularly from the viewpoint of the last 20 years where the established industrial patterns of the past have been breaking up in all sorts of organizations. The most fundamental disadvantage, though, has been obvious for much longer than that. This is that by such a functional division, those staff responsible for technical processing are, almost literally, in a back room, physically and mentally far away from the demands and needs of the customer of the library. This problem was debated extensively in the United States in the 1940s and 1950s, and in Britain in the 1960s and 1970s. It became apparent that a culture, particularly in cataloguing, of technical perfection for its own sake had grown up. Because the discipline of constant and immediate contact with readers was lacking, librarians could easily build up collections of material which no-one really wanted, and which was accessible only by applying rules that no-one but the professional practitioner really understood. I quote the philosopher F. M. Cornford's guide to academic politics in Cambridge at the beginning of the century:

> 'Books are the sources of materials for lectures. They should be kept from the young; for to read books and remember what you read, well enough to reproduce it, is called 'cramming', and this is destructive of all true education. The best way to protect the young from books is, first, to make sure that they shall be so dry as to offer no temptation; and, second, to store them in such a way that no one can find them without several years' training'.[2]

In the debates of 15 years ago the argument that technical processing had become divorced from user needs was perhaps overstated, but there was more than a germ of truth in it. More stressed today is the psychological aspect, that the easy identification by staff that a particular part of the library is *their* department is bad, because the goals of the library as a whole can easily be lost sight of, with undue concentration on one limb of it only. This can occur with reader services staff, who fail to appreciate the essential nature of technical services operations, just as easily as with staff in the latter departments. Inevitable ebbs and flows of work and resources lead to the creation of backlogs in particular areas which harm the library as a whole, but, in the traditional structure, is a problem for one department only.

Structure by subject discipline

The subject divisional library was the alternative approach to the strictly functional. Strictly applied this means that even when all library services are on a single site, within one building, the organization of staff should be split by subject, with services and processing entirely subordinate in the structure to this basic subject division. Many academic library buildings of the 1960s and 1970s were designed around this principle. By and large the strong points of the approach are the mirror image of the disadvantages in the functional alternative. The most significant advantage of the subject divisional structure is that all library staff are brought into contact with those they are serving, and over-concern with the minutiae of cataloguing rules is as obviously esoteric as it actually is. Almost as strong an argument is the subject expertise built up by the staff, around the bibliography of the discipline, the needs of the practitioners, and regular contact with them. Against the subject approach is that, at least when a single building is involved, it can lead to duplication of stock and services, and be more costly to staff in consequence. It is this last factor which has led to many of the bold new experiments of the 1960s being superseded and by a return to the more functional approach. It might be asserted that the subject versus functional division argument is not worth pursuing, being based on fashion rather than essentials. More genuinely fundamental has been the shift in what is regarded as the heart of professionalism in academic librarianship. The fairly recent emphasis on service to readers, rather than on cataloguing, is a genuine advance, not merely a self-interested re-definition of professional mysteries.

There are other rationales applied to academic library structures. Type of material, for example archives and rare books, where physical form is overwhelmingly important in dictating how the library should organize itself to handle it, is common. Official publications are another example. Another division, usual in North America but less common in Europe save in very large libraries, is the clear separation of undergraduate and other course student services and stock, from the research library. Another debate that has ranged over decades has been on the desirability of such a separation. Use of the academic library by the undergraduate is clearly very different in nature, level and kind than use by the research scholar. Those against undergraduate libraries have argued that by divorcing material on reading lists from the rest of the stock librarians are impoverishing education by depriving students of the easy opportunity of wider reading. I personally believe that this divide is highly desirable for both sides, efficient teaching on the one hand and effective research on the other.

Those academic libraries that are providing information services to a user community other than their own students and staff, and charging for those services, are increasingly recognizing this distinction in their structures. A separate departmental unit, clearly funded from the income from these services, avoids the moral and practical dilemma of which service has priority, that to the institutional community or that which is being directly paid for by outsiders, who obviously expect value for money.

Automation and its impact

The introduction of computers into academic libraries is a major reason why the debate between functionalism and subject organization has been by-passed. Modern libraries almost inevitably have hybrid structures. Record systems can now be accessed by terminal wherever located. This does not mean that all library tasks can be decentralized without an economic penalty, but automation has freed technical service functions from the tyranny of the duplicate card catalogue, the shelf and accessions registers, and all the other impedimenta of manual library record processing. Conversely, a reference librarian can check directly from his desk such information as when a book was ordered. There can be functional integration of procedures even though they are being carried out in physically discrete or even distant parts of the library.

There is an additional imperative which is particularly useful in a library context. This is, no individual should be expected to work continuously at a terminal for more than about 40 minutes in each hour. Work has to be broken up to avoid this, so that tasks that involve talking with people, or book handling in one way or another, can be deliberately interwoven into the work pattern. Technology has reduced the time necessary to carry out one of the most tedious parts of a librarian's work, record creation and manipulation. It has made virtually no difference to the labour necessary to manhandle books in day-to-day operations. But both the need and the opportunity for greater face-to-face contact between library staff and library users, the most rewarding part of non-professional as well as of professional work, have been increased by automation. It is now far easier for every member of staff, wherever employed in the library, to be convinced that the objective of his department is to provide services required by users, and the techniques being employed are just that, means to an end, not the end in themselves.

Signs of stress

However, the fact that technology has given us greater organizational and spatial freedom does not mean that an ideal structure is within grasp. There is, of course, no such thing, only one which, for the time being, appears to be performing well in a particular place. What are the signs of a structure that is not working well? First, conflict between members of staff or between departments. Occasional disputes are inevitable in any organization; if they are continuous, revolving frequently around the same sort of issue, it is likely to be the fault of the organization rather than necessarily of the individuals involved. Does the library react adequately to solve local crises, from the breakdown of the computer system to the illness of the person rostered to carry out late night duties? Is the trades union structure constantly being invoked to solve problems which management has failed to tackle? Do members of the library staff feel part of the entire library rather than just one fragment of it? Do they take coffee and lunch across departmental boundaries, and thus communicate informally the information that must be passed on if the library is to run well? Faulty structure, of course, is not the only cause of problems such as these, but taken as a whole their occurrence is a fair indication that something is fundamentally wrong.

Organization theory

Over the last two decades it is not only electronic technology that has transformed the ways libraries work but also a better understanding, on the part of librarians, of good management practices and how they might be adapted to suit the particular environment of libraries. There is far greater understanding today (even if this understanding is not necessarily applied) of how organizations work and how to encourage productivity to useful ends. All human beings are goal directed; they need to have an object in view, and will work best in pursuit of goals they see as relevant to themselves. The organization structure should aim at bringing together institutional and individual objectives. To do so is by no means easy, hence the massive interest in western writing on the subject, both learned and popular, in Japanese methods and culture. The route to 'library goodness' is the establishment of long term goals, and more immediate objectives, by proper planning.

A significant consequence of greater understanding of contemporary management theories on the part of those who administer libraries has been a move away from very strict hierarchical structure of any kind. This move has been assisted by pressure from those at the bottom of old hierarchies for more say in how the organization works – 'participative management'. This has taken very varied forms. In North America, particularly in the period following 1968, there were structures which effectively denied the chief librarian the authority to manage. For obvious reasons, most experiments in this direction were short-lived. A 'faculty' structure, where all professionals of whatever management position are theoretically equal, existing parallel with the hierarchical structure, is still followed by some libraries. More usual has been the blurring both of strict departmental lines and of the division into line and staff functions. These

'organically oriented systems [are where] authority and power are delegated and dispersed, and managers are not viewed as omniscient any more than omnipotent. Communication is horizontal and diagonal as well as vertical, and consists more of advice, information and suggestions than of direct orders. Collaboration and consultation are emphasized and the organization chart features a wider span of control: i.e. each supervisor has responsibility for a greater number of subordinates and, as a result, the number of management levels is reduced. Finally, individual staff members are encouraged to take responsibility for solving problems'.[3]

It has also to be said that a very obvious consequence of such organic systems of management is that one's colleagues are never at their desks; they are always in meetings!

Training the academic librarian

In talking about organizational structure we are of course also talking about individual people. A normal professional career will begin after tertiary education and initial training at around the age of 24, and go on for 30 or 40 years. Individuals have talents, skills, handicaps. They change, develop, or perhaps degenerate. Over so many years there are bound to be enormous changes, in the library, in the parent institution, in the world.

In British librarianship a professional librarian is one who has a degree, usually after three years' full-time study, in an academic discipline, followed by a postgraduate diploma in librarianship awarded by a university or another tertiary institution, normally by one year's full-time study. An academic library will usually require its professional staff to possess an honours degree of quality. Schools of librarianship face an extraordinary range of problems. Thirty years ago there was concensus that education for librarians should be based firmly on the techniques of bibliographical description and book handling, against a cultural background of book trade history. There is no such concensus today. Education for all so-called professions is in a state of uncertainty, but in librarianship 'crisis' might be a better term, so many traditional skills having become near-redundant because of changes in information and communication technology. What are the qualities and skills that we require in a professional librarian in a modern academic library?

First, he or she should have acceptable personal characteristics, intelligence and drive, and good interpersonal and communication skills. Second is a requirement for knowledge of the particular library itself, the books and other information sources within it, the academic community being served, and even the individual information needs of certain key people in that community. All of these skills are either inate, or can be best, or indeed only, learnt on the job.

Other skills can be taught before the career begins, by for example a first degree in an academic discipline, which may or may not be relevant to tasks carried out in a particular library. A degree in, say, chemistry, is not a vital prerequisite for working professionally in a chemistry library. The value of education in the discipline is obviously considerable, but unless complemented by the other skills of a librarian it is not enough on its own; and adequate knowledge of chemistry can be acquired by an intelligent and enthusiastic librarian with a degree preferably in another scientific subject whilst working on the job. There must be training in information handling, including the techniques of bibliographic description and of how to work using computer systems and other pieces of electronic technology; the economic structure of the book trade and the physical characteristics of books; management theories and application, including marketing, costing, and public relations. It is an awkward and inconvenient mix, very difficult and unsatisfactory to fit into a single year's course. What is quite clear is that education should continue throughout a professional career, both because the facets of librarianship are so multifarious that one always needs further training in one or other of them, and because the mechanisms of information handling are changing so rapidly. This is another major argument for flexibility in staff structure.

Promotion and mobility

There are two final points. The first is in the form of a dreadful warning, applicable only in those countries where there is an over-supply of individuals who have passed through university and library school, and are desperate for a job in a library. Such people will apply for non-professional positions in libraries, where the duties are intended to be largely clerical or simple book handling. For underfunded libraries these qualified but unemployed people are a tempting source of cheap labour. There is a great temptation to employ them on a lowly salary scale, but to make use of their skills and give them duties which should be carried out by more highly paid professionals. There are few more divisive steps that can be taken to ruin a staff structure. Particularly when the individuals concerned are good, they may be given more responsible tasks than less able individuals who are comfortably employed as professionals. Desperation rapidly changes to deep discontent in such circumstances, a flourishing soil for low morale which can corrupt a whole organization.

The last comment concerns staff mobility. In Britain there has been a substantial reduction in job opportunity in academic libraries over the last decade, as there has been in universities generally. The number of professional jobs available has fallen considerably. Compared with, say, philosophers, opportunities remain for academic librarians simply because it is necessary for each university to have a library, and senior staff to manage it. As some two thirds of the chief university librarianships in Great Britain have fallen vacant and been filled over the past five years, there has been considerable movement at the top, which has moved down the staff structure a little way, but only a little way. The abolition of every non-essential position has been forced by economic pressure. Marked regional differences in the cost of accommodation have combined with few job opportunities to bring about near-stagnation in the movement of professional staff from institution to institution. For younger professionals, at any rate, it is crucial that they be given the opportunity, and if necessary pushed, to change jobs within the library in which they work. Many years spent in the same job are good neither for the individual concerned nor for the library. Variety of experience is more important than specialization in a single area, whether functional or subject-based, however considerable the academic qualifications of the librarian concerned.

Funds for academic libraries from traditional sources are declining. Information technology is providing more opportunities for libraries, and increasing demands from customers. There will necessarily be continuous change in the nature of library services, and organizations, to survive in spite of all the constraints, must be flexible enough not merely to cope but to prosper. It is a daunting challenge. The role of library management, of the chief librarian, becomes even more crucial than it has been in the past. The so-called organic systems of organization are the way ahead, but because of their very fluidity they put more load on the manager than strictly hierarchical structures.

References
1 Cotta-Schönberg, Michael von, 'Automation and academic library structure'. Paper presented at the IFLA Conference in Sydney, 1988.
2 Cornford, F. M., *Microcosmographia academica, being a guide for the young academic politician*, Cambridge, Bowes & Bowes, 1908.
3 White, Herbert S., *Library personnel management*, New York, Knowledge Industry Publications, 1985.

22

Staff development and appraisal

David M. Baker

Introduction

We are − or we should be − in search of excellence.

'For their continued success in terms of educational provision, well-managed establishments of further and higher education must be effective at gathering information, marketing their services, monitoring the quality of their services and bringing the best out of the people who work within them. Excellence in these areas guarantees that colleges have, firstly, the knowledge on which to base their strategies and allocate their resources; secondly, the ability to identify and meet the demands of clients; thirdly, a range of techniques for evaluating the success of what they do and, fourthly, policies, mechanisms and skills for reviewing and enhancing the motivation and performance of their staff'.[1]

This paper concentrates on the fourth requirement, relating to personnel management, and on two particular aspects: staff development and appraisal.

Development and appraisal in context

Personnel management is a complex subject with a number of elements; staff development and appraisal have no practical existence in their own right − they have to have a context.

Inevitably, the type of library (its external and internal organizational framework, its history, philosophy, ethos, management style, structure, users) will have an important bearing on the way in which staffing policies are formulated and introduced. In a university library, for instance, staff selection policies (at least at senior levels) will emphasize academic achievement as well as − possibly as much as − managerial competence and experience. Similarly, in many such institutions, the emphasis has traditionally been on personal professional development, with little 'interference' from management. How can an appraisal scheme best be introduced in such an environment?

In particular, the library's overall policy governs virtually all aspects of management. Is the emphasis on collection building or user education, on reader or technical services? Where does the organization wish to be in 5/10/20 years' time? Where it is now? A completely different organization? What kind of staff, with what sort of qualifications, experience and training, will be required in future?

Certainly, over the last ten years, automation, whether of housekeeping activities or information storage and retrieval, has had a profound effect on libraries in Europe and North America and on their staff recruitment and development policies and objectives. Major changes in organization and method have been experienced and the library workforce has, in many respects, been de-skilled and re-skilled over a short space of time.

Those are some of the major variables that inevitably affect the way staff training and development are carried out. But there are other, more specific, ones. While promotion and disciplinary procedures are (or should be) separate from appraisal schemes in particular, they are essential prerequisites of a good staff development programme; if such procedures do not exist, how can the workforce be sure what is intended when, say, a new training plan is introduced — will people not wonder whether there are hidden motives?

At some point then, and especially when introducing a new scheme, whether of training or appraisal, it is essential that senior management defines the parameters:

How does the scheme relate to the overall aims/objectives of the organization? What are the aims/objectives of the scheme itself? What will have been achieved at the end of a given period of time? (Updated staff, changed methods, new routines, etc.?)

Will individuals have anything to expect/fear from such a scheme in the way of promotion/demotion?

There is no single correct answer to these questions, no single set of ideal objectives, sure long-term plans or safe assumptions and, certainly, no unique perfect model, either for an academic library in general or its staffing policies in particular. My point is simply that the specific library/institutional/staffing context must be considered when a staff development and appraisal programme is being introduced, and that the links between such a programme and the basics of personnel management — appointment, probation, terms and conditions of service, promotion and dismissal — should be clear from the outset.

Why develop staff?

We have already begun to answer this question. It is important, for instance, to identify the skills which will be required for an institution's long-term strategic plans with the minimum of disruption and discontent and the maximum level of effectiveness and concord.

That is one specific kind of, and reason for, development — preparing people for the future — and effective and efficient management should always be ready to prepare others as part of a continuous process of change and improvement.

There are other reasons. A section from the University of East Anglia Library's staff development policy statement reads as follows:

'By enabling staff to become better informed, more skilled, more versatile, better prepared to accept and cope with change, we are making better use of an essential and costly resource. By providing opportunities for broadening their experience and deepening their knowledge, we help to improve their motivation and to increase job satisfaction. By breaking down seemingly impenetrable barriers between departments or activities, we help to increase their understanding of and commitment to the Library's objectives.'

This paragraph links back to the quotation reproduced at the start of this paper: the message is the same — staff development as a way of improving performance of the individual, the section, the library. And such an approach is based on the belief that knowledge brings understanding and understanding brings satisfaction and commitment. As the policy statement goes on to say:

'We must invest in our staff. They are an essential element in the long-term future of our organisation. As librarians, we are in the business of building our collections — and maximising them. We must ensure that we do the same for the library's personnel. The concept of 'conservation' is seen as of increasing importance in relation to library materials; the concept of library staff training and development at all levels should gain similar currency . . .'.

Staff salaries account for the bulk of expenditure in academic organizations, and even in the library/information unit, where there is usually a sizable non-payroll budget, up to 50% (or possibly more) of the total cash allocation will be spent on personnel. As senior managers, we need to make the most of our staff as well as our stock.

The preamble to UEA Library's training policy statement (drawn up by a small working group, excluding the librarian but including staff drawn from all levels and departments), headed 'Why train?', includes the following telling statement:

'Training must always have a purpose. We must be clear about our aims or we run the risk of training being perceived as a costly indulgence at a time of financial stringency by those in charge of the purse-strings; as a disruptive intrusion by those trying to keep services or processes going; as an empty gesture without visible benefits by those undergoing training . . .

'Training has resource implications, both in time and money. Resources of both kinds are — and are likely to remain — limited . . . Training must be seen as a worthwhile investment for both the Library and its staff.'

Staff appraisal — the formal approach

The basis for a good staff development programme has already been identified. It is essential that the organization has a clear view of its overall aims and objectives and of the ways in which staff training and development fit in with these objectives; any developmental programme must also have its own set of aims and objectives.

Assuming that the parameters have been defined, how does staff development actually take place in practice? Firstly, we must attempt to define staff development. The following list may be helpful:

1 Planning for the long-term future of the individual and his/her place within the organization.
2 Setting and achieving individual/group aims and objectives.
3 Identification of skills/resources required to meet the requirements posed by 1 and 2.

4 Identification of training needs resulting from 1 and 2.

5 Helping and allowing staff to achieve their full potential through 1 to 4.

There are a number of ways in which this list could and should be applied. Note that training is only one element in the process of staff development.

How does one plan for the long-term future of the individual within the organization? In many libraries (and other institutions), there is an informal developmental network. Senior managers 'talent spot' their staff; they notice who is good at particular kinds of work, whether relating to finances, techniques, services or personnel. On the basis of what they see, they may plan (or at least have some thoughts on) a future for their staff.

It is essential that a manager knows his or her staff. If you do not know them, how can you find out who is good at doing what, who has particular talents and how best to exploit them? But there are, perhaps, dangers in adopting too informal an approach.

In recent years, there has been much debate in British higher education about formal staff appraisal schemes as an adjunct to the kind of informal staff development discussed above. There are various forms of staff appraisal, but Scribbins and Walton summarize it as 'the structured assessment of an employee's performance of the work which he or she undertakes. That work may be different from the employee's contractual duties'.[2] They continue by enumerating what are generally perceived as being the positive advantages of staff appraisal schemes:

● the opportunity to discuss problems at appraisal interviews.
● greater clarity about the role of management.
● better knowledge about the people being appraised.
● expectation of support, particularly when facing difficulties.
● a realization that one's efforts are being noticed and, where appropriate, appreciated.
● a chance to discuss and set objectives for the future.
● a greater sense of departmental and organizational unity, coupled with improved understanding of priorities and of the system itself.
● improved communication.[3]

It could well be argued that many of these advantages should already exist in a well-managed library and that there is therefore no need for a formal staff appraisal scheme. Certainly, the need for good communications, support, feedback and setting of objectives are all elements of a positive managerial style and the 'sense of departmental and organizational unity', for instance, is an important aim of any staff training and development programme. What staff appraisal schemes can and should give both employer and employee is a mechanism for open and constructive discussion, criticism, feedback and future planning. Continuous, informal staff development is all well and good but there is room for bias, assumption and misunderstanding, which can be largely eradicated in a good appraisal scheme.

A study of the literature of appraisal schemes suggests most strongly that, to be successful, it must be clear to all concerned what relationship (if any) there is between appraisal, promotion and staff discipline. This is true of staff development programmes in general but nowhere is it more important to gain the support of staff than in what is, inevitably, a particularly sensitive area − appraisal of staff as individuals.

There are various models for a staff appraisal scheme; some are, perhaps, more appropriate to an academic library than others. Scribbins and Walton identify two basic kinds − 'hard' and 'soft'.

Hard means that the outcome involves:

Taking decisions which are: preventive
                       corrective and drastic
      and which: connect with cash rewards and disciplinary action.

Soft means that neither sanction nor reward is the outcome. The fundamental aim is to offer:

encouragement
self-appraisal
an awareness of current performance and
objectives for the future.

The trend in institutions of higher education in Britain is towards the second kind of scheme, for a number of reasons. Firstly, the collegiate nature of such organizations militates against the 'hard' approach, as does the fact that there is a separate control on standards of performance through professional associations such as the Library Association. Secondly, a scheme based on remuneration and reward is unlikely to work effectively where firm grade and incremental structures are in use, as is the case in most universities and polytechnics in this country.

The techniques of staff appraisal will vary from organization to organization and will depend to a certain extent on the style adopted and the links between the scheme and promotion and disciplinary procedures. 'Harder' styles will tend to encourage the use of rating scales and results-orientated appraisals. In educational institutions, where individuals tend to have a high degree of autonomy and much is expected in the way of personal initiative, the goal-setting implicit in the remunerative schemes is unlikely to find much favour.

What may well work in an academic library environment is the kind of scheme where appraiser and appraisee establish mutually agreed standards of performance in a range of areas where the person appraised is expected to be capable of operating. Clearly, staff will not be expected to excel in every area but to reach a minimum level of competence in weaker areas. A review of the literature suggests that a combination of structured self-analysis, appraisal and counselling interviews and periodic formal and informal feedback are likely to be required.

There is no ideal appraisal scheme. As Scribbins and Walton summarize:

'Key objectives should be to achieve and maintain a good and constructive relationship between the appraiser and the employee and not to allow appraisal to degenerate into a form-filling exercise with the information being used solely for personnel records and annual returns. Above all, the clear message is: keep it simple'.[5]

As in all aspects of staff training and development, it is important to create a hospitable climate within the organization and to engender positive attitudes amongst staff. This is especially true of appraisal, which many may perceive as threatening, however 'soft' the model. The success of staff development and appraisal schemes depends, to a very large extent, on the level of commitment shown by senior management. Does senior management get appraised? Clearly, training of appraisers and preparation of those to be appraised is also important; so too is the development of those staff who have a more general training function.

Above all, however, successful staff development and training schemes rely on the provision of adequate resources and a proper training infrastructure. Without adequate time and funding, for instance, a staff appraisal scheme will founder. There is simply no point in, say, identifying an individual's training needs, if those needs cannot be met, either because funds are not available or the organization does not have an appropriate, well-developed training programme.

There are a number of other factors which contribute in a significant way to the effectiveness of staff development and appraisal. Effective staff recruitment is one; the existence (or otherwise) of a structured approach to staff probation, induction and preliminary training is another. Put more crudely: if the wrong appointment has been made, there is a limit to the extent to which training, development and appraisal can rectify that mistake.

Staff appraisal can be a performance indicator in respect of an institution's personnel management style and strategy. The more successful the scheme, the greater the maturity of the organization, the better the preparation and the training infrastructure, the more serious the commitment, the clearer the aims and objectives at all levels. Involvement and good planning and implementation will be much improved by the creation of a steering group for development and appraisal programmes, while the existence of a training officer with the authority and resources to implement programmes will provide a solid base on which to build.

'We did it ourselves' – the informal approach

Staff appraisal schemes centre upon a one-to-one relationship between appraiser and appraised and, while the results of the appraisal process may have implications and benefits, either for the organization as a whole or a specific sub-group or department, the emphasis is upon the development of the members of staff. Clearly, this is an essential aspect of staff development but there is a broader level, which cannot rely solely, or even primarily, on formal approaches.

Appraisal may identify areas where further staff development is necessary and training can improve relative weaknesses in performance. But librarianship is about living in the 'real world', about managing and motivating real people in live situations. Very few staff work in isolation; most work in groups or teams. And it is behaviour in (and contribution to) such teams where an individual's attributes and skills are likely to have most effect. It is essential that staff work well together in groups and, while training and appraisal can help individuals to find ways of making the most of their role (having once defined it), practical team building is essential.

Increasingly, libraries are using inter-departmental groups to complete special projects – projects with specific goals to be achieved – and which draw upon particular talents and expertise. Such an approach should allow the members of the group to diversify from, and add to, any more functional or operational roles which they might have. Leadership of such groups is clearly important and formal training may be necessary for those put in charge of such groups. However, it is the practical training which comes from involvement in planning and implementation and from the interaction with others which is likely to be of most value. Given the previous comments about staff development in a 'professional' environment, it is important that such groups have a measure of freedom in their actions, within appropriate overall boundaries. A measure of self-determination is likely to lead to improved job satisfaction, aided by a sense of achievement when goals are reached and individuals appreciate for themselves the importance of working effectively in a group. 'We did it ourselves' should be the comment.

End-note

In sum:

- We are in search of excellence.
- We can find excellence only through our staff.
- We can develop staff only in the context of our overall aims and objectives.
- We must develop them if we are to succeed.
- We can do this through a combination of formal and informal means, having:
  - (a) defined the relationship between training/development/appraisal and probation, promotion and disciplinary procedures;
  - (b) created a climate and an infrastructure conducive to constructive development and appraisal;
  - (c) demonstrated a firm commitment to development and appraisal;
  - (d) ensured that our staff are our number one priority − 'Who cares wins'.

References

1 Melling, Geoffrey, *in* Scribbins, K. and Walton, F., *Staff appraisal in further and higher education*, Bristol, Further Education Staff College, 1987, vii.
2 Ibid., 1.
3 Ibid., 3−4.
4 Ibid., 31.
5 Ibid., 34.

23

Training for management

Alan F. MacDougall

Introduction

This paper examines training for library management in the context of a rapidly changing environment in which the drive for innovation, cost effectiveness and cost benefit is increasingly apparent. The demand for 'value for money' is assuming central importance in organizational thinking. The expansionist days when additional resources were obtained by managements with relative ease have been replaced by the requirement for rigorous explanation and defence, not only for more resources but also, more significantly, for the protection of existing resources. The educational world has not been exempted from this trend, and increasingly across continents education has been the subject of a crusade for lower unit costing while at least maintaining and at best improving standards. The quest for the most efficient use of tax-payers' money is not confined to national boundaries.

In the information world the impact of electronic publishing is beginning to offer new perspectives and increased sophistication of computerized database retrieval systems is contributing to increased demand in services – all at a time when inflationary pressure and underfunding result in less finance to provide an effective service.

The library service within the academic community is having to come to terms with these developments. Consequently librarians, and their libraries, are required to be more accountable for service provision and expenditure. In such circumstances librarians will have to be more forward-looking and proactive, as well as responsive to external requirements; this requires imaginative, innovative and well-trained management. To meet this challenge there is an increasing need for staff at all levels to become more effective managers. No longer will the acquisition of a formal library and/or degree qualification, supplemented by occasional on-the-job training and occasional short course, be sufficient. There is now a requirement to think in the longer term and plan suitable training programmes which include the subject of management.[1]

This paper does not therefore use the narrow definition of training, namely 'the systematic development of a pattern of knowledge skills, attitudes and behaviour requirements in order to perform adequately a given task or job.' A wider definition of training and continuing education which 'builds on the foundation of basic education, updates and extends perception and understanding, and maintains a flexible and fresh approach to work' seems more appropriate. For the purpose of this paper it is the intention to consider training and continuing education as one term. The educational aspect of qualifications such as those awarded by library schools are not addressed.

Management training

There is a danger in a management paper of this kind of becoming too didactic and pedantic, for example by giving lengthy explanations of what exactly management means. For the sake of brevity a theoretical debate is not pursued.

There are a myriad ways of viewing management. For example, it can be thought of purely in human terms, that is getting things done through people, (sometimes observed as manipulation); or it can be regarded as a more exact science which concentrates on formulae and modelling approaches with definitive measured outcomes. For the purpose of this paper it is defined as 'the organization of total resources of the system towards an objective.'

This definition permits a wider consideration of the various aspects of management, but what exactly are the functions of management? Fayol's four areas of planning, organizing, coordinating and controlling are perhaps not sufficiently detailed for the purposes of this paper. Therefore the following, devised by Anderson[2] and updated for this discussion, are listed as the basis of management activity. It is emphasized that there are many ways of grouping and delineating management activity and the list is proposed as only one of the many ways in which the subject could be considered.

Management function and library and information work activity

● Policy formation Policy analysis Decision making	Book selection Periodical selection Collection building (i.e. collections of special materials) Stock withdrawal Use of commercial services (e.g. abstracts, citation indexes, etc.) Target setting Allocation of resources
● Planning	Financial planning Budgetary control Corporate planning Manpower planning Staff development
● Co-ordination	Bibliographic services Editorial services Cataloguing Classification Indexing Abstracting Information handling work

- Systems design   Profile production/updating
  Systems control   Information retrieval
  Operations analysis   SDI
                               Computers/automated systems and processes (including computer appreciation)
                               Purchasing procedures
- Work study   Clerical procedures and routines (e.g. overdues)
  Work measurement   Reprographic services, etc.
  O & M   Design and management of internal records (e.g. order forms, workcharts, etc.)
                               Statistics
                               Periodicals control
                               Performance measurement
- Resources management   Handling of printed materials
  Marketing   Handling of non-book materials
                               Exploitation and promotion of stock
                               Information systems
                               User-community services
- Communications   Interdepartmental coordination
                               Liaison with parent body
                               Liaison with outside organizations
                               Staff structure and administration
- Staff management   Selection and interviewing techniques
                               Training
                               Supervision
                               Relating people to jobs
                               Personnel management.

Types of training

What effective management training could be given? A simplistic answer would be to implement a programme of cognitive learning associated with the above headings. This is a detached way of learning which imparts information perhaps through formal lectures or through reading a book. This assimilative process, important as it is, is by itself insufficient.

Of more relevance to effective management training is the requirement to acquire a range of management skills. These skills could then be tested, developed and evaluated in practical training sessions, for example by means of group seminars and discussion, management exercises such as case studies, role-playing etc.

Katz[3] proposed the grouping of the necessary types of skills under three headings – technical, human and conceptual. Technical skills imply an understanding and proficiency in a specific kind of activity, particularly those involving methodology, processing, procedures or techniques. Essentially it is working with things. Human skills involve acting effectively as a group member (or leader) and building cooperative effort. Essentially it is working with people. Finally, conceptual skills involve the ability to see the enterprise as a whole.

The level at which these apply, or have increasing relevance to different grades of staff, would be determined by local circumstance. For example, the acquisition of technical skills may assume more importance at lower levels of the organization and relatively less at the more senior levels. On the other hand, the acquisition of human skills could be considered equally important throughout the organization but requiring more concentrated efforts in certain areas at particular levels of responsibility. Conceptual skills, it could be argued, assume greater importance for higher placed personnel in the organization. In this instance the importance of job rotation and exchange as a way of understanding the institution assumed importance, along with management exercises, group discussion etc.

The precise forms of training and the appropriate level will depend on an examination of needs, wants and demands of the individual and the organization. The creation of staff profiles will be a priority (appraisal schemes will be of assistance in this respect) in forming a view of the requirements.

Limitations

Inevitably a paper such as this can only skim over some of the important considerations. The requirement for management training and skills can be identified, but it is impossible to propose a programme of training applicable to all academic libraries in every country.

The types and level of skill acquisition will depend on local requirement, circumstances and existing knowledge; in many instances management training has been given serious consideration only for professional staff.

Naturally there is a variance in training provision not only between countries but also within academic libraries within the same country. Major problems could include unsuitability of courses, cost, duration, geographical location, lack of direction and coordination, courses organized only to meet demand rather than need etc. Consequently staff embarking on the improvement of their managerial skills may be faced with what appear to be intractable problems. These very real obstacles can be further complicated by a whole range of perceptions. According to research carried out in the UK[2] there appears to be a wide variety of perceptions. For example, employers maintained that although there was a definite need for management training, there were widely differing views as to what constituted management. Employee perceptions varied with their position in the organization; library assistants identified the need for interpersonal skills, numeracy and organization of their work, but there appeared to be an inability to communicate these points to senior management.

The way ahead

What can the busy manager or individual do, given the very real possibility of encountering these various obstacles? The ability to pursue or implement will depend on the individual circumstances and inclination. The following options are proposed as possible ways of moving forward:

Within the institution:
- Designate a librarian with specific responsibility for training.
  Ensure that the trainer is trained. Consider, where the organization is measured in several hundreds of staff, the employment of a professional trainer rather than a librarian.
- Compile staff profiles — this can be done partially by the operation of staff appraisal schemes.
- Define overall training needs of the organization.

- Evolve skills programme for management training. Where possible utilize expertise within the institution.
- Link management programmes with incentive schemes, for example additional increments or possible promotion.
- Establish a programme of evaluation.

Outside the institution:
- Where possible seek external expertise within the geographical and financial restraints. Experts can be contracted to give management training at the institution or can be hired to offer consultancy expertise concerning management training.
- Establish cooperative training groups to utilize existing expertise at cost effective prices.
- Establish modular programme of management training.
- Establish national forum for the establishment of management training requirements utilizing where possible good practice from the business and commercial world.

The future

A number of options has been advanced; solutions will vary according to the individual circumstances. The value of management training has to be sold to employers as the key to effective and efficient deployment of resources − the occasional *ad hoc* lecture on management is no longer sufficient. Now there is an urgent requirement for systematically planned training programmes for all staff which include the acquisition of management skills. Their successful development and implementation though must be underpinned by the ability to reward successful completion. In such circumstances academic libraries will be in a healthier position to meet the demands of the rest of this century and beyond.

References

1 Library and Information Services Council, *Professional education and training for library and information work*, London, Library and Information Services Council, 1986.
2 Anderson, U., *Management training for librarians. Report of an investigation into post-experience management training for librarians and information scientists, evaluation of courses and summary of perceived needs*, London, Library Association, 1977. (LA Research Publications, 18; British Library R & D Reports, 5327).
3 Katz, R. L., 'Skills of an effective administrator', *Harvard business review*, **52**, 1974, 90−102.

24

The concept of 'library goodness' : user and library perception of quality and value

Maurice B. Line

Introduction

What is a good library? Goodness is always difficult to define, and even more difficult to describe. It is tempting to approach the topic of library goodness by defining and describing a really bad library and then leaving readers to work out the opposite. However, this would not work, because *effective* badness may require positive qualities such as courage, persistence and intelligence; an effectively bad library might require a great deal of planning and leadership. I will try and approach the question directly and see if we can arrive at some consensus of goodness, or at least some common qualities that constitute goodness.

I make some assumptions. The nature and goodness of academic libraries must depend to a fair extent on the nature of higher education, which depends in turn ultimately on the nation's culture, society, economy and politics. I shall not attempt to examine these underlying aspects, although higher education in some countries appears to be undergoing changes in its fundamental principles and approach. Higher education and academic libraries are however inevitably interrelated, and even relatively minor changes in one affect the other. For example, if students are required to read less, or to study less on their own, the burden on libraries is reduced. Conversely, libraries with smaller stocks could lead to shorter reading lists and more direct instruction.

If the question 'what is a good library?' were asked of users 30 years ago and now, probably different replies would be made − not because users' needs have changed but because circumstances have changed, opportunities have changed, and expectations have changed, both positively and negatively. *There is no absolute perception of goodness*. Librarians would also give different replies, as would different users − staff and students, and users in different subjects.

It would of course be possible to find out what users think constitutes a good library by asking them. It is a little odd that this appears never to have been done directly; it is different from asking them whether they think their own library is adequate or inadequate, or good or bad. Also, users might have some difficulty in distinguishing between their own wants and true quality, and their initial reactions might be different from those arrived at after due consideration. Nevertheless, the question might be worth asking.

Librarians' perceptions of goodness

In the absence of such information, I am reduced to guessing. I am even reduced to guessing what librarians think is a good library, though I would be fairly sure that the answers would vary and that they would vary according to the nature and age of the library (and possibly of the librarian). As with users, the initial reaction of librarians might be different from their considered reactions. However, I will make a crude attempt to say what I think different types of librarian would regard as a good library. For simplicity, I am deliberately taking opposite extremes.

My first librarian is a librarian of a traditional university − well established if not very old, with extensive research collections, including some old and rare books and probably quite a few that are uniquely held in the country. His ideal library would:

- be collection-oriented − rather than user-oriented;
- have as large a collection as possible;
- have a collection that is 'rounded', that is balanced as far as possible in view of the subjects covered by the university;
- have a research collection that is not only rounded but carefully selected to stand the test of time, not merely to serve immediate needs;
- be well preserved, and kept in a condition that will make it usable in two or three centuries' time;
- be thoroughly catalogued, in the sense of detailed and accurate bibliographic description;
- be kept secure against losses, mutilation, etc.

One might summarize this kind of library crudely as an 'eternal' library. From the users' angle, it is probably not easy to use, partly because of its size, age and complexity; large portions of the stock are almost certainly not on open access; and services are weak − not only direct information services, but online access to databases, interlibrary supply, and the other add-ons to major research collections. This is not to say that such services will not be given, but they are given with the staff and money left over from building and recording a research collection.

My second librarian is one of a fairly ordinary polytechnic. This library:

- is service-oriented − that is, its main rationale is to serve users with what they want as thoroughly as possible;
- has a collection built to serve mainly current needs, so that little retrospective purchase is done, and no great qualms are felt about discarding stock;
- is indexed to serve basic bibliographic needs, not to a high level of bibliographic perfection, and places special emphasis on subject access;
- provides rapid and comprehensive access to external resources, since its own stock is inevitably limited;
- provides bibliographic reference services, especially by the use of online databases;
- provides positive information services where required − SDI etc.

This library might be called for simplicity the 'ephemeral' library. The user will not find in stock much of what he needs, but he should be able to get most of what he wants without having to go to great efforts.

Users' perceptions of goodness

I will follow my caricatures of librarians by two caricatures of users. Users will probably have difficulty in distinguishing between what they want and true 'quality'. There is an easy and superficial equation of goodness with size − a confusion of the goodness of the *collection* with the goodness of the *library*. I propose to consider what I believe they want rather than what they would necessarily say.

My first user is a humanities user. He probably wants:

- a very extensive stock − the range of potentially useful material is much wider in humanities than in other subjects;
- extensive current acquisitions, especially books;
- browsing capacity − the ability to wander among the stock and pick up material and information here and there; he likes to do his own hunting rather than have it done for him (but we know extraordinarily little about the value or even the true nature of browsing);
- good catalogues from the viewpoint of bibliographic description.

For the humanities user time is of little object, and it follows that speed of access is not very important.

The science and technology user on the other hand has quite different wants:

- good access to databases, especially by subject − the library catalogues are generally of far less interest to him than external databases;
- extensive current accessions of periodicals for him to scan and keep up to date with his own field and marginal fields − but browsing through an extensive non-current stock on the shelves is of relatively little importance;
- rapid access to documents, whether they are in stock or not − the precise location is not generally vital;
- a library that is easy to use, and does not require extensive 'training' in the use of catalogues or the need to find his way through a labyrinth of a massive older stock;
- information services as required, though he may not know how useful they are until he receives them − he often prefers to be served rather than to serve himself.

Midway between these two types of users, but more in the direction of the humanities than of science and technology, is the social scientist. There are of course other divisions of users, most notably the researcher and the undergraduate; researchers, in whatever field, want good access to a wide range of literature, while students generally want immediate access to books required for current study.

Assuming − and it is rather a large assumption − that users know what they want *and* that they want what is good for them, can humanities and science, or researchers and undergraduates, all be served by the same 'good' library? Some desirable qualities are barely compatible, for example a very large stock and easy and fast access. This is a question that will be considered again later.

As for librarians, they ought to want what users want − or rather, what is good for users. What is good for users ought to be good for librarians; but here we need to consider whether we are talking only about today's users or about future users. This brings us back to my distinction between the 'eternal' and the 'ephemeral' library. Some librarians would be willing to sacrifice present users for the unknown users of the future. I believe this to be a very dangerous practice. There is no evidence that books selected for tomorrow's users actually serve tomorrow's users any better than books selected for today's users, though a fair range of reference and other works that fall into the gaps between immediate departmental needs may be desirable. Whatever librarians and users may think is 'good', it is not really satisfactory to define goodness in terms of what users want or think they want. It is much better to define it in terms of what they *need*, whether they are current users or future users; and this raises the question of whether librarians are better judges of what users need than users are.

Goodness, quality and value

Two of the key writers on library goodness are Richard Orr[1] and Buckland.[2] Orr first distinguished between *quality* and *value*, concepts used and developed later by Buckland. *Quality* is defined as 'capability' — how good is the library? According to this concept, the library that is able to meet a very high percentage of needs is a very capable library, and therefore one of high quality. *Value* on the other hand is defined as 'beneficial effects' — what good does it do? If we use this distinction, it is tempting to put the traditional librarian and the humanities user on the side of quality and the polytechnic librarian and science and technology user on the side of the value. However, the kind of collection perceived by a traditional librarian or humanities user as 'good' is so perceived because it has specific value and benefits for them.

I am doubtful about this quality/value distinction. Most 'quality' can be expressed in terms of 'value'. Even in the case of, say, diamonds, which may be of high quality but do not do anyone any good, one can argue that they have great financial value and possibly some aesthetic value. A collection of medieval psalters may have no immediate value to the users of a particular library but considerable value to society at large.

In any case, the quality of a collection is difficult to measure at all objectively. Conspectus is one attempt to measure quality, but it has a large element of subjectivity. It may be that librarians in different libraries happen to use similar subjective criteria or to assess their collections in similar ways, but there can be no guarantee of this. Another way of measuring the quality of a collection is to compare holdings against standard bibliographies, but this also can be arbitrary and it makes various assumptions; for example if a bibliography is truly comprehensive (as few of them are) and a library has 70% or 80% of the items in it, are the 30% or 20% that are not held of key importance or of no importance? If the bibliography against which the collection is checked is not comprehensive, we are dependent on the quality of the bibliography. In any case, what do the results mean? If a collection is 'good', good for what?

It makes more sense to talk of direct versus indirect value — or perhaps immediate and direct usefulness versus long term or wider benefits (see figure 1). We can then think of two kinds of value (1 and 2 in the figure): the long term, the indirect, the wider benefit to society — perhaps very simply described as 'benefit'; and the short term, the direct, and the useful — 'effectiveness'.

VALUE

1. *Benefit*
     long term
     indirect
     wider benefit to society

2. *Effectiveness*
     short term
     direct
     usefulness

3. *Cost effectiveness*
     value for money

4. *Cost benefit*
     long term/indirect/wider benefit for money

Fig. 1

The measurement of value

Effectiveness or usefulness is not much easier to measure than so-called quality, although many attempts have been made. First, objectives have to be clearly defined against which usefulness has to be assessed. *Value measures* could include user surveys of perceived satisfaction, but these depend a good deal on expectations. They also tend to be rather vague, and *performance measures* have become more common in the literature (not only of course library literature) and increasingly in practice. Performance measures require a more precise definition of objectives, indeed of targets. Performance measures demand a whole paper to themselves; I will merely make one or two observations. One of the commonest and easiest is immediate *availability* of documents. Even this apparently simple measure is fraught with difficulties, since what is asked for is partly if not largely a function of what is expected, which is in turn affected by past performance. To some extent this particular hurdle can be overcome by first rate 'bibliographic exposure' — providing users with all possible references to their subject, from which they can then select according to their wishes. Performance then depends on the bibliographic service, and on the selection the user makes from the references he receives — which can hardly avoid being affected once more by his expectations. Effectiveness in serving demands has to be distinguished from effectiveness in serving needs; and one performance measure should certainly be the volume of demand attracted by a library, without which its availability performance means very little.

Much the most difficult performance measure is also the most important: *What is the actual benefit to the user's work, research, teaching or output?* Various attempts have been made to answer this question, and although there have been a few indicators of likely or possible benefit, the question remains unanswered. One looks at a country like Japan, which does not have good libraries in our sense at all, but has had the most astonishing technological and economic success since the war. Few would argue from this fact that poor libraries lead to economic success, but it is virtually impossible to prove that 'good' libraries confer any ultimate benefit on society, much though individuals may benefit from them (perhaps since society is composed of individuals, the cumulative influence of individuals who have benefited from libraries could be identified, but this would be a hard task).

Once we start asking about benefits to users, we need to ask *which* users — undergraduates, teachers, researchers? Also, are we talking about immediate educational benefit (that is, curriculum-based), longer-term educational, social, political benefit — or what? These different benefits cannot quite be categorized under my two kinds of value. It is probably simplest to say that while certain aspects of value can be measured, value in its general sense cannot, partly because it comprises several subconcepts.

If we cannot measure value absolutely, can we measure it relatively? It is tempting to suggest that we can cut straight through the complications by asking whether a researcher at, say, Birmingham University, which has a very large library, is better or worse off than one in the same field at Aston University, which has a small library but is more oriented to service, and if so in what ways and how much. It would not in fact be difficult to state a set of criteria according to which such a comparison could be made: for example, number and quality of bibliographic references provided, speed of access to documents, significant information picked up by browsing, and so on. A study of this kind would not be very difficult to carry out, and although the results would not be in any way conclusive, this applies to all library research; at least some good indications should emerge. One would of course expect the results to differ according to subject. At the very least, some of the assumptions we fondly make could well be challenged — for example, browsing capacity, which is almost universally believed to be of much value, but whose precise value has yet to be established.

Value for money

In considering library goodness, librarians and users are not the only people to be taken into account. Academic institutions, the University Funding Council (formerly University Grants Committee) and the Polytechnic Funding Council (formerly National Advisory Body) — or their equivalents in other countries, and the Government have also to be considered. It would not be helpful to present the Government with a platonic ideal of a good library; few governments are interested in virtue for its own sake. They are generally against sin, but may prefer it in specific cases if it comes cheaper than virtue. They cannot be expected to have much interest in abstract notions of quality, though academic institutions quite probably do, at least if it is a source of institutional pride. Governments are not even particularly interested in value in itself, though here again institutions probably are.

What governments *are* interested in is *value for money*. So to our two previous kinds of value we can add another one: value for money, or 'cost effectiveness' (3 in figure 1). If governments are interested in it, we have to be too. Indeed, we may reluctantly be forced to subordinate our concepts of value to theirs, or at least to think in terms of theirs in order to protect ours.

Librarians too of course want value for money, in the sense that they want to optimize the use of the resources they have. This is not the same as what the powers that be want, which is to have a justification of the money librarians have asked for. This comes back again to our perception of goodness, our idea of what the library should be; and here we add a fourth and final type of value (4 in figure 1), of long term or indirect or wider benefit for money — 'cost benefit'. The Bodleian Library could probably make an excellent case for its cost benefit in this broader sense, in a way that would be difficult for, say, Lancashire Polytechnic. 'Value for money' in a narrow sense could lead to certain kinds of distortion in a library, or at least in some kinds of library. For example, it may be difficult to justify high quality binding in terms of immediate value or immediate usefulness — indeed, it may be a nuisance to users if periodicals go off to be bound at the period of their maximum use; but in the longer term this could well be justifiable. A utilitarian 'value for money' approach might mean selling off 100 rare books because no-one uses them or because (to take a recent example in the UK) they are 'duplicates'; this might be quite a reasonable option in some libraries, but it could do damage in reducing the visibility and notability of the library, and possibly even do some damage to the status of the university. It would be foolish to ignore the perceptions of an academic institution or of the world at large in one's attitude to one's collection, since this could result in actual economic damage to the library. Simple market criteria will not work because for academic libraries there is at present no real competition — though there might be in the future — and because academic users do not generally pay directly for library and information services. (It is actually rather interesting to speculate what would happen if they did, and how it might change their, and our, perceptions of goodness).

In spite of necessary reservations about a 'value for money' approach, this line has to be pursued if only in self-defence. As stated above, proving that we have 'quality' (whatever that is) will not help us; even proving that we do useful things may not help us; but proving that we give value for money can help us, especially if we can show that *a small increase in money can give a larger increase in value*. We are all familiar with the law of diminishing returns: that after a certain point you have to double your expenditure to achieve a 5% or 10% increase in effectiveness. However, this effect begins to operate only over a certain level; below that level the converse is true — that to take 10% off resources given to the library can reduce effectiveness by 20% or more (see figure 2, where this occurs below the 50% effectiveness level). To the best of my knowledge, this effect has never been demonstrated, but I believe that it could be, providing that the demands of users do not automatically sink with the library's resources. Certainly, below a certain level of resources, a library cannot fulfil its responsibilities to the institution, and without a certain level of resources students, researchers and teachers cannot perform their jobs properly.

Tensions in the concept of goodness

Implicit in much of what I have argued above is that there are various tensions or possibly conflicts in the concept of a good library:

Humanities and social sciences *versus* science and technology
Archival library   *versus* service library
Long term value   *versus* short term value
Intrinsic value   *versus* value for money.

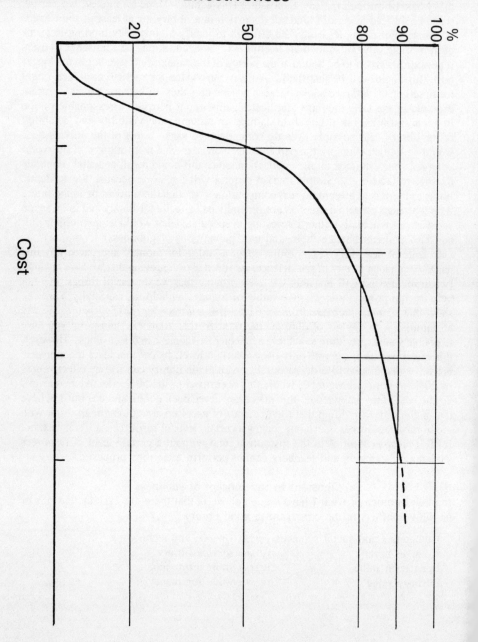

Fig. 2

Does each library have to choose between these, or can a single library do or be all of these things by resolving these tensions in some way? Libraries must certainly serve immediate needs, and some must also serve longer term needs. The question is whether one or the other should be dominant, or whether some balance should be sought, and if so what (a matrix is shown in figure 3).

	'ETERNAL'	'EPHEMERAL'
HUMANITIES AND SOCIAL SCIENCES		
SCIENCE AND TECHNOLOGY		

Fig. 3

In some cases the answer may be fairly straightforward; the Bodleian Library would obviously be biased towards the left-hand side of my division, a technological university library to the other (figure 4). But in other cases the tensions may be so severe that it is almost impossible to have a single library that is 'good' for all these things. This is recognized implicitly by the existence in some academic institutions of separate undergraduate libraries, or of separate science libraries (figure 5). Even within a library, is it possible or sensible to distinguish between 'permanent' and 'impermanent' parts of a collection?

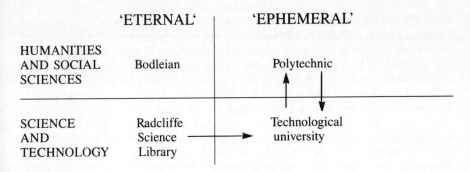

Fig. 4

	'ETERNAL'	'EPHEMERAL'
HUMANITIES AND SOCIAL SCIENCES	'Main' Library	Undergraduate Library
SCIENCE AND TECHNOLOGY		Science Library

Fig. 5

A core goodness?

Is there some core goodness that can apply to any academic library? With some hesitation I put forward my own view of such a 'good' library. It tends to be service-oriented rather than collection-oriented, but in order to achieve good service for, say, a historian there has to be an extensive collection. No collection, however 'good' in itself, can constitute a good library unless more attention is paid to the user than is sometimes the case. An academic library that is not easy to use and that does not offer personal assistance as required, possibly to a high level, that does not provide efficient online services and interlibrary access services, cannot in my view be considered a good library.

I would add an 'X' factor. Anything that is barely efficient is not effective, and a skeletal library cannot be a living library. The good library should aim to go beyond narrow value for money, immediate usefulness and direct satisfaction of requests. It should have additional material, it should aim to give wider exposure, it should go beyond the curriculum − it should even have some surprises. If it is to serve its function fully, a library cannot be purely functional, any more than a public park or cathedral or symphony orchestra can be purely functional.

Conclusion

I stated at the beginning that effective badness has some positive aspects. *Negative* badness has none. A truly bad library is the negative, weak, feeble library, with no discernable qualities at all. Conversely, a library in order to be good must be a positive, strong, powerful library. Strength is not enough, and can be abused; it can also be used in various ways, which may be valid at different times for different users. A positive library should also be a *visibly* good library. It is no good being good if we don't make it obvious to everybody that we are good. One way of doing this is by proving that we give good value for money, but we also need to have much more aggressive public relations than we do at present. I have long had reservations about educating people in library use, but I have none about educating them in the sense of opening their eyes to perceive our goodness. This is no longer an optional extra: it is an essential element in our strategy for survival. Personal sanctity may be associated with poverty; library goodness is not. Library goodness has to be paid for, and we have to use all means at our disposal to persuade our lords and masters to make it necessary payment.

References

1 Orr, R. H., 'Measuring the goodness of library services: a general framework for considering quantitative measures', *Journal of documentation*, **29**, (3), 1973, 315–32.
2 Buckland, Michael K., 'Concepts of library goodness', *Canadian library journal*, **39**, (2), 1982, 63–6.

An earlier version of this paper appeared in *UC&R newsletter*, no. 20, November 1986, 3–8.

25

Performance measurement

A Graham Mackenzie

What is performance measurement?

This paper attempts to point out some of the advantages of using performance measurement, and at the same time to warn of some of the dangers inherent in the whole concept; it will describe some of the various techniques available, and give some examples − both good and bad − of their construction and use.

What is performance measurement? Not merely simple statistics ('Last year I spent £300,000 on purchases; 75,000 books were borrowed by 6,000 readers'). Such figures are very easy to collect, and they may look impressive to a lay person, but they do not mean very much by themselves; even if you have a series of figures from successive years, or compare them with data from other libraries, they tell you very little about how your system actually *performs*.

Performance measurement may be defined as 'the systematic measurement of the extent to which a system (for example, a library) has achieved its objectives in a certain period of time'.

None of the words in that definition is simple in practice. Take 'objectives': clearly this has to be our target as managers − something which we are trying to do, and therefore something which we have to define quite rigorously before it can be of any use to us. But in management theory the term must be given a more specific meaning: not only do we have to define it carefully, but at the right level, because there are at least three different levels of 'target' within any given system.

Buckland[1] has a helpful discussion of objectives, not least because his examples are drawn from the world of academic libraries. He points out that usage has not been consistent in the past: some writers use the same words in directly opposite senses. He starts with the top level, which is very general: a 'mission statement' is a broad definition of what business the library is in, what is its general area of work: 'To meet the informational requirements of the total university community'. This may sound very obvious; but it is surprising how few organizations ever bother to state their mission explicitly. Presumably they believe that it is so obvious in each case that it is not needed. But this is not always so: shortly after I went to St Andrews, a senior member of my Library Committee told me 'This is a research library; it does not concern itself with undergraduates'. This statement aroused a great deal of debate: but in the end, the committee refused to agree with him, and supported my

196

efforts to produce a better level of stock and service for the undergraduates, who had up until then been seriously disadvantaged (for example, the formal library policy was to acquire only one copy of any textbook, however many students needed to use it).

A mission statement is not of much use even in planning, let alone in day-to-day management; for these you need something more detailed, a comprehensive list of objectives representing the activities that the library tries to carry out in pursuit of its mission. Buckland includes

- to assess the informational requirements of the university community on a continuing basis . . .
- to select from available information that portion most applicable to the requirements of the university community
- to acquire, organize, and arrange these informational resources in a manner and a physical setting most conducive to their use
- to study the operations and services provided by the library to assure effective use of available resources
- to anticipate and plan for future developments in the informational needs and services which are likely to affect the university community.

These are only a few examples; any university library must have many more objectives.

Even statements at this level of 'objectives' do not easily lend themselves to measurement. Something less abstract is needed for this purpose, the 'performance goal', relating not to the library as a whole, but to a more convenient (and usually self-contained) subsection of it. For example, one goal for a periodicals unit might be 'to check in and distribute all current serials on the day they are received'; for a service desk 'to reshelve all returned books within four hours'; for a cataloguing unit 'to continue the revision of the catalogue, aiming to complete letters D-F by the end of the academic year'. It is easy to see that goals of this type can be exactly defined in terms of yes, no, or partly, and that numbers can be attached to them to give precise measures; even if they are not totally achieved, the extent of failure can be seen − perhaps over a week only 88% of returned books were shelved within four hours, or by the end of the year 19% of the planned catalogue revision still remained to be done. To this extent success or failure is performance measurement in practice. Nevertheless severe problems still remain, if we want to set measures for the system as a whole.

First, the library is itself part of a larger organization, the university/polytechnic/college; and this too may never have seen a need for a statement of missions, objectives or goals. If this is the case, the library is in difficulty, because it has to be sure that its own mission does not conflict with the institution's, and also that its own statements actually contribute to achieving those at the higher level. Secondly, both objectives and goals, the most specific part of the performance measurement system, have to be drawn up so that they cover the whole set of the library's activities. Thirdly, goals must remain relevant and comprehensive: if the goals/objectives/mission structure only comes to mind every few years, when a formal measurement is in progress, it is only too likely that it will be totally forgotten in the periods between, and that alternative, and wholly unofficial, targets will be constructed at the middle or bottom level of management in order to meet immediate needs.

Finally, goals belong to sub-units; these tend to be managed by people who are not deeply or closely involved at the overall policy-making level. There is thus a tendency for goals to migrate upwards, to be seen at unit level as (firstly) objectives, and then (if care is not taken) as mission statements for the unit concerned. This is why, if you ask someone why a particular task is done in a manner which seems irrational or unduly complex, the answer is often "But we've always done it that way'. I was once involved in a consultancy in another country, on behalf of an international organization; at one point I was talking to the staff of the cataloguing section in a university library, and suggested to them that instead of typing 10 or 12 complex catalogue cards for each book it would be easier, quicker and cheaper to make only one card, duplicate it by machine — there were few library computer systems in these days, but there were other types of copying available — and type in extra author, title or subject headings as required. 'But' they said 'if we do this there will be no more work for some of us, and we will lose our jobs.' This is a classic case of a goal which was quite clear to the managers (to produce catalogue entries as cheaply and effectively as possible) being converted into an objective for a sub-unit (to retain the present system) and then into a mission (to reduce the national unemployment figures!).

In spite of these difficulties, in theory, and if the specification has been drawn up correctly, all the goals added together make up the totality of the objectives; and all the objectives together cover every aspect of the library's activities and mission statement.

Why performance measurement?
There are two main reasons why a librarian might wish to introduce performance measurement in his library; one is internal, the other external. He could — indeed should — be interested in making his systems work better (and we shall come back to the differences between efficiency, effectiveness, cost-effectiveness and cost-benefit); in this endeavour he needs to have at his disposal as many management tools as he can find — though he will not, if he is wise, make indiscriminate use of them all on every occasion. Externally, he will need to adopt some form of performance measurement when he is trying to justify a budget to his institution. You will have a better chance of getting what you want if you say 'Please give me enough money to employ one extra assistant; if not, I will be forced to close the library one hour early each evening', and if you can provide evidence, in the form of figures, to prove it. Then, if you do not get the money, you can come back the next year saying 'I told you so!'; it will not help the library in the short term, but it can strengthen your case in the future. You may of course get the money, and still find that you have to close early; in this case you have scored an own goal.

Ashworth's very perceptive paper[2] makes this point well: by the mere act of defining your objectives and goals you are entering on a very 'political' activity, and you are handling a sword with two edges which may either defend you against your enemies or inflict a nasty wound on your own body, if you are not very careful.

Buckland[3] gives an example drawn from real life: you believe that students in your library cannot get access to enough textbooks; you therefore decide that one of your objectives must be to improve this position. You measure something that you call 'availability' (the exact details do not matter for the purpose of this example), and establish that it is 60%; you then decide that your immediate goal is to improve this figure to 85%. Let us assume that you are able to achieve this goal, by changing the period of loan, or by buying extra copies. You have therefore succeeded in your objective, and the service to readers is very much better as a result.

Next year, however, you take the same measurements again, and find, with surprise and horror, that availability has fallen back to 60%. Clearly something has gone wrong; or has it? A new factor has entered the equation: you have successfully changed one side, the *supply* of books; but the readers themselves have changed the other side also, because they have individually recognized that they now have a much better chance of getting the book they want, and therefore the *demand* on the system has increased to the point where you can no longer provide the improved service. Yet at the same time, readers have found out how good a library can be; you will be blamed for not continuing to give the better service. Your only hope is to change your goal rapidly (though not your objective of providing a better service); you state, publicly, that your improvements have not increased availability permanently, but that many more books are nevertheless being borrowed.

Qualitative or quantitative measures?

As we have seen, goals tend to be quantitative, and it is often possible to measure whether the library has reached them or not. Objectives, on the other hand, are normally qualitative, and it is difficult to attach a numerical value to them, except (sometimes) by inferential reasoning. This will be possible only if the goals have been carefully designed to cover together every single part of each objective. This, however, is very difficult; we simply do not have enough knowledge of the many possible complex interactions between various parts of the library system, and even if we did, we would also have to be able to identify and analyse the wide range of reactions by readers − who form the other side of this equation − to the actions of the library itself. When we are analysing functions and structures, goals, objectives, and missions, it is easy to forget that we exist only to provide a service for present or future readers.

We therefore have to be very selective in the measures we choose to evaluate our systems. Some may be quantitative − 'what proportion of the potential readers visited the library last month?', and some qualitative − if a sample of readers are asked to indicate, on a scale of 1-10, how good they think the library is, what is the mean score? (Note that this question assumes that respondents understand what is meant by a 'good' library, and that their terms of reference are identical − neither is usually true. Note also that this particular performance measure is qualitative, in spite of the fact that it produces an apparently quantitative result).

The difficulty in choosing between quantitative and qualitative measures is easily described: the hard facts you need to tell you whether you are meeting a quantitative objectives are very difficult to collect; on the other hand, a qualitative objective is much more fuzzy round the edges, and reaching it or failing to reach it tends to be much more a matter of opinion and interpretation.

A hierarchy of quality measures in a library service

Efficiency is doing something well

Effectiveness is doing the *right thing* well

Cost-effectiveness is doing the right thing as well as possible *within a given budget.*

These are all measures internal to the library; the next, however, depends also on extraneous factors, and is only partially under the librarian's control:

> *Cost-benefit*, which is getting the best *overall* result for the community within *its* total budget.

The meaning of this terminology may be shown by a simple example. A library that did not allow its readers direct access to the stacks might be proud of delivering 95% of books requested within 10 minutes; it could be argued that this is very *efficient*, but not *effective*, because readers might well get their books more rapidly if they could go to the shelves themselves. It might also be the opposite of *cost-effective*, because extra staff are needed and this policy therefore costs the library more than the self-service solution. Finally, it produces a poor *cost-benefit* ratio: the end-result for the reader is not optimal, since he cannot browse on the shelves, and the total cost is higher than it need be. To put this in another way: doing the wrong thing, even if you do it very efficiently, cannot be good for the community (the institution) by any standards; and even to do the right thing very well *may* be damaging if the cost is high, since the money spent could have been spent on more useful things. The normal way to describe this concept is that every action you take has a specific 'opportunity cost' — you are 'paying' for taking action A by giving up your chance to use the same money to take actions B, C or D.

Data and their validity

How then do we try to measure whether the library is giving value for money? Every library collects statistics of one kind or another: usually these include the amount of money spent on staff, on purchases of books, periodicals and other items, and on services bought in from outside — for example interlibrary loans or binding. It is also common to count the number of books bought and catalogued (not always the same thing!), issues to readers, even the number of people who enter the building; and we all have figures for the number of books on the shelves, even although this figure is both meaningless in terms of the library's performance and, in all probability, wildly inaccurate. Mosts of these figures tell us something — if nothing else, how well the library is being supported financially by the institution, and how much activity it generates; or that the total cost of running the library divided by the number of readers, the average cost of supporting one reader, is (say) £300. (We can ignore, for the moment, the fact that the *real* cost of providing service for a first-year undergraduate may only be £30, but that for a professor it could well be £3,000.) We can also tell how these figures change from year to year — useful information, if perhaps not spectacular.

The theoretical problem is, however, that *input* figures (like those for expenditure) do not tell us anything at all about *output*, or *impact*, the effect that the library is having on readers, or what good it is doing, the benefit side of the cost-benefit equation. The figures we can easily collect as a matter of routine cannot be used for this purpose; but the figures we need to answer the really important questions are not readily available without a great deal of effort, and they can usually be produced only during a specially funded research project.

The problems of measuring benefit are very severe. In 1973 Ford said[4] that nobody had ever succeeded in proving that libraries have any effect on anything; this is still true today, in spite of the many man-years of effort expended on the subject since then. The nearest we can come to a measure of impact is to count our activities, in the hope that these output figures bear some relationship to, and will act as a surrogate for, the impact or benefit which we hope we are producing. And we must remember two things: first, even if we could measure impact or output accurately, the library's contribution to the total objectives or mission of the university is relatively small (the average expenditure on a library in the UK is less than 5% of the total institutional spend); and, second, that our output statistics are merely part of the overall picture, so will not be taken too seriously, except perhaps locally. Thus my cataloguing section's output figure is part of the library's process figure; library books lent are my output, but the university's process.

Moreover, facts about activities (our output figures) may tell us little about benefits (impact). Let us take two incidents: in the first someone borrows a book for three months, and in the second someone takes a periodical from the shelf, looks at it for a few minutes, and puts it back. It is 'obvious' that the three-month loan is much more 'valuable' to the community than a mere ten-minute scan. However a book may be borrowed and returned in three months, but we have no way of telling if the borrower has even opened it, let alone read it; if he has not, this must be a *disbenefit* to the community rather than a benefit, since for three months it has been away from the library and not available for other readers. Equally, something may be taken from the shelves and consulted for ten minutes only, to give a researcher a key fact or an idea which forms the basis of a completely new theory or a marketable invention. Counting loans cannot give any kind of reliable measure of the amount of, let alone the benefit of, this type of library use: perhaps ten times as many books as are borrowed may be consulted within the building, and in an open access library there is no way of recording these numbers. One substitute for a total count of such things is to use sampling techniques; this is the approach favoured by SCONUL (the Standing Conference of National and University Libraries) in compiling the 'activities' section of university library statistics: readers are asked, on one day each year, to specify the number of books which they took from the shelves, but did not borrow, during each visit to the library. The philosophy is that there may well be small, or perhaps even large, inaccuracies in the figures which appear; but even inaccurate data are better than none at all when we are working in an area which holds so many other uncertainties.

The collection of university library data in the UK

SCONUL has been collecting and publishing detailed statistics of expenditure in university libraries since 1981;[5] for the past three years it has also been producing figures for library activities, with the aid of a research grant from the British Library.[6] Data are collected for about 40 different categories of expenditure, and there are 12 more sets for numbers of different categories of staff and students; in the activities section, there are over 80 separate headings for data of various kinds, including library accommodation and stock as well as activities in the strict sense.

The published figures are not merely tables of raw data; these are of course included for each library, but in addition sets of ratios are produced, in an attempt to put the figures in context. For example, expenditure on acquisitions is also given on a per-student basis, and total staff costs as a percentage of total expenditure. The activities section includes not only the number of loans, but the number of loans per student, and the ratio of in-house use to loans, as estimated by sampling on one specific day.

In addition to figures for each library, summary tables are produced, grouping libraries together by their type or size; for example, a single table is produced giving the maximum, minimum, mean and median values for all the ratios in technological universities, and another for all universities with 3,101–4,400 students.

There are several difficulties in this kind of exercise. One is to decide exactly what information is required, for if we ask for too little the result is not going to be useful in management terms; but if we ask for too much some libraries will refuse to put the required effort into collecting data, and the response will be poor (at the moment, only two of the libraries SCONUL asks to collaborate refuse). Another problem is that a great amount of effort has to go into making sure that the data are collected in exactly the same way by all the 60 or so libraries involved: on any other basis it would be impossible to make comparisons between them, or even within the same institution from one year to another. This means that very careful definitions must be prepared in advance, and also that they ought to remain unchanged from year to year (this is even more important because we may wish to make some quite different analyses of the data in the future). The preparation of definitions is helped, to some extent, by the fact that all UK university libraries operate within the same financial and accounting conventions; the libraries in the Republic of Ireland, which also contribute data, find that their different financial framework sometimes makes it impossible to answer all the questions. These difficulties are to some extent theoretical; but as the editor/operator of the Part 1 database on expenditure, I have been very much aware also of the practical difficulties. No matter how carefully the questions are asked and the definitions framed, there are always some who misunderstand, some who reply carelessly, and some who miss out vital information. The telephone bill at St Andrews grows alarmingly during the month in which I am editing and processing the data (I use a standard statistical package, SPSS-X, on the university mainframe).

The Centre for Interfirm Comparison approach

A different approach to costing (one essential preliminary to establishing value for money) was taken a few years ago in a research project funded by the British Library. Following its work on public libraries the Centre for Interfirm Comparisons (CIFC) undertook a study[7] of a sample of 12 academic libraries, selected from universities and polytechnics. In each, the managers were asked to analyse their total costs by headings which, taken together, represented all the work done by the library: cataloguing, acquisitions, issue of books, reference enquiries etc. The major cost in most categories was, of course, staff salaries – in the UK these are typically between 55% and 60% of total library expenditure – and in the end this was the weakness of the technique: because many staff work at a number of different jobs at different times, it proved very difficult to allocate their time to the various categories of work with any accuracy. This is at least part of the reason why the CIFC work was not continued; but perhaps more important was the effort involved in collecting the data, and the judgement of many of the librarians who took part in the study that the results, which needed a great amount of local interpretation, did not justify this effort.

The Committee of Vice-Chancellors and Principals and performance indicators

In 1987 the Committee of Vice-Chancellors and Principals (CVCP) responded to an initiative by the University Grants Committee (the official body which allocated funds to universities in the UK until April 1989, when it was succeeded by the Universities

Funding Council) by producing a set of performance indicators (note, not 'measures') to compare the efficiency of various institutions as well as to serve the purpose of improving internal management.[8] Few would object to this in principle; but in practice the indicators adopted for libraries (in spite of severe criticism from librarians) proved to be totally inappropriate. They number seven:

- library expenditure as a percentage of total expenditure
- publications (by which they mean acquisitions) and pay expenditure as a percentage of library expenditure
- library, book and periodical expenditure per FTE (full-time equivalent) student
- library expenditure per FTE academic staff.

It is clear that none of these figures is in fact a performance measure, or even an indicator; they are all, quite simply, measures of input to the library, and tell us nothing at all about its performance. Many of the figures merely reflect decisions that may have been taken many years ago, and cannot easily be changed to meet the new circumstances which call for greater economy. They do not even say anything about the performance of the university itself: there are no standards for library provision against which these figures could be measured, and each university has different needs. No account is taken of the effects of scale, which indicate that if everything else is equal a large university can have the same standard of library service for a lower percentage of its total expenditure than a small one can.

Even if we could accept a set of indicators with such theoretical weaknesses, there are still major problems, in the CVCP's definitions. The very first item, library expenditure, is quite different from the true cost of running the library; it excludes, for example, all costs of cleaning and portering, heating, and telecommunications. On the other hand, it includes all expenditure on books and periodicals within the university, even when this has no connection at all with the library, because of the accounting conventions which are in use.

The whole document is crude in the extreme, as far as it refers to libraries; it cannot supply valid comparisons between institutions, it is open to very simplistic interpretations which can only damage libraries individually and collectively, and it shows once again that those responsible for compiling it have ignored professional advice over the years, that measurement is a very complex operation.

Developments in the USA

The Association of Research Libraries (ARL) in the United States has given a great deal of attention to performance measurement. For many years it also has produced very extensive statistical tables, but more recently it commissioned Kantor to construct a framework of 'objective performance measurement' for the use of its members. The report of this project[9] is well worth reading for the insight it offers into these questions, and for its suggestions for a possible path into the future. I particularly liked the discussion of book availability, and of the simulation technique by which he deduced the current success rate of readers in finding a specific sought-for book: each step of the process depends on success at the previous step, and at each step there is a finite probability of failure (the library may never have acquired the book; it may be wrongly catalogued; the reader may not find it in the catalogue, even though it is in the right place; it may already be on loan, etc.). Even if the probability of failure at each step is only about 10% (and this would represent good performance by each of the sub-units concerned), cumulatively these failures mean that overall the reader has less than an even chance of getting what he wants!

Nevertheless, I have reservations about the practicality of the approach Kantor proposes, however elegant it is in theory, simply because it demands a great amount of effort to put his monitoring schemes into practice. One of the important factors about any performance measure proposed is that it must be possible to collect the necessary data within the normal routines of running a library; libraries in the United States may still be able to devote their uncommitted manpower to such a project, but we certainly cannot do it in the UK unless external funding is made available, and I suspect that this is true for most other countries.

'Library goodness'

Performance measurement is a tool, and by itself can make no value judgements; I have said little about the factors which make a library 'good' — or, for that matter, 'bad' (see Maurice Line's paper in this volume). As he points out, his view is not the only one. Goodness cannot simply be a factor of all the goals, objectives and mission statements, because these (as we have seen) relate to matters which are imperfectly understood, and there is no theoretical model which could tie them all together into a single measure of goodness. I suspect that there is in fact no absolute quality of goodness, that in each library it must relate to local circumstances to a great extent, and to the needs of each group of users. Nevertheless there are certain qualities which we could all agree will be present in a good library, and absent in a bad one.

Orr's classic 1973 paper[10] differentiates between two aspects of goodness: quality, defined by the question 'How good is it?', and value, 'How much good does it do?' (these might equally be phrased — as Lancaster has done[11] — in terms of effectiveness and benefit). He points out, however, that these two qualities are closely interrelated, in that a library which does good to its users will tend to increase its outputs, which in turn will justify greater resource being given to it, which in turn will tend to improve its quality further. Line does not accept this distinction between quality and value on either theoretical or practical grounds.

Whatever the arguments adduced, it is likely that this discussion will be with us for many years. Librarianship is not yet a science — how could it be, when it embraces so many disparate elements of human life? — and there is room for many more theories before any certainty can be reached.

References

1 Buckland, M. K., *Library services in theory and context*, Oxford, Pergamon Press, 1983.
2 Ashworth, J. (Introductory address) *in* Harris, Colin (ed.), *Proceedings of a Conference on Management Information*, 1986. London, Taylor Graham, 1987.
3 Buckland, M. K., *Book availability and the library user*, Oxford, Pergamon Press, 1975.
4 Ford, G., 'Research in user behaviour in university libraries', *Journal of documentation*, **29**, (1), 1973, 85–106.

5 Standing Conference of National and University Libraries, *University library expenditure statistics*, London, SCONUL, 1981 – .

6 Standing Conference of National and University Libraries, *Statistical database, Part II: Library operations*, London, SCONUL, 1986 – .

7 Centre for Interfirm Comparison, *Inter-library comparisons in academic libraries*. London, British Library, 1984. (British Library Research & Development Reports, 5763).

8 Committee of Vice-Chancellors and Principals *and* University Grants Committee, *University management statistics and performance indicators in the UK*, London, CVCP, 1987 – .

9 Kantor, P. B., *Objective performance measures for academic and research libraries*, Washington DC, Association of Research Libraries, 1984.

10 Orr, R. H., 'Measuring the goodness of library service: a general framework for considering quantitative measures', *Journal of documentation*, **29**, (3), 1973, 117 – 34.

11 Lancaster, F. W., *If you want to evaluate your library* . . . , London, Library Association, 1988.

Further reading

Brophy, P., *Management information and decision support systems in libraries*, Aldershot, Gower, 1986.

Ford, G., 'Performance measures: principles and practice', *IFLA journal*, **15**, (1), 1989, 13 – 17.

Goodall, G. L., 'Performance measurement: a historical perspective', *Journal of librarianship*, **20**, (2), 1988, 129 – 44.

Hamburg, M. *and others*, 'Library objectives and performance measures and their use in decision making', *Library quarterly*, **41**, (1), 1972, 107 – 28. (This whole issue was devoted to the operational research approach to libraries, and contains several other seminal papers.)

Layzell-Ward, P., *Performance measures: a bibliography*, Loughborough, The University, Centre for Library and Information Management, 1982. (CLAIM Report 15).

Morse, P. M., *Library effectiveness: a systems approach*, Cambridge, Mass., MIT Press, 1968.

26

Monitoring and management information

Lynne Brindley

Introduction

The subject of this paper is to be interpreted broadly, namely the collection, analysis and presentation of information useful in the management of library operations and/or supporting decision-making relating to the academic library. Other papers deal in more detail with related topics of financial management systems, budgeting and costing, and performance measurement. In one sense I regard these as part of the wider question of the role of management and the place of information in management, at a variety of levels.

It is important, perhaps, to avoid the label 'management information systems' (MIS) for this paper, for again the topic is wider in concept, and management information systems have gathered rather a bad name as being too theoretical, too costly, and of limited use where the data is derived as a by-product of the automated control of library operations. Instead, I will adopt the view that management information is, in principle, everything that the manager calls on to make a decision. This can be extensive both in volume and kind.

Kinds of information

Sandra Ward, one of the UK's leading industrial librarians, has said,

> 'The department measures quantity and efficiency but cannot always determine effectiveness. Of course, much of the strategic information required for planning must by its nature continue to sit outside any formal information system — the marrying together of the analyses of present services with external developments and with corporate needs for managerial decisions is the manager's art'.[1]

This highlights a significant point, that there are two kinds of management information, the formal and the informal, both of which are derived from sources internal and external to the academic library; however, informal or 'soft' information is more often found externally, among the user public and the administrators who govern budgets. It is the senior library managers who have to develop a nose for administrative and planning data of this elusive kind, and the professionals working direct with user groups who should feed back 'soft' information on user attitudes and changes which are likely to affect demand for library services. One practical problem for this paper is how to express the totality of relevant information for decision making.

Awareness of this complexity of inputs to a management information system explains an apparent conflict. Those who research or construct an MIS, principally the manufacturers of turnkey automated library systems, or theoreticians, claim that librarians pay mere lip service to the need for such systems, whilst being unprepared to pay realistic prices for them. This school sees librarians as concerned with internal professional goals like collection building and the quality of services, and ignoring the management imperatives of customer satisfaction and cost-effectiveness.

The other point of view is taken by senior librarians who see their function as a kind of opportunism in getting resources, or even avoiding cuts, based on an unquantifiable feel for the motives and pre-occupations of those set in authority over them. This political dimension of decision making is fundamentally important, and political awareness, through a network of contacts, an intelligence network, and an awareness of the hidden power structures and loci of decision making, is an essential skill for senior managers to acquire. The sceptical, if not cynical, attitude towards rational decision making based on management information systems and their use is well summed up by the Vice-Chancellor of Salford University,[1] who tells the story about a medieval king asking a peasant 'What is the golden rule?' 'It's quite simple', came the reply, 'them as had the gold, rules'. To be fair to this school of thought, one must agree that information and analysis only *support* decision-making, which must always be based on judgement exercized in the face of a degree of uncertainty. That is what risk taking and higher management are all about. In an ideal world, what we should be aiming to do in academic libraries is to fuse the two approaches together to improve the quality of decision making in all its manifestations and at all levels.

LEVELS OF INFORMATION

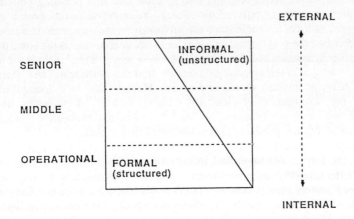

Fig. 1

As I am a qualified optimist about the value of rational argument and the eventual development of more effective MIS in academic libraries, let me at this stage agree that the informal and formal sources of information both have a vital part to play in management. It is important, however, not only to distinguish between formal and informal, but also to see the needs of library management on three levels, a pyramid of operational supervisors, middle managers, and senior managers. These levels and their various concerns obviously overlap, and in some cases may be undertaken by the same person, especially in smaller libraries. Nevertheless, the distinction remains a generally valid one, in terms of information need. At operational and some middle levels, formal information, systematically provided with short term time comparisons, forms the bulk of what is required. Higher up the pyramid, unstructured information, much of it external, is a more significant consideration; also, the more senior librarians will want only shapshot or selective sets of data derived, for example, from operational systems and university budgets. They may, however, require long time series for trend analysis, and this presents difficulties in our present situation of flux. For one thing the information has not been collected in the same way, if at all, and more importantly, the whole environment of the parent institution is changing rapidly and in some cases adversely.

The managerial environment

Moving on from the general points about the kind and levels of information, it is now worth considering the managerial environment within which information is to be used. The academic and library managerial climates in the UK have altered considerably in the past few years, under the pressure of declining resources from public funds and a very critical, if not hostile, political attitude towards higher education, at least in its present rather conservative manifestations. The implications of this are instability and unpredictability, except for the safe assumption that it is no good sitting it out in the hope that retrenchment and restructuring will go away. In the context of academic restructuring, with in some cases the loss of whole disciplines from institutions, there is a need for the library as a support service to justify its use of scarce resources, and also to show that it is pursuing policies in support of the university or polytechnic strategy for survival in this future.

Peter Brophy, at a recent conference on performance measurement in academic libraries[2] described the polytechnic sector as in a state of turmoil, listing some dozen major changes polytechnics and their libraries are now facing. These include the move to corporate status, increasing emphasis on non-traditional students, new learning methods, CNAA accredited status, and so on. He saw this as a context which necessitates the development of clear and reliable methods of evaluating library services and measuring performance, not least to be able to demonstrate the quality and relevance of library products in a situation of major change.

Management information needs

Having made the general points about kinds and levels of information and the balance of external and internal information, it is possible to construct a more detailed profile of management information needs. A schematic model may help to highlight the relevant areas. This perceives the library as an open system taking in resources — people, money, materials, and providing services — loan of books, information, study spaces, as an outcome from a variety of operating processes — cataloguing, shelving,

MANAGEMENT INFORMATION NEEDS
MODEL

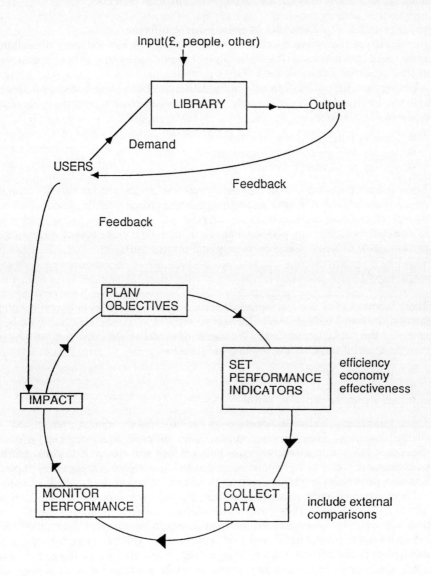

Fig. 2

publication, and so on. It also links the inputs and outputs to a feedback loop from users of services, which in turn leads in to the whole planning cycle of setting objectives, performance standards and monitoring performance in terms of both efficiency and effectiveness (figure 2). What is clear is that the design of a management information system to cover all these needs is a daunting task, and in virtually all libraries there exist only partial elements of this kind of model.

Examples of management information

Having, if you like, given a top-down view I would now like to move on to giving some more concrete examples of management information that goes to making up at least a partial picture of the library's activities.

Let us turn first to performance information available from *automated library systems*. I will use, by way of example, some of the statistical reports available from our own Geac system.

- account purchase order summary
- vendor performance by elapsed time
- vendor performance by order type.

These three reports are used at the operational level by the acquisitions librarian to ensure financial control of order and commitment expenditure; fulfilment rate of orders by type of material from each library supplier and the number of days a supplier takes to satisfy orders; and performance information on average cost of volumes and percentage of orders initiated by faculty and library staff.

- hourly transaction statistics
- usage statistics of OPAC.

These reports can be used as input to determining such things as optimum opening hours and counter staffing levels. The second report can be used in deciding the best siting for the public terminals and the nature of access to the catalogue, which can then be a useful input to any training programmes.

- circulation statistics
- circulation totals
- circulation statistics by patron.

These reports give useful information on the different circulation transactions – charge, discharge, fines and reservations, in the different loan categories. A daily list is used as input to a dynamic loans policy which will change loan status and/or purchase more copies of an item, based on demand for material. Through these reports it is also possible to establish changing trends in collection use by kinds of users.

There are many more examples possible, but these are indicative of the kind of information provided. They have drawbacks as management tools. The first is presentation – in many cases the information has to be extracted and manipulated before it becomes meaningful, and a report generator, which can take this raw data, manipulate it, and present it in a meaningful way, is essential for anything more than operational needs. Frequently the reports comprise a pile of indigestible printout, a complete turn-off for any serious analysis and requiring significant amounts of time to use. Secondly, the effective analysis of historical data is difficult because of the lack of historical information fields and easy direct comparison with a similar period in a previous year.

I have used examples from my own system, but I think it is no more or less good in the provision of information than other automated systems. In other words most of these systems have been designed with MIS as only a background consideration. A few libraries have developed their own management information enhancements, and I would draw attention to the work of Sussex University Library in this respect.[3] This library has developed a system for book stock management, decision support, and management information, by modifying its Geac system. It manages the stock by moving books between loan categories and by provisional withdrawal to storage and final withdrawal, and adjusts purchasing and budget allocation in the light of book use. The system gives assistance in book stock management, covering the complete life span of each item.

In summary, whilst the data and statistics available from most turnkey library housekeeping systems are of some value, they are partial and laborious to use, and generally useful only for lower level management, unless subject to further processing and analysis. They do not easily provide longer term trend information useful for strategic planning. In addition they need supplementing with statistics collected manually, on a regular *ad hoc* basis, covering the full range of library activities.

Let me move on now to the area of *financial management information*, a crucial part of an overall MIS, most of which cannot easily be derived from existing systems. It concerns the way in which resources are being distributed and utilized. Again I will work from some examples used in my own library. One of the most important areas is management information on inflation, especially for books and periodicals. This is gleaned from a variety of external price indices — Blackwells Comparative Index to Periodical Prices, British and US academic book prices being the main ones. These data are matched with our own subject profile of expenditure and country of origin profile of purchasing and used to produce an index of book and periodical prices reflecting our overall price increase. This is required input from the Finance Officer as part of an annual budget preparation cycle, and its professional compilation and development by the Assistant Director has resulted in full inflation cases being accepted for the past two academic years.

Once we have a budget for the year the need for management information switches to budget control, devolved to both cost centre and subject managers. This information is collected from a variety of automated and manual systems and is produced monthly in the form of a spreadsheet. The figures are accompanied by reports from each cost centre manager, commenting more subjectively on the way the budget is going, any potential problems of over- or underspend, and expected outcome. The subject reporting for book acquisitions works in a similar way. This kind of reporting is fairly adequate for budget control purposes, especially as it is supplemented by real-time control of acquisitions expenditure at a broader level, an essential feature towards the end of the year.

However, what it does not provide is any indication of whether and how the funds are being used, and whether they are being used wisely and linked with objectives. This requires an approach which brings in the use of performance indicators (PIs). This poses considerable difficulty, not least because of the need to start with clear objectives, and the ability to define appropriate and meaningful PIs, both qualitative and quantitative. The cynical observer might suggest that the action of librarians indicates an underlying assumption that it is important to spend as much as possible, issue as much as possible, store as much as possible in as large a building as possible, with as many staff as possible! It requires a considerably better set of objectives to gain usable PIs.

The approach we are taking at Aston to this work is to start by drawing up a service and activity matrix, which embraces all our work, and is covered by our stated objectives (figure 3). Where anomalies have been discovered there is usually some fuzziness in our thinking on overall objectives, so the very classification process itself has helped management thinking. This identifies activities and sub-activities and gives a framework for the development of performance indicators of all types and levels. It also provides the basis for the development of service costings, which attribute the direct and overhead costs to each element of the service, something which is not necessarily inherent in the more functionally oriented budget control process.

We are then pursuing a rigorous analysis of the key performance indicators under each activity and examining critically the range of statistics kept to see how far they support these PIs, or how far they are still being collected only because they always have been although no-one takes any notice of them.

ACTIVITY/SERVICE MATRIX

MATERIALS PROVISION	1 Monograph provision	1 Book ordering	Objective "to provide ... a limited range of material in support of the University's teaching, research and service programmes".
	2 Serial provision	2 Serial ordering	
		3 Serial chasing	
		4 Receipt of materials	
		5 Processing	
		6 Binding	
		7 Payment of invoices	
BIBLIOGRAPHIC ACCESS	1 Record provision	1 Create, add, amend delete records	Objective "to provide ... quick and easy access from its own stock".
	2 OPAC provision	2 OPAC development	
		3 Catalogue maintenance	
		4 Reading list provision	

Fig. 3

ELEMENTS OF AN MIS

ENVIRONMENTAL INFORMATION
    academic plan
    profile of institution
    higher education trends
    IT developments
    publishing trends
    political factors

LIS PLAN
    functions and objectives
    services
    activities
    priorities
    criteria for evaluation

FINANCIAL INFORMATION
    inflation factors
    staff costs/distribution
    budget control
    buildings
    equipment

PERFORMANCE INDICATORS
    external comparisons
    unit costs
    service delivery times
    space utilisation
    stock turnover
    cataloguing throughput/backlots
    speed of supply

STATISTICS
    number of items purchased
    number of enquiries handled
    number of online searches
    use of library
    opening hours

USER SATISFACTION
    consumer group information
    complaints
    staff-student committees
    questionnaires
    surveys of use
    knowledge of services
    perception
    market research

STAFF MORALE
    sickness rates
    recruitment success
    training time

Fig. 4

This is a large task, and we have been able to appoint a project officer to lead the project, involving staff as appropriate in devising sensible indicators for their own areas of work and moulding this with the needs expressed for higher level indicators from senior management. For many activities it is possible to go a considerable way on internal indicators of performance and statistics from our systems, but this falls down in a range of services whose outcomes are less tangible products than (for example) a document or book supplied.

This brings us in to the area of user satisfaction, and the need for getting feedback from users on their perception of services provided and their needs. Most of this work falls outside any by-product collection of information from systems or elsewhere and usually involves some kind of sampling and user survey work. We supplemented this by regular attendance at and feedback from staff and student consultative committees, regular meetings of the consumer group − representatives of students giving their opinions of services, and so on. We have been able to take advantage of the constant need for student projects to run some one-off questionnaires and surveys of particular groups.

Conclusions
I conclude by repeating that any information useful in making decisions relating to the academic library is potential management information. In an ideal world I would like to be able to tape into a system, ask the health of my library, and be able to pull out all the relevant information to make an evaluation. However, it is really not like that at all. Much of the really valuable information is not available as a by-product of systems; much useful information is imprecise or open to a wide range of interpretations. We have to take from all of these sources and mould them into an overall picture of the performance of the library. A single MIS for academic libraries does not exist, but its key elements can be identified and pulled together (figure 4).

References
1 Harris, Colin (ed.), *Management information systems in libraries and information services*, London, Taylor Graham, 1987.
2 Performance measurement: can you manage without it? LIRG conference held on Nov 18−20 1988. (Publication forthcoming).
3 Peasgood, Adrian N., 'Towards demand-led acquisitions? Experiences in the University of Sussex Library', *Journal of librarianship*, 18, (4), 1986, 242−56.

27

Financial management systems

John Fletcher

One of the major problems with our profession is that the more we are promoted, and the higher we rise in the profession, the further we leave behind our reasons for joining the profession in the first place. This is not an uncommon problem — it happens in many professions; architects, teachers, even policemen, become administrators or managers above a certain level of promotion. For most library managers books are things which cost money and occupy metres of shelving, and readers are people who wear out carpets, ask questions and occupy seats in libraries.

The problem arises in the management training we receive, or rather in the lack of it. Chief librarians manage an operation with a very substantial financial budget. Even a relatively small academic library serving 6,000−8,000 students has an annual budget of over one million pounds, and many have much larger budgets. Yet it is unusual for their librarians to be qualified in financial management, or even have received any formal training in accountancy, but they are expected to manage substantial budgets. They all have to learn by experience, and this can be a painful and very inefficient process. With this in mind, this chapter takes a rather basic approach to financial management systems, and the author apologizes in advance to those readers who already have expertise in this area.

At its simplest level, a financial management system is merely book-keeping — controlling the amount of money spent and ensuring that it does not exceed the amount available. This operation must be carried out methodically and accurately at the institutional level, for all institutions and their constituent departments' heads are accountable to those who fund them, whether this is central government, regional government, or private bodies.

The same financial control can, and usually does, apply at lower levels of the institution: the total institutional budget is allocated to various departments, services and functions, and the heads of these divisions control expenditure within their own budget.

This is a very simplistic view of a financial management system. More information than total commitment and expenditure against a starting budget is needed if the future operation of the university or polytechnic is to be planned, if the limited financial (and other) resources available are to be used in the best possible way. More than this basic information is needed in order to know what is going on in the libraries

215

in financial terms and to manage them well.

This implies a much more commercial view of educational and library management than has perhaps been expected in the past, but in Britain it is becoming commonplace for such a commercial attitude to be applied. In this context British higher education institutions are becoming more like the larger privately funded American colleges and universities. Certainly, a much more sophisticated approach to financial management is called for, though with the power of even small modern computers that does not necessarily mean that it needs to be either complicated or expensive. What is required is a well thought out financial management system, which should include other measures of the institution's activities, and provide a **financial management information system**.

The first part of this chapter considers the higher education institution as a whole, and the way in which a good financial management information system can provide valuable data to help its managers. This is especially important at the departmental level. The library is looked at as part of the total institutional system, and in more detail.

It is advisable, before proceeding any further, to put down some definitions. Librarians are not as familiar with the terminology of finance as with that of their own profession.

A **financial management system** is an accounting system, usually now in computerized form, which handles all the financial transactions of the institution and parts of the institution.

Allocation is the amount of money earmarked for a specific purpose during a given period of time. Thus the university may allocate a certain sum of money to the library for the purchase of books and periodicals during the coming financial year.

Budget gives the overall picture of the various allocations (for expenditure) and the expected income, and will include funds in hand at the beginning of the period, and intentions to add to, or subtract from, those reserves during the period. The term 'budget' is also used to denote the financial allocation for a specific purpose or purposes during a given period. Thus there will be reference to the library's materials budget, or equipment budget, which is the sum of money allocated for this purpose.

Commitment is the money within the allocated sum which has been set aside by ordering goods and services which have not yet been delivered.

Expenditure is the amount of money already paid out for goods and services which have been delivered.

Balance is the amount of the total allocation less the sum of the commitment and the expenditure. Cash balance is the allocation less the actual expenditure. The balance is thus the amount of money which remains to be used.

Revenue account is the budget for the current financial year. In some financial systems all of the total revenue budget must be spent within the financial year — what is called 'carry-over' is not permitted. In other systems, carry-over, and even overspending within defined limits, are allowed.

The **capital account** is non-recurrent money allocated for the purchase of capital goods. 'Non-recurrent' signifies that it is a one-off grant, for a specific purpose, and that normally it must be spent within a specified time. Capital goods are defined as fixed assets, items which will last many years, such as new buildings, furniture and equipment. The related term, 'consumable goods', means those goods that will be used up over a relatively short period of time, such as stationery, computer discs, pens and ink. These are normally purchased from revenue funds.

It is fortunate that a recent report on the needs of British higher education institutions for a financial management information system has recently been published. At the same time British universities were seeking to review their financial control systems.

The Coopers and Lybrand report *Information for independence*, published in 1988, was commissioned by the Committee of Directors of Polytechnics and the Standing Conference of Principals of Colleges.[1] These higher education institutions in England became, on 1 April 1989, independent corporations, free from the control of the local government authorities which have supervised them for so long. They now receive funds from the Polytechnics and Colleges Funding Council, a central government body, similar to the Universities Funding Council (the successor to the University Grants Committee) which now controls the funding of universities.

Until now the polytechnics and colleges have followed the financial regulations laid down by their local authorities, but now they must devise their own financial control systems. The Coopers and Lybrand report is therefore an up-to-date review of what such higher education institutions need in the way of financial management information, and the systems that are available to meet those needs.

The report begins with the conventional division of inputs, processes and outputs:
Inputs are students, staff, buildings, and equipment;
Processes are courses, research, catering and accommodation;
Outputs are qualified students, research products and reports, and 'other entre-
preneurial activities'.
It is perhaps interesting to note in passing that library stock is included as 'equipment'. By extension, this could offer librarians a new approach to library finances: if the bookstock is equipment, such a category of asset normally has a rate of depreciation, and has to be replaced after a number of years. Should librarians perhaps be thinking of their book funds as the preservation and replacement cost of a depreciating capital asset as well as the cost of increasing the size of that asset? Such an approach could have a significant impact on the way in which libraries are funded.

The report then goes into considerable detail about the data which could or should be collected about all aspects of these main groups. Most, but by no means all, is financial information.

The great advantage and benefit of a financial management information system is that by bringing together various financial transactions and other data into one system some products of one part automatically form the raw material for another part. For example, staffing data, essential to calculate the payroll costs, are also necessary to work out the feasible student numbers for specific courses. Student numbers, and by extrapolation class sizes, are raw data for planning building provision and utilization. Such integration of data can produce enormous benefits for the institutional and departmental manager.

It is not easy to discover the financial management system used in many British universities and polytechnics. Many finance officers are reluctant to discuss them except in highly technical terms comprehensible only to a qualified accountant. The only guaranteed approach is through the summary data which both types of institution have provided publicly − the universities to the University Grants Committee, and the polytechnics to the Polytechnics Finance Officers' Group. In both cases the data is aggregated into fairly broad headings, such as 'salaries and wages', 'libraries', 'premises', and 'central university computers'. These are clearly aggregations based on much more detailed data series collected in the institutions, and are summarized for the purpose of national reporting. The problem in such aggregation is always the same: do the responsible finance officers follow the definitions accurately, or to put it more fairly, do they all interpret the definitions in the same way? There is some evidence that they do not, which inevitably casts doubts in the minds of non-accountants about the comparability of the resulting data.

I will turn now to the methods which might be used to produce the data. Generally speaking, the structure of an institution's financial system reflects the structure of the management of the institution. With the increasing emphasis on financial control, institutions are thinking more and more in terms of 'cost centres', even 'profit centres' in some cases. These are departments or sections of the institution which have a common purpose, and to which greater financial autonomy may be given.

The organizational chart of a typical university or polytechnic may look something like this:

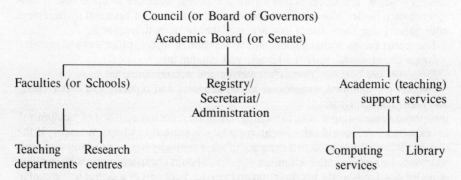

Each of these may be treated in financial terms as a cost centre, with its own budget, and with the head of the section or department as the budget holder with control of the expenditure of his or her given allocation. Heads of department may well divide the total allocation into smaller budgets, for specific uses, and delegate responsibility for the control of these allocations to members of their staff. To quote from the Coopers and Lybrand report:

'financial management should be delegated to the lowest practical level of management activity . . . This requires the facility for financial activity to be recorded at that level, and presupposes a sufficiently flexible accounts coding system'.[2]

The method of achieving this is logical, and fairly simple. To simplify it even further, it is useful to concentrate on the right hand side of the structure chart, since this is the most relevant to the academic library's interests.

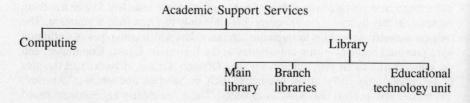

218

This structure shows similarities to a decimal classification scheme, with which all librarians are familiar: if the Academic Support Services are the 200s, then Computing can be the 210s, the Library the 250s, and the Main library 251, the Branch libraries 252–255 and the Educational technology unit 257.

Each of the Libraries, and the Unit, can now be regarded as the columns of a matrix chart, and the rows of the chart can be the various expenditure headings which we use. By prefixing the row numbers (which themselves are decimalized to give a hierarchical structure) by the column numbers, individual code numbers are created:

		Main Library (251)	Branch A (252)	Branch B (253)	Ed Tech Unit (257)
Books	(10)	25110	25210	25310	25710
Periodicals	(11)	25111	25211	25311	25711
Online	(20)	25120	25220	25320	25720
ILL	(21)	25121	25221	25321	25721
Lighting	(31)	25131	25231	25331	25731
Equipment	(40)	25140	25240	25340	25740
Repair & maintenance	(45)	25145	25245	25345	25745
Staff	(90)	25190	25290	25390	25790
professional	(91)	25191	25291	25391	25791
clerical	(92)	25192	25292	25392	25792

etc.

This simple matrix gives the key to a very powerful financial management information system. Each order going out of the library, each invoice coming in, and each payment being made must carry the five-figure coding for the individual cell derived from the matrix. It is then possible to see from the accounts at any time the costs of specific activities, purchases, and outstanding commitment, and compare these with the initial allocation.

It is also possible to sum the columns and get, for example:

a total of all Main library costs   25100 to 25199
a total of all Educational technology unit costs   25700 to 25799

In modern computing terms this is usually achieved by asking for the code 251** or 257**, where * is any number from 0 to 9.

It is possible to aggregate across the chart to find, for example:

a total of all periodical costs   25*11
a total of all R & M costs   25*45

This is a simple coding system now widely adopted by financial management systems, which gives managers greatly enhanced information about the costs, expenditure, commitment and overall budget situation.

It is a fundamental necessity for the cost centre approach to financial management, which is increasingly being adopted in higher education in this country, following the pattern of industrial companies. There is considerable debate resulting from this movement on how far such disaggregation of budget control and responsibility should go. Devolution, for example, to the level of the cost of books and periodicals, or of buying and running the library's computer system, is clearly valuable, even essential. There is less agreement on the need to allocate to cost centres such detailed expenditure as cleaning, security, telephones or lighting. These may best be regarded as overheads, costs which have to be incurred if the Library is to function at all. If detailed data are required for these operations they can be worked out as one-off calculations for a specific purpose, rather than going to the expense of continuous cost monitoring.

This, then, is a simplified outline of a financial management information system for a higher education institution. It can produce valuable financial data at departmental or section level which, if combined with non-financial data, can give valuable management information on, for example, the cost of producing a graduate in mechanical engineering compared with that of a biologist or an economist, and the total library cost of running a library service for the engineering or politics departments (but only if they have their own departmental libraries).

All this is at the institutional level. Most departmental managers, and all librarians, require more detailed information about running their departments. It does not seem reasonable for managers to expect their institutional financial control system to handle the more detailed cost information which they need as managers. One would expect a departmental manager to monitor this level of detailed activity, and its costs, internally within the department. Such a financial monitoring system should however integrate with the institution's financial management information system, complementing it but not replacing it.

What I shall describe now is the financial management system which I have at the Lanchester Library of Coventry Polytechnic, not because I think it is ideal, and it certainly is not perfect, but because I think it is fairly typical of the small-scale system we can all devise to meet our own needs, which can be run very simply. It uses a spreadsheet software package on a microcomputer, and was developed in-house.

The polytechnic allocates the library's annual revenue budget, excluding staff costs, under five headings. They are:

- Equipment
- Repair and maintenance
- Subscriptions
- Travel and subsistence; and, of course,
- Materials.

To meet my management needs we divide some of these into smaller categories:

Equipment is intended to cover all items, so we divide this into two, hardware and consumables;

Repair and maintenance is for all equipment, so we separate the costs of the main computer system from other costs;

Subscriptions is an unusual category: the library is responsible for all memberships of organizations held by individuals within the polytechnic if the institution pays the subscription; this we do not divide;

Travel and subsistence is for all travel and conference fees for library staff, and also pays for any costs related to training of staff; again this remains one category;

Materials are all books, periodicals, binding, non-book items such as films or videotapes, online searching, and interlibrary borrowing. This category is divided partly by type of material and partly by subject, and is the most interesting part of the system.

First there is audio-visual media: audio and videotapes, cine films and slides.

Online is all online searching charges made by hosts, and by British Tele-communications. We carry out a few online searches for outside people and reclaim the costs, so this is off-set as income.

Binding: we divide books from periodicals (at Coventry binding is all done commercially − we do not have our own bindery − but a division between in-house and commercial binding could be made here if required).

We also separate out interlibrary borrowing costs, and the small amount of income we receive from interlibrary lending.

This leaves books and periodicals. We separate these from each other, then divide both by subject. At Coventry the detail of the subject areas covered by one fund varies considerably, but they are subjects, not departments; thus, if a civil engineer wants a book on the law of safety on building sites, it is purchased from the law fund, not the engineering fund.

In addition to the subject funds we also have several general funds: general reference, and general funds for each faculty for books which span several subjects; we also separate duplicate copy purchases. Finally there is a contingency fund to enable us to deal with unforeseen problems during the year.

These subjects are aggregated into the faculties, but this must, by definition, be somewhat inaccurate in terms of expenditure per student, since readers from one faculty may, and do, use books and periodicals from another faculty's subjects.

As in the polytechnic's main financial control system, all orders (that is commitments) and invoices (that is payments) are set against the allocated budget for that subject or type of material. At present this is a manual operation, but we hope to implement this part of our computerized ordering system later this year.

Each month, and more frequently towards the end of the financial year, we produce a printout on the microcomputer which gives, for each budget heading, the allocation, the expenditure, the outstanding commitment, and the remaining balance. The total expenditure and outstanding commitment are also shown as a percentage of the original allocation. This enables us to monitor on a regular basis the rate at which the allocated funds are being used up.

Monthly printouts are circulated to the senior professional library staff who have responsibility for the control of their subject funds, and this enables them, and the librarian, to monitor expenditure throughout the year, and amend allocations (which are under the librarian's control) as necessary.

It is important to notice that the aggregations of the various internal library fund allocations match the allocations in the polytechnic's financial management system. This means that on a monthly basis, or whenever required, the internal financial data can be checked against the finance office data, and the two sets reconciled. There is an inevitable time-lag here, and that needs to be allowed for, but generally speaking this reconciliation of the two sets of financial accounts works well.

221

At various levels, other data collected by the library and/or the polytechnic enable calculations to be made of a variety of ratios related to, for example, expenditure and use by subject area, inflation rates on book and periodical purchases by subject, the running costs of the library's computer system, etc.

What has been described above is not sophisticated, not complicated, and not expensive. It is a simple manual and microcomputer system, developed in-house using conventional accounting methods allied to a basic spreadsheet software package. It provides easily available and up-to-date information on the current state of the library's budget. It also provides additional data on the financial aspects of the library's operations which can be related to other non-financial data to give good day-to-day management information.

As institutions of higher education become more self-supporting, more responsible for their own economic and financial viability, so librarians will have to become more aware of such financial control and information systems. Increasingly heads of departments are becoming more like departmental managers in commercial organizations, and need to have, or acquire, the financial expertise to control their budgets accurately and wisely. As a group senior librarians must accept this challenge, and learn the skills necessary to create systems which will allow them to control satisfactorily the financial affairs of their libraries.

References
1 Coopers and Lybrand, *Information for independence: financial management information systems for polytechnics and colleges*, London, Coopers & Lybrand, 1988. 2 vols.
2 ref. 1, vol. 1, para. 2.19.

28

Revenue earning and cost recovery

Nigel Macartney

Why earn extra income?

Academic libraries in the UK are under pressure from a number of sources to earn extra revenue. Firstly the UK Government has made it plain that universities and polytechnics are expected to supplement their allocations from the two Funding Councils by income-earning activities;[1] this thinking is evident in much of the present Government's approach to the public sector, and the public library is not exempt either.[2] Secondly, there is often pressure from the institution itself on the librarian. I have experienced myself several times the suggestion that if cuts in the Library's expenditure estimates are to be minimized, the income estimate should be increased. Currently the Director of my own institution is discussing with each dean of faculty and head of centre his or her plans for income earning over the next three years. Finally, the librarian as a manager is more and more seeking alternative sources of finance to create a greater flexibility and a greater financial independence.

There are other benefits which can follow from income-earning activities. Spare capacity or resources can be effectively deployed; for example, a special collection which is under-used by students or academics might be of interest to external users who would be willing to pay for services based on it. Equally, a member of staff might be underemployed and could be released to spend time on revenue-earning services.

It may also be appropriate to develop fee-based services in support of the institution's consultancy or sponsored research activities; the library may also be asked to cost its support of a commercial or semi-commercial venture. If the institution begins to think commercially, its library will need to respond.

A positive approach to income-earning can help to reverse the traditionally poor image of libraries and librarians; additionally, at a time when academic institutions are subject to a number of different pressures, such an approach can earn the library useful internal status and respect. A further advantage is that those activities which involve services externally put the library in touch with the outside world, making it less isolated and providing new opportunities for making useful contacts.

What is the scope for revenue earning?

At first the range of possibilities may seem rather limited, but librarians have proved

223

themselves inventive and imaginative over the years and there are more opportunities than many observers might think. There has been recently in the UK a greater willingness on the part of academic librarians to talk about their income-earning activities and to a limited extent even to disclose accounts. However, it must be said that most academic librarians are fairly secretive about their revenue-earning activities, partly in an attempt to conceal from their institutions how much they make and partly, I suspect, from a feeling of sheepishness, that their efforts are not models of good practice. More recently, some librarians have been cagey about their financial successes as they wish to preserve their commercial secrets.

Table 1 lists potential and actual sources of income for academic libraries. Fines and other charges to library users can represent a substantial income, but, of course, the charges for lost books are often more than offset by the cost of replacing the original item. Income from fines may well reach a plateau at which attempts to raise extra money by increasing the level of charges fail as readers return items on time. Moreover, many institutions and libraries are wary of turning to students and staff as a source of income and wish to avoid the risk of alienating their readers.

Table 1 Actual and potential sources of income in academic libraries

1. *Charges to library users*
   Fines
   Lost books
   Lost tickets

2. *Sales to library users*
   Photocopies
   Microfilm copies
   Photocopies supplied for retention from external sources (in place of inter-
   library loans)
   Examination papers
   Binding
   Typing
   Withdrawn books
   Withdrawn library furniture and equipment

3. *Retail sales to library users*
   Bookselling
   Stationery
   Audiovisual materials
   Refreshments

4. *Publications*
   Bibliographies
   Newsletters
   Course publications
   Facsimile reproduction from the library's collections (e.g. rare books)
   Institutional press
   Joint publishing ventures

Table 1 (continued)

5. *Services to faculties and other internal users*
   Computerized information retrieval searches
   Photocopying service (staffed)
   [Cost centre approach]

6. *Services to external users*
   External borrowers' tickets
   External membership (includes interloans, etc)
   − group membership
   − contract libraries
   − document supply
   − information and enquiring services
   − desk research and reports
   − consultancy
   − research
   Management contracts for other library services
   Sale of space on automated systems
   Exhibitions
   Short courses
   Conferences

7. *Charitable and related investments*
   Donations
   Deposit collections
   Endowments and bequests
   Sponsorship
   'Friends of the Library'

Sales to library users offer considerable scope since visitors as well as registered members form the market. However, most librarians would probably admit to inadequate promotion of their sales and services and a reliance on photocopying for their income in this area. Investment in equipment which is reliable and of good quality will pay for itself in photocopying, microfilm reader printers and other areas. Equally, ease of access to self-service machines and appeal to impulse buying through good displays are important.

Publications can be sold to an even wider market as they can be promoted nationally or even internationally. However, the true profitability of much institutional publishing must be in doubt; librarians tend to hide these costs from themselves, as can be seen from the example in Table 2, which came from my own library.

Re-charging faculties for their use of staffed photocopying services and online services can act as a deterrent, which may be appropriate for photocopying but is less so for online. Additionally, it is doubtful whether the time cost of such services can be recovered from faculties; indeed the cost of invoicing and ensuring that payment is made is often a significant overhead in itself.

Table 2 *Education review: a case study* [1]

Financial analysis 1985

Expenditure	per copy	Annually
	£	£
Printing	32.00	800.00
Indexing forms	7.70	192.50
Postage	16.51	412.75
Sub-total	56.21	1405.25
Professional staff time		
8 hrs at £5.50 ph [2]	44.00	1100.00
Clerical staff time		
9 hrs at £2.70 ph [2]	24.30	607.50
Total	68.30	3112.75
Income		
Subscriptions		2303.99

1. a fortnightly index of articles covering further and higher education published by HERTIS at Hatfield Polytechnic.
2. calculation includes 16% overheads in respect of employers' costs.

A superficially profitable publication becomes a loss-maker when staff time is taken into account. Marketing drives were only partially successful and the publication ceased at the end of 1986.

Services to external users represent some of the most promising areas for revenue earning. Besides the fairly common approach of offering library services to firms, the librarian can attempt to operate off the campus by running other library services on a contract basis, as my organization does, and by undertaking research or consultancy contracts in information and records management.

We should not forget that libraries can act as charities and solicit gifts of money and books and seek sponsorship. Such activities can be more rewarding than commercial activities, which may consume much staff effort for relatively little gain.

What are the demands of revenue-earning services?

It may seem to be a relatively straightforward matter to introduce charges or fee-based services, especially for internal users. However, the following considerations will apply to many income-earning activities and should be borne in mind at all times, but particularly at the planning stage.

Quality and reliability

If users and other clients are to pay a realistic price for library products and services, the clear intention should be to aim at good quality and reliability. In the case of enquiry services, that will mean fast responses and a continually staffed telephone.

Photocopiers and other equipment should be proven and durable, and there should be good maintenance arrangements.

Calibre of staff
Equally, library staff seconded or appointed to these services must be motivated, able and hard working; these requirements may mean the librarian uses his or her best staff on a venture, clearly a decision that is not easily taken.

Impact on users
Librarians will need to be prepared for reaction from readers to new fee-based services, even if the effects are only indirect. For instance, a loans service to external borrowers may well bring concern about books important for research or course work being lent outside the institution. These and other concerns should be sympathetically listened to and any serious inconvenience to academic staff and students mitigated.

Impact on library staff
Here the librarian may have an even more difficult task, since it is important that all staff should support and appreciate the reasons for new initiatives. From time to time, for example, there are tensions between my own colleagues in the polytechnic library and those working in our Information for Industry Unit, usually over questions of money; in general, however, the two groups get on well. However, many staff will be unhappy with a 'commercial approach' in the academic library and the issue will need to be handled with care.

Finally, the scheme will almost certainly turn out to be more expensive to operate than you have imagined.

Costing and charging

Be realistic
A realistic approach to costing is essential for the reason just given. Hiding costs from yourself as well as others is a mistake which can prove expensive; you do not *have* to pass all the costs on to the customer, but you should be aware when you are subsidizing a service or a product. When costing a project, the following must be included:

- staff salaries (including overheads such as insurance and pension scheme contributions)
- consumables (e.g. online costs, photocopying expenses etc.)
- telephone, postage
- typing and other clerical expenses
- travel expenses
- training budget
- marketing (including publicity)

You should also consider:

- office rent, heating, lighting
- taxes (e.g. VAT, local taxes)
- charges for the use of institutional facilities (e.g. conference rooms).

- overheads levied by the institution (variously rated between 40% and 150% in UK universities and polytechnics)
- surplus or profit.

The example in Table 2 illustrates this approach.

Establish a pricing policy

There must be a thoughtful approach to pricing the service or product.

Firstly, does the identity of the customer make a difference; for instance, will students or teachers be able to claim a discount on a publication? It is, however, difficult to argue that some customers, companies for instance, should be charged more merely because they are likely to be able to afford it.

This brings me to my second aspect of policy; a careful analysis of various degrees or levels of service might be appropriate. This approach implies that customers of chargeable library services or products who require them to be in a particularly convenient form or delivered rather than collected at the library will be willing to pay more. Table 3 illustrates examples from the 'levels of service' approach, on which we at Hatfield have recently carried out a research project for the British Library;[3] the focus of the study was information services to business and industry and we found the concept of higher levels of service, of convenience and of 'packaging' was readily accepted by customers of various library services, as were the accompanying higher levels of charging.

Other factors may also help to determine a pricing policy; for instance, the British Copyright Act has required since 1956 that charges to all users for photocopies of copyright material legally made under the Act include a contribution to library overheads. If demand is high for a service or product, pricing may well be pushed higher, while what competitors charge is also influential; an example of that is that we charge for our mailing list services at Hatfield at the level of our most expensive competitors, but not above that level.

Methods of charging

Charging systems should be as convenient as possible to both the customer and the library. The handling of substantial numbers of small sums is expensive in staff time; invoicing in small amounts is particularly expensive in this area, but bank charges, debt recovery and record keeping also cost money. While our study showed that business customers of information services would, on the whole, prefer to pay as they use the services, most questioned recognized that their own businesses found paying small invoices inconvenient and costly.

Among the systems which I have found effective over the years are the following

- annual subscription
- deposit accounts
- vouchers bought in advance.

There is occasionally talk of the use of a 'credit card' for information, an idea on which no doubt we shall soon see developments.

In enquiry services, there is evidence of a move towards charging by time as many buyers and accountants do; my Information for Industry unit is developing this approach which, once the office recording system has been set up and staff adapt to it, has the advantage that enquiry services are easier to cost.

The librarian as entrepreneur and financial manager

Retention of revenue

The first problem that librarians contend with is concerned with retaining the revenue they have earned. Some hide the income away in cash boxes, if the money raised is fairly small (e.g. minor charges or fines). Institutional finance departments are becoming more effective in recording income and the auditors will also often enquire into procedures; sooner or later such hidden trickles of income will need to be declared, though some form of agreement may be negotiated whereby such moneys are credited to the book fund and spent by the library. If the library has an agreement, written or unwritten, which allows it to spend the income it earns, it would be foolish to disturb this arrangement. But if the library loses all or some of the income it earns to the central accounts of the institution, it is worth drawing the attention of the academic community to it. The present climate in my institution is that income is *either* shared between the department which earns it and the polytechnic central account *or* that it is credited against the cost of the department. This latter arrangement may not seem particularly satisfactory but in practice it can help shield the department from cuts in funding imposed by the institution; the department which cannot or will not contribute to its own keep may be seen as a burden on the rest of the institution and become a target for economies to be imposed.

The true secrets of retaining income are twofold. Firstly, the librarian should ensure that he or she is involved in the budgeting and estimating process and that potential income is underestimated; this is good practice, since overestimates lead to financial difficulties, but additionally the librarian should be able to arrange to spend the extra income earned over the targets. One way of achieving this is to monitor the flow of income closely and to allocate expenditure (e.g. books, equipment, overtime) to the project to use up the extra resources before they become too obvious.

The second is to set up what the British Library calls 'service envelopes', where income and expenditure associated with a particular activity are effectively kept as a special account; the librarian can negotiate to collect profits on these accounts at the most auspicious moment. The 'service envelope' concept means that the institution agrees that as the take-up of a particular service grows extra resources needed for the service can be spent from the income it has raised.

Flexibility

The entrepreneurial librarian will seek as much flexibility in funding and staffing arrangements as possible to make his or her income-earning ventures successful. Staff may need incentives of various types, whether extra payments (e.g. while seconded to a project) or even the prospect of useful experience in undertaking new work. The ability for the library to take on casual or contract staff without cumbersome negotiations with the institution is invaluable; one way of doing this is to place an order with a private information broker for a particular piece of work to be undertaken, thus not making any call on the institution's staffing budget.

229

Table 3   Levels of service in LIS (Derived from Margery Hyde.[3])

1	2	3	4	5	6
User borrows book in person			User rings up for book to be posted	User rings up for book to be sent by courier	
User reads journal article in library	User photo-copies article personally		User rings up for article to be copied and posted	User rings up for article to to be faxed	
User reads document	User photo-copies document personally	User asks library to copy document	User rings up for document to be copied and posted	User rings up for document to be copied and faxed	
User compiles list of references or products/companies in the library		User asks library to compile list and print it	User asks for list to be posted	User asks for list to be faxed	
User asks a quick reference enquiry		User asks a substantial enquiry		Short deadline on substantial enquiry	User contracts with library for a report to be written on the enquiry

Access to development funds and reserves is also vital. In my work with CIMTECH (the UK national Centre for Information Media and Technology), which is self-financing, I and the director, Bernard Williams, have found that the large reserve fund the Centre has built up over the years has been invaluable; in bad years the fund covers any loss, while it can also provide resources for marketing drives, new equipment or pump-priming for a new service. The institution will often recognize the need for such a fund in self-financing services and can be persuaded to respect it as inviolate.

Financial control and information systems

In most libraries, the financial control system will be operated by the institution, though libraries often have more local independence in ordering and paying invoices than other departments because of the scale of their financial operation. We have calculated at Hatfield that the library pays as many invoices as the rest of the polytechnic departments put together. Librarians should use the financial control system to monitor expenditure on income-earning ventures, which is as important as monitoring income. Equally, though, we have found that a growing effort has had to be put into issuing invoices and ensuring that they are paid. The time-consuming pursuit of small sums is particularly wasteful, because it is not cost-effective to take non-payers to court; consequently deposit accounts or quarterly invoices are preferable.

Company structure and joint enterprise
These two approaches are currently fashionable in UK librarianship and a few academic libraries, including Hatfield Polytechnic, have tried them both. Company structures are inappropriate unless there is a proven record of good profitability for an enterprise or the prospect of a private sector partner who will inject risk capital into the venture. A joint venture may be particularly attractive in an area such as specialist publications where the expertise and distribution system of a private sector partner are important.

Starting up
The foregoing may put off colleagues from income-earning ventures if the rules are taken too literally. If we are honest, librarians who have generated extra income successfully have often 'fudged' the accounts to start up a service or a product and 'hidden' the costs; once the activity became successful these subterfuges have been abandoned. However, I am quite sure that the most successful librarians have known by how much they were subsidizing such services in their early stages.

Conclusion
I started by stating why libraries try to earn extra income. I must finish by sounding a warning. While undoubtedly the entrepreneurial library stimulates and develops its staff and delivers extra services to its users there is a narrow line between the enterprising and the tawdry, the academic and the commercial. The dangers were well described recently in the press, in the context of the way Britain's leading museums, art galleries and indeed libraries are responding to the enterprise culture:

> 'The plethora of cafes, museum shops and general moneymaking razzmatazz invading what were once rather remote, inspiring places of discovery and learning, force one to examine what are indeed the priorities prevailing at the Victoria and Albert Museum and comparable institutions'.[4]

References
1 Department of Education and Science, *Higher education: meeting the challenge*, London, HM Stationery Office, 1987. (Cm.114).
2 Office of Arts and Libraries, *Financing our public library service: four subjects for debate*, London, HM Stationery Office, 1988. (Cm.234).
3 Hyde, M., *Library and information services to business and industry: study on levels of service, related costs and charging systems*, London, British Library, 1988 (British Library Research Paper 48).
4 MacCarthy, Fiona, 'Playing cheap shots in Sheffield', *The Guardian*, January 22, 1989, (part two), 9.

29

The IT-based manager

Mel Collier

Introduction

The aim of this paper is not to discuss the management of Information Technology – IT – but the impact of IT on the management of the library. Management should therefore be interpreted in both its senses: as a discipline, and as the group of people practising the discipline. When IT impacts on management it impacts on what we manage; whom we manage; how we manage; and on ourselves as managers in the skills that must be developed and the techniques that must be learned. At the same time it is often difficult to separate thinking about the impact of IT on management from management of IT, as they are clearly very closely interlinked. There is a large literature on the management of IT in libraries, a small sample of which is included in the recommended reading at the end of this paper, and the literature often touches on the implications of IT for management. However, there is relatively little written specifically for librarians on the impact of IT on management. One work well worth reading is *The information payoff* by Strassmann, which is all about information management in the electronic age; the word 'library' is never mentioned!

The market for IT in libraries

An understanding of the market for IT is essential for an understanding of its potential impact. Library automation is now a small but lively sector of the information systems business and as a vertical market has shown phenomenal growth over the last two decades. There is, however, a strong imbalance in the spread of IT into libraries, most noticeably a geographical imbalance and to a lesser extent an imbalance between types of library. These imbalances will tend to disappear as the market for low cost microcomputer-based systems expands rapidly into smaller libraries and information units and into new geographical areas. The study of the market for library IT is still in its infancy and little coordinated analysis has been carried out. Some initial work has been done by Blunden-Ellis, who analyses the market by maturity, potential size, variety and number of product and by customer sophistication. Mature markets are still few: USA, UK, Scandinavia, Germany, Holland, Belgium and Australasia, for instance, with France, Spain and South East Asia developing very rapidly. The maturity of the market impacts heavily on the management of the individual library. Increasing maturity brings a proliferation of products and professional imperatives which apply pressure to automate.

Types of product

In discussions about library automation there is an understandable tendency to concentrate on the specialized applications of library automation such as circulation, cataloguing, acquisitions, interlibrary loan, and periodicals control. These were the first types of application to be automated because they are the high volume transaction-based applications, but also and more interestingly they present much more structured problems; that is to say, they are more amenable to systems analysis and systematic solutions. Such specialized library systems also tend to be backed up by an extensive infrastructure of national networks, bibliographic utilities and commercial vendor support.

However, as a result primarily of low cost computing becoming available to libraries, there is a rapid development of automation of activities that have not been considered before because automation has not been hitherto cost-effective. These activities include office automation applications: word-processing, spreadsheets, database management; information retrieval packages, messaging, teaching and study packages and desk-top publishing. Significantly, these applications are also more unstructured than the transaction based applications. They bring automation out of the specialized areas and the domain of the systems specialist and will pervade the work of the entire organization. It is the pervasion of these applications that will change the fundamental nature of library and information work and, as Strassmann says, the principle challenge of IT is how to deal with unstructured work.

Impact on what we manage

Even a small library or information unit is a big information system: most academic libraries are extremely large information systems. Every librarian knows that libraries and information systems tend to slide into disorder without constant adjustment and maintenance to prevent that slide. The experience of the first 20 years of library automation has shown conclusively that IT is now the principal tool at our disposal for avoidance of the slide into disorder. At the same time, experienced managers of IT in information work will acknowledge that a poorly managed IT-based system will drift towards chaos even more quickly. The manager of an IT based library is responsible, in very broad terms, for the following:

- acquisition of information
- storage and delivery of non printed information
- storage and delivery of printed information by automated means
- telecommunications
- management information
- human resource management
- project management
- equipment and infrastructure.

All these activities are IT-based or backed up by IT. One of the most interesting and challenging aspects of managing in this environment is the demands placed on managers by rapid technological development. In a mature IT environment the manager will be handling a wide range of systems in various states of novelty or obsolescence. Obsolescence applies to both the product and the state of the art of the application. Obsolescent applications which might be still perfectly serviceable include batch circulation systems and COM or computer-produced card catalogues. Stable applications, those where the application is well understood and development has slowed down, are online circulation, serials control, cataloguing and most commercial information retrieval. Dynamic applications are those where products are being taken up by the market but where development continues apace and new features are constantly appearing; they include OPACs, acquisitions, accounting, management information, interlibrary loan, messaging, and office automation. Emerging applications are those which are still in the reserach and development stage; they include intelligent or expert systems, decision support systems, distributed databases, electronic information transfer and online book supply systems.

The IT-based manager must understand the volatile and sometimes subtle dynamics of research, development and the market-place at many levels. Obviously the dynamics will affect decision making at the initial procurement stage, but consideration of this question does not stop there. The dynamics affect recurrent decisions on maintenance, budgeting, upgrading, training and many other aspects of human resource management.

Impact on whom we manage

Impending change has great potential for the creation of uncertainty and stress among staff. Some stress is probably inevitable in a period of change but its degree will depend on the skill of the manager in introducing change and the existing attitudes of the staff involved. The challenge is heightened by the fact that change brought about by or through IT is often rapid, even sudden, and may introduce emotive issues such as de-skilling. In extreme cases the whole nature of the job could change. It is a debatable point whether the problems arise more from the introduction of IT or from the imposition of change itself; despite common stories of computer phobia I incline toward the latter view. Certainly new staff coming into an IT-based environment knowing what is expected of them seem to have relatively little difficulty in adjusting to the new environment. Existing staff who feel they are in control of new development or who are enthusiastic to try something new also appear to adjust relatively well.

In a mature IT-based environment the manager is much more noticeably concerned with skills management. Most of the conventional office and information skills are still required, but additionally a wide range of skills is acquired by staff. Staff therefore have a greater variety of skills than before, and these skills are high value skills. Staff will therefore be attracted more rapidly to promotion or improved positions elsewhere both within the profession and in other lines of employment where their skills are equally appreciated. The manager therefore is faced with a challenge of managing turnover, coping with recurrent skill shortage, and improving pay, conditions and job satisfaction in order to retain valued staff. At the same time staff will constantly find that they require to update or improve their skills which requires effective programmes of staff development, training or, possibly, redeployment.

Skills required in this environment include at the practical level office automation skills such as keyboarding, database management, messaging and spreadsheets. At the broader professional level the education and continuing education of qualified information personnel should include development of understanding of the information society, innovation in publishing, information management, systems analysis and management, information infrastructures and human factors.

Impact on how we manage

Introduction of IT into the library brings an increase in the range of skills of staff, activities, products and outputs which places considerable demand on the versatility of the manager. The atmosphere of change inherent in an IT-based environment imposes further pressure. The manager must be sensitive to the effects of these pressures on the staff, on the quality of the product and on the performance of the manager himself or herself. The manager should therefore be reactive and flexible in rapidly changing situations but cannot rely on reactive responses alone. If the whole process is to be under control and the staff and management are to be comfortable in such a dynamic environment the manager must be proactive and prepared for new development in advance of its occurrence.

A major effect of the proliferation of IT-based systems in libraries is the increased importance of management information systems (MIS). The relevance of MIS to libraries has been the subject of professional debate for many years, but professional practice has been slow to develop. The amount of transactional data available from automated systems now adds additional pressure to utilize and organize management information in decision making. Other imperatives are also coming from government, funding bodies and institutional managements for application of performance measures and much more detailed accountability. From the MIS discipline the concept of decision support systems (DSS) is now emerging; this will require the successful library manager to be personally adept at operating and specifying IT-based information systems.

Finally, the manager of an IT-based library is concerned for a substantial proportion of his or her time with management of new projects as opposed to routine or day-to-day line management. The routine management still has to be done, of course, but is likely to be delegated or carried out more efficiently in order to release time for new projects. Project management requires a different discipline on the part of the manager. The manager is working to tighter deadlines often imposed by factors outside the manager's control, and the project will often involve persons with whom the manager does not normally interact or over whom there is no direct control. The manager will be acquiring new skills in the process and developing new skills in others. Most importantly the manager is working, by definition, in a field or area of activity which is novel to the participants and where success depends on the skills applied to the project management process rather than on experience of the activity itself. The new pattern for library managers concerned with innovation is one where a significant proportion of time is spent on project management until the new project has become sufficiently stable to be delegated to others, for whom it will provide a new challenge and so on down the line. Meanwhile the manager has embarked on the next project! The bonus of this policy is a lively and proactive staff development environment in which benefits can flow to the whole organization.

The impact of IT on management is change

Change occurs in the library in a number of different ways: it is introduced by library managers of their own volition in order to fulfil their management objectives; it may be imposed by senior management as part of institutional programmes; it occurs in a natural and evolutionary way often as part of the process of development by junior staff; and it occurs as a result of professional or technological imperatives. What is clear is that the information society is creating a dynamic working environment in which change is always present: it is the norm rather than the exception. Library staffs must therefore be selected for their ability to survive and thrive in such a climate; their professional education must reflect the dynamic nature of the field, and the manager above all must be trained and must be personally suited to the management of change.

Further reading

Adams, R. J., *Information technology and libraries: a future for academic libraries*, London, Croom Helm, 1986.

Blunden-Ellis, J., 'Library automation systems: the UK economic marketplace', *Program*, **21**, (4), 1987, 317–32.

Clayton, M., *Managing library automation*, Aldershot, Gower, 1987.

Collier, M., *Telecommunications for information management and transfer*, Aldershot, Gower, 1988.

Leeves, J., *Library systems: a buyer's guide*, Aldershot, Gower, 1987.

Strassmann, P. A., *Information payoff: the transformation of work in the electronic age*, Glencoe, Ill., Free Press, 1985.

30

Marketing

Nigel Macartney

Introduction

What is marketing? This is the first question those of us from publicly-funded institutions will ask when confronted with this word from the seemingly alien world of commerce and industry. Hitherto we have usually looked after the interests of the library by developing expertise in dealing with bureaucracy and fighting our battles in a world populated by committees and academics. Now we are increasingly told that we must 'market' the library.

The *Oxford English dictionary* defines marketing as 'the action of selling; also of bringing or sending to market'.

However, it is usually agreed that the modern concept of marketing is more sophisticated than this definition would suggest. The Institute of Marketing defines the term as 'the management process responsible for identifying, anticipating and satisfying customer requirements profitably'.[1]

My view is that this definition is a little too glib, and certainly does not often reflect the view of the individual at whom marketing is directed. I prefer the more detached statement in a recent dictionary of economics: 'a term used to cover those activities of firms associated with the sales and distribution of products. Broadly speaking, it covers such activities as sales promotion, advertising and market research'.[2]

Marketing, thus, is not merely promotion and publicity or selling, but refers to the approach to the product or service from the design stage through to after-sales service. Marketing issues are often ill thought out or even ignored, but they are important in a highly competitive world.

But why should the academic library market itself? After all, the library has traditionally been seen as the heart of the university, the source of inspiration as well as the repository of human knowledge. Perceptions are changing; librarians can no longer rely on such clichés about their role, and most are recognizing that it will be dangerous fully to rely on past assumptions about the centrality of the library in the academic institution. Indeed it is necessary to get over the messages that the library *is* changing with the times and that it *is* cost-effective.

Moreover, the librarian and his or her staff may want to institute change themselves. New services may be on offer or new facilities may be required, while other services may need to be phased out. At Hatfield, I had to 'market' the idea that the new

237

Polytechnic Library building was not at the centre of the campus, but on the periphery, by giving presentations which emphasized the improvements that readers would find in the new building, e.g. a more comfortable environment, more space, better facilities; I even had to conduct trial journeys to show that the extra distance that academics would need to walk would take, at most, three more minutes!

Finally, the library will need to put over various 'messages' to its users from time to time; for instance, academic libraries frequently run campaigns to persuade their readers to avoid over-using the interlibrary loan service because of the cost. Careful marketing of the library's overall services can be effective in realizing this type of objective, as a recent item in SCONUL's *Hints and queries* shows.[3]

The marketing plan

Most of us go about marketing without any formal planning; indeed we may not even consider what we do as 'marketing'. However, in an increasing number of contexts, a plan of some description is useful or may be even required by senior management, especially if it is an external service that is under consideration. The library development plans produced by UK academic libraries often include sections on marketing.[4]

The planning process has been well described by Cairns.[5] It can be divided into seven stages:

1. Defining the service or product
2. Studying the users' needs and demands
3. Analysis of the present position
4. Establishing detailed objectives
5. Producing the market plan
6. Allocating resources
7. Review and evaluation.

Defining the service or product

There should be an ability to summarize both aims of the library and the services it offers to achieve the aims. Such statements should be kept brief; the aims of the Hatfield Polytechnic Library, for instance, are stated on a single page (Appendix A). Brevity encourages reading! A statement of aims is as important for library staff as for users or paymasters; if staff understand what their key aims are their morale and sense of purpose are better.

Studying the users' needs and demands

It is now generally recognized that librarians must put more effort into researching the needs of their users. This market research is clearly vital in any consideration of library plans and library management, but it is not quite as daunting a prospect as some might fear. After all, there is a wide range of sources of information on users' preferences; the librarian can turn to, for instance:

suggestion books
meetings with students
meetings with academics
feedback from user education sessions
feedback from enquiries
feedback from subject librarians.

Additionally statistical information from library computer (and manual) systems can provide useful data, for instance on the most heavily used stock. Of course, questionnaires and surveys are often carried out on specific topics, preferred opening hours for example. The process of evolving development plans should include participation by users; this participation adds to the legitimacy of such plans.

Analysis of the present position
It is important to have a good appreciation of the general standing of one's library's services, their usage, and the cost as well as users' level of satisfaction. It can be helpful to approach it by the SWOT (strengths, weaknesses, opportunities, threats) analysis. An example in Appendix B illustrates the idea, which is to highlight the critical issues. It is also useful to consider alternative strategies for achieving the library's aims here; for instance, costly services might be dropped in favour of cheaper alternatives, or of releasing staff to provide a new service.

Establishing detailed objectives
The next stage is to construct a strategy designed to meet the problems and opportunities that have been identified. Some problems may have fairly obvious solutions which can be tried out, while others need in-depth study.

All objectives will need to be discussed with the library staff to ensure that they understand the reasons for the objectives and support them. For instance, at Hatfield we were under pressure from some readers to open in the evenings during vacation in order to help students who were at work during the day. A trial period of evening opening was proposed to measure the demand, and staff were involved in discussing the proposal before they willingly committed themselves to working late in vacations.

Producing the marketing plan
It is important to commit to paper a formal programme or plan; whether or not it is published outside the library, it is vital that the librarian and his or her senior colleagues work methodically and to a schedule. If action points are not executed effectively and consistently much of the original effort in analysing and planning will have been wasted. I will discuss a detailed marketing plan for an external service later in this paper.

Allocating resources
Managers often do not allocate sufficient resources in both staff and money to carry out a marketing plan. It is interesting to observe the large sums being spent on marketing departments in universities and polytechnics as these institutions realize they have to compete to attract the declining population of school leavers. Libraries are not able to commit resources on such a scale but need to make sacrifices elsewhere so that a marketing drive can take place.

Review and evaluation
It is essential that the results of any marketing plan are reviewed and their effectiveness evaluated. It will prove difficult to assess the success of some targets; for instance, improving the image of the library with a particular client group cannot be accomplished overnight, and there are few criteria against which to judge improvement. Nonetheless, some form of assessment must be attempted.

I now wish to comment on three areas:

- marketing the academic library within the institution
- marketing the academic library to the external community
- marketing the academic library's commercial services.

Within the institution

The priority for an academic librarian must be to ensure the success of the library within the university or polytechnic. While I cannot speak for British university librarians, almost all of their polytechnic counterparts have produced 'development' or similar plans in recent years, and most produce annual reports; while many of these documents will have been commissioned by the institution, it is also likely that librarians were keen to review their services and plan for improvements in performance and relevance. I have observed a considerable reduction in the volume of promotional and publicity material for basic services in academic libraries in recent years; this is in part due to the high levels of demand that most librarians are facing, but also because it has been realized that promoting services for the sake of it is unnecessary and the marketing drive of the library should be in certain clearly defined priority areas and to particular client groups.

The librarian must also understand the concerns of his or her institution, and the direction of its own marketing plans. Such plans are increasingly formalized in the UK and available to senior staff in the institution; to ensure the support of the vice-chancellor or director the librarian needs to tailor his plans to match those of the overall organization. The needs and wants of readers are also central to the marketing of the library. Many academic librarians have discovered that most readers want a comfortable environment with good opening hours and refreshment facilities; while the availability of books is central, surveys at Hatfield have underlined that environmental considerations are at least as important. The installation of a coffee bar has been strongly welcomed and has gone some way to counteract the effect of moving the library off the centre of the campus, since readers find it less necessary to leave the building in search of refreshment.

Having set revised objectives, and determined how to implement them, the librarian should ensure that the marketing plan is carried out by allocating staff and other resources. Some of the marketing will be effected by the librarian in person; for instance he or she might arrange a series of meetings to explain to academic staff and others the library's new plans. Other staff will also need to be deployed on marketing activities; several institutions have research and development librarians (e.g. Newcastle Polytechnic) while others see their reader services librarian as the professional in charge of user studies and what commercial organizations call 'customer relations'.

Finally, it is important to review the success (or otherwise) of the library's marketing activities. The staff should ask themselves questions such as

- what have been the most successful and least successful ways of putting over the library's message?
- what changes in services have been successful and least successful?
- in what remaining areas is the library not meeting demand from staff and students?

To the external community

The academic library's relationships with the outside world are becoming almost as important as those with its internal readers. Visitors will frequently come to the library and many will wish to use it in a personal capacity. The librarian may find himself or herself invited to meet and talk to people of influence: politicians, senior civil servants, directors of large companies, representatives of grant-awarding bodies and even government ministers might be among the visitors to the institution or involved in meetings at which the librarian is present.

It is important that he or she has something constructive to say and a clear idea of the message which should be put over. The role of the library is service to the external community and its contribution to that community must be analysed and put on a firm basis.

Since British academic institutions obtain most of their funding from the government I have found it is useful to coordinate my thinking on how to present the library's problems and prospects with colleagues from other polytechnics and universities; in fact, COPOL has set up a working group to research evidence on the funding position of polytechnic libraries and to suggest ways in which we can best project its case nationally and locally. It has become as important to show that libraries are cost-effective and have much to give as to complain about lack of money. A positive and constructive approach is vital if the librarian is to win the goodwill of those he or she is addressing. In Britain in the 1980s it is vital not to be accused of 'whingeing'.

The message should be not only by word of mouth, but by imaginatively written and produced publicity materials. Dry figures can be enlivened by interpretation into common language; for instance, I am always asked by the editor of the polytechnic prospectus to say how many miles of shelving there are in the library as this seems an impressive figure, while the fact that there are half a million visits to the library annually recorded on the gate counter is also striking to the non-librarian. The institution's press officer may be able to place the occasional news item about the library in the local newspaper. A friendly, hospitable welcome to important visitors (accompanied by lunch in the refectory where appropriate) reflects well on the library. The many approaches from external readers who would like a borrower's ticket should equally be greeted with a pleasant and polite reception even if your current policies are not able to help them; you never know who is likely to apply!

The library's commercial services

An even more professional approach to marketing is required if the library is selling information services; if it is acting like a business it should operate like one. The main differences between marketing the academic library to its commercial users are that:

- financial profitability is the objective (or at least breaking even)
- clients are not usually on the campus, and are therefore more difficult to communicate with
- a substantially longer commitment in money and staff time is required.

Appendix C contains three documents relating to the HERTIS Information for Industry unit, which offers fee-based services from the Hatfield Polytechnic Library. The aims and objectives, which were agreed with the staff, laid down the way the unit would operate. The marketing plan is divided into a long-term strategy and a short-term strategy covering the period 1985–1988.

The financial and business plan, which is not reproduced here, also included the target of raising the number of firms taking out membership subscriptions from 270 to 420. It is interesting to look back and analyse how well the unit performed in terms of its marketing plan. While progress has been made in virtually all of the short- and long-term strategies, we lacked the staff and the money to carry out the plan in full.

More recently we have allocated substantially greater sums (a minimum of 7% of turnover) to marketing and publicity and are using freelance colleagues who know as well how to undertake marketing initiatives on specific services. Even now most of the marketing falls on the shoulders of the unit's manager and to some extent on myself as chief librarian; in many respects it seems to me that one of the main roles of the librarian is to market his or her service while the day to day management is delegated.

Libraries can no longer expect to be unquestioned, essential and 'a good thing' in the academic institution. It is our job as librarians to regularly review our services and project them as

- relevant
- good value
- high quality
- in the forefront of change
- adaptable.

We must know our customers, understand our paymasters and promote our skills. This flexibility and responsiveness does not mean that we abandon the basics of the academic library concept, rather that we keep it up-to-date.

References

1 Chartered Institute of Marketing – official definition.
2 *Macmillan dictionary of modern economics*, London, Macmillan, 1986.
3 Davies, A., 'Limiting inter-library loans', *SCONUL hints and queries*, no. 5, December 1988, 1–2.
4 Council of Polytechnic Librarians, *Working papers on development plans and position papers*, COPOL, 1985.
5 Cairns, J. D., 'Preparing a marketing plan', *in* Roberts, S. A. (ed.), *Marketing strategies for the academic library*, London, Library Association Colleges of Further and Higher Education Group, 1986.

Appendix A

Aims for Hatfield Polytechnic Library

1. **Fundamental principles**. There are three main principles
   1.1   The role of the library is to support and contribute to the aims of the Polytechnic
   1.2   The function of a library service is the storage, retrieval and dissemination of documented and recorded information and ideas
   1.3   The library is inter-dependent with other libraries and information units in the region and as such plays an important role in the community and in the profession

2. **Aims**
   2.1   To identify user needs, individual or group, expressed or unexpressed and respond to them. Changing circumstances in the Polytechnic require this identification to be a continuing process
   2.2   To provide information media and services to support the activities of the Polytechnic
   2.3   To make library services as simple to understand, easy to use and economical of users' time as possible
   2.4   To promote the use of library services and facilities
   2.5   To develop awareness and understanding of information sources and the library within the Polytechnic
   2.6   To provide comfortable and well equipped study and reference facilities
   2.7   To coordinate the work of the library with that of other Polytechnic staff, and to maintain formal links with all bodies in the Polytechnic at various levels, and especially other support services such as Media Services and the Computer Centre
   2.8   To plan for the use of the library's resources by the regional community and for drawing upon the information resources of other libraries in exchange
   2.9   To maintain access by the regional business and industrial communities to the library and to provide specialized services for them, at least recovering all costs, through the HERTIS Information for Industry
   2.10 To maintain an innovative approach to new information technologies and techniques and to contribute to their development in the information professions
   2.11 To manage the staff, financial resources and other assets of the library with efficiency and an entrepreneurial approach.

Appendix B

SWOT Analysis

Extract from the marketing plan of a commercial unit at Hatfield Polytechnic

4   REVIEW OF THE CURRENT POSITION

(a)   *Strengths*
(i)   An existing body of expertise in operating the various instruments and analysing the result.
(ii)   Geographically well placed for industrial contacts.
(iii)   Due to sandwich courses, contact with a wide range of industry.
(iv)   A pool of junior technician support from higher degree students.

(b)   *Weaknesses*
(i)   Split location.
(ii)   Uncertainty over the future funding and management of the Unit.
(iii)   No accepted renewal/replacement plan.
(iv)   No marketing plan and information leaflet.
(v)   No clerical backup.

(c)   *Opportunities*
(i)   The more commercial attitude being taken by the Polytechic.
(ii)   Increasing numbers of small firms are being created which should increase the market potential.
(iii)   Offer of help from Mr N Macartney, Library, for market research and contacts.
(iv)   A research grant in Materials is providing a part-time post for marketing who is including our facilities in his approaches to industry.
(v)   In the current re-allocation of space it is possible to rehouse the Unit on a single site.

(d)   *Threats*
(i)   Possible breakup of the Unit under inter-School and inter-Division rivalry.
(ii)   Increasing competition from external providers of similar services which could limit external earnings.
(iii)   Increasing pressure/work load on internal academics who may decide to devote less time to our activities.
(iv)   Impending breakdown and obsolescence of equipment.

Appendix C

Aims and objectives of HERTIS Information for Industry Services

1. To provide a range of services to meet the information needs of industry and commerce in Hertfordshire and also its surrounding region.
   1.1 To provide access to college libraries for reference use by industry and commerce.
   1.2 To provide postal document supply or lending services as well as technical information services to members in exchange for appropriate payments and subscriptions.
   1.3 To endeavour to create and maintain information files or publications where no adequate alternatives already exist.
   1.4 To keep abreast of new developments relevant to information services to industry and commerce.
   1.5 Any service will be introduced, maintained or phased out according to the level of demand and the ability of HERTIS to provide that service effectively and economically.
   1.6 To maintain adequate contact with both subscribers and the industrial and commercial communities of Hertfordshire in general; this will be achieved by personal contacts, meetings, and newsletters or circulars.

2. To ensure that all enquiries and requests are answered speedily and accurately.
   2.1 To staff enquiry points adequately so that enquiries or requests received in person, by telephone or by letter are answered promptly and the necessary action undertaken within the time agreed with the client.
   2.2 To ensure that care is taken that any information provided comes from a reputable source which is identified to the client; and that relevant qualifications to that information are also conveyed to the client.
   2.3 To take active steps to ensure that clients who are referred to another agency by HERTIS, are in touch with the other agency before HERTIS staff cease work on the enquiry.

3. To use local and regional resources and expertise whenever appropriate
   3.1 To exploit the resources of the Hatfield Polytechnic and the Colleges of Further Education in answering enquiries and providing services.
   3.2 To cooperate with other Hertfordshire County Council information-providing services, especially Hertfordshire Library Service in answering enquiries and providing services.
   3.3 To play a constructive role in cooperating with other Hertfordshire or regionally-based agencies which provide recognized information services to the industrial and commercial communities.

4. To ensure the service is run as effectively as possible
   4.1   To keep accurate and appropriate statistical records.
   4.2   To monitor trends in demand feedback so as to keep the service as responsive as possible.
   4.3   To assess costs and income accurately.
   4.4   To build up the financial independence of the service through subscriptions and sales (commensurate with monitoring the quality of the service identified in Objective 2 above.)

Annexe

Marketing Plan for HERTIS Information for Industry 1985–1988
The Business Plan for IFI sets out the aims for the period to 1988 largely in financial terms. The next step is to outline how these aims are to be met in terms of product planning and market development.

Discussions on future developments of the products, that is services and activities of the Unit, are under review with the BL/CPI reports on co-operatives providing a focus. It is hoped by the end of 1985 IFI will be able to make a clear statement of the product offered now together with plans for both short term and long term developments.

At the same time, a planned approach for identifying and reaching potential customers is necessary to ensure that services offered are relevant and visible to potential clients. In order to increase client numbers consistently it is also necessary to ensure that the service offered can meet and maintain the quality promised. Repeat orders and personal recommendation are the most effective form of marketing.

LONG TERM MARKETING STRATEGY

Objectives
1. To develop/maintain a high profile in the local business community.
2. To identify geographical and/or activity sectors, match services and marketing to these sectors.
3. To attract clients from out of county areas where similar services are not available.
4. To develop a reputation for information related project/consultancy work.

Methods
Objective No. 1
1.1 Continued development of relationships with local press, radio, HERTS288 Prestel channel, business organizations, academic institutions, etc.
1.2 Supply of effective publicity material.
1.3 Provision of speakers and displays for local and national events.
1.4 Continue to upgrade and exploit the Business Databank; possible development on a regional basis.
1.5 Joint marketing with 'Polyfield Services' (the Polytechnic's trading company).

1.6 Programme of courses and exhibitions for the business community, possibly in cooperation with Polytechnic departments, colleges and business organizations.

1.7 Contact with final year students or prior to industrial training.

Objective No. 2

2.1 Geographical areas identified by business parks/industrial estates or by concentrations of industrial population.

    2.1.2 Use local networks, organizations, exhibitions and the Business Databank to contact potential members. Involvement of local HERTIS colleges whenever possible.

    2.1.3 Possible involvement of HERTIS members in industrial locations to provide accommodation for promotional meetings.

2.2 Identify target activity/industrial sectors by comparison of the county's industrial base with

(a) existing HERTS members and (b) HERTIS resources.

    2.2.1 Match services to specific sectors, e.g. Patents service; British Standards service.

    2.2.2 Reach potential clients as 2.1 plus trade and research associations, and trade press.

Objective No. 3

3.1 Direct mail to specific areas , e.g. Science Parks.

3.2 Business and trade press, submission of articles.

3.3 Presence at National Exhibitions, possibly as part of a group made up of cooperatives, information services, etc.

Objective No. 4

4.1 Maintain a register of skills available from HERTIS staff or freelance brokers. Possibly develop a referral scheme for freelance workers wishing to sub-contract or pass on work.

4.2 Publicize capabilities in business and information press.

SHORT TERM MARKETING STRATEGY

Objectives

1. To maximize information available for use/non-use by HERTIS members, and potential member enquiries.

2. To improve communications between HERTIS members/potential members and IFI.

3. To strengthen links with local agencies.

4. To identify one target sector in order to increase membership and gain further experience from a controlled marketing effort.

Methods

Objective No. 1
1.1 Analysis of enquiries to determine:
    1.1.1 quality of service; success rate; supply time; help provided by subject librarians, etc.
    1.1.2 type of enquiry and relevance of service.
    1.1.3 type of member and relevance of service.
1.2 Monitor use by members. Contact those firms not using the service to obtain feedback, need for a visit or suitability of service.
1.3 Monitor potential member enquiries for source of interest, e.g. leaflet, poster, meeting, word of mouth, subject librarians, academic staff etc.

Objective No. 2
2.1 Increased frequency of HERTIS News sent to members, plus extra mailings when sponsored. Annual printed copy as advertising via Hertfordshire Businessman (8000 circulation). Use of HERTS288 Prestel channel for HERTIS News items.
2.2 Programme of visits.
    Priority of order 1. Agencies, organizations
                     2. Potential clients
                     3. Clients using service infrequently
                     4. Established clients
2.3 HERTIS 'event' to encourage members and non-members to visit IFI.
2.4 HERTIS/Polytechnic Industry Year Event.

Objective No. 3
3.1 Visits to identified agencies and possible inclusion in the programmes of a number of them during the following 12 months, and participation in Industry Year Events.

Objective No. 4
4.1 Possible target areas – Stevenage, Letchworth, Watford, Lea Valley. Cooperation and help to be sought from local colleges, HLS, business centres, advice agencies, etc. Links strengthened with local press. HERTIS events to be planned for local venue with 'Industry Year' logo. Use of shopping centres for publicity to be explored.

GENERAL
The above comments are couched in general terms and no effort has been made to identify 'gaps' in the market or to quantify demand. It is anticipated that the discussions on the development of services, the work involved in planning those services, and feedback from the market place will lead to the inclusion of specific marketing proposals, with supporting evidence, in future plans.

31

Public relations and publicity

Lynne Brindley

Introduction

'Why should as worthy an institution as the library have to resort to marketing and public relations? Is it not beneath the dignity of a profession to engage in these commercial tactics?' These quotations from Kies[1] indicate, as late as 1987, the ambivalence, to say the least, of the profession towards public relations and publicity, nowhere more so than in academic libraries. Why this should be so perhaps lies in the traditions particularly of university libraries in times of plenty, where they could operate with a fair degree of autonomy, focussing on collection building, in some cases as much for the future as for the present. All that has changed, in parallel with a more general public sector awareness of the importance of satisfying customer needs, as libraries find themselves in an environment of diminished institutional resources and in increased competition both for funding and as service supplier.

There seems to be more fundamental questioning of value for money given by the library, and a need for much more forthright defence of service provision and stimulus of it, through greater awareness of possibilities, greater attention to what users really want, and a thorough realization that the library only exists to serve its community of users, not for the professional edification of its staff. In this changed environment, the librarian needs to employ a full range of marketing and public relations skills to keep a central position in the teaching, learning, and research process. Failure to maintain good relations and communication with the constituency of users as part of the management process will ensure ignorance of service offerings and performance, and will most likely adversely affect the library's operating budget. There is no room for complacency.

Relationship of marketing and public relations

Marketing and public relations are commonly misunderstood and confused terms. Another paper deals with the wider concepts of marketing, including its various definitions. These need not, except briefly, detain us. Suffice, as a context, to say that marketing aims to attract optimal resources to the library, by providing a range and quality of services best adapted to the perceived needs of the community. This requires the identification and analysis of user needs, together with the organization, resource allocation and services to meet these needs. All this comes before promotional activities, whose purpose is to maximize relevant demand and support for the library's activities, through public relations, advertising, publicity, and so on. The most fundamental requirement in staff thinking is to consider customer needs and their satisfaction rather than think in terms of products and services and their promotion. In practice, of course, one enters a living situation in the context of which evolutionary change must be achieved. For the purposes of this lecture, it will be assumed that the other aspects of marketing are being taken care of, within an overall planning approach.

It is important to bear in mind that not only is the library becoming more marketing oriented, but so too are other parts of the institution, and quite likely there is also a corporate focus for relating to the outside world, through an information office, fund-raising efforts, business parks, schools liaison office, and so on. If there is corporate image or promotional effort associated with these activities, it is important to view the library service within this overall framework of policy and communications media, both as a vehicle for corporate development, and as a way of promoting the efforts of the library.

Promotion and public relations

What then are public relations and promotion? These can be considered as the focus for communicating to the user community, the funders and governance of the institution (including senior administrative as well as senior academic colleagues, and members of Council, especially lay members), and relevant external publics, a positive and convincing message that the library is fulfilling its purpose; together with a statement of what is needed to enable services to be delivered adequately. A related function is to obtain feedback from those concerned about their wishes and perceptions of the library service. Public relations is therefore not simply about promotion, publicity, and advertising, but the stress is on this two-way communication.

Such functions need to be directed by the senior management of the library, as one of its most important duties. If it is not led from the top, largely by example, then the library is in a disadvantaged position. Equally, it is my view that promotional activities need to be regarded as a basic and pervading responsibility of every member of staff, from the librarian to the porters and the shelvers. We are all in the public library service and the public gaze, whether on or off duty, and the wrong impressions given by the lowliest of our staff can be seriously detrimental to the library's image and its perception by users. This has been well recognized in a variety of well-publicized private sector turnarounds, such as Scandinavian Airlines, and in customer-focussed companies, such as Macdonalds. In libraries, I still have the impression that much training and staff development are required to ensure both attitudinal change and necessary skills of public relations and promotion, and I suspect this is hindered by professional pride and status. In large libraries there is obviously a case to be made for PR specialist(s), but even here I would conceive the role as coordinating and seeking opportunities, rather than replacing the need for awareness and relevant action by all members of staff.

Another fundamental tenet of public relations and publicity is to stay in reasonably close touch with the truth, for one's boasts will find one out, at least eventually. It is easy for senior staff in any service organization to be unaware of detailed failures and of under-performance at the delivery level, unlike the users, and it should be remembered that the same tools can be used in situations of failure or problems, as well as successes and new projects. There is no need to be continually washing one's dirty linen but sometimes a failure becomes so acute or so public that only a frank disclosure of what went wrong *and what is being done to put it right* will allay loss of confidence in the library as a whole. The phrase 'reasonably in touch with the truth' is used deliberately, for there is often an important element of confidence building within the staff themselves as well as customers through promotional efforts. There is a cumulating belief in what it is possible to achieve through good promotion, making success an increasingly self-fulfilling prophesy.

Promotion and public relations techniques

There are many communication and promotional techniques and local circumstances, budget and attitudes will largely determine the mix of activities used for such communication. Probably the most limiting factor is our own imagination and the inhibitions of our professional culture and training. The range of options is wide and includes printed communications, such as press releases, newsletters, annual reports; verbal and visual communications, such as media spots, speeches and presentations; written and oral communication, such as letters, memos and conversations. All available media need to be exploited to get the message over, not least the publicity of word of mouth recommendation by satisfied customers.

In a sense, every report and every document emanating from the library is an expression of public relations and publicity. Presentation is very important; a professional service needs professional service literature. Desktop publishing software and printing facilities are bringing such ambitions within the realm of possibility for more libraries and for everything that the library publishes.

In a deeper sense, every communication from the library, and even its inarticulate expressions through buildings and their organization, all are saying something about the library beyond the intended message, creating an image. The medium is part of the message. That is why the library staff need to get around, to see and be seen, and to report back on new trends or developments. The librarian needs to promote intelligence gathering beyond the operations of the library itself, and through the more effective informal routes, as well as the formal, committee-based activities.

Experienced library managers are well aware that institutional life is a game in which credibility is built up, or lost, and credits and debits are logged on an unwritten balance sheet. Professional integrity requires high standards of service from everyone of course, but sometimes more junior colleagues can be obstinate about a piece of service which seems to them marginal, or to favour senior university functionaries unduly. These are perhaps one of the few occasions on which it is justifiable to overrule in the long-term interests of the library.

In addition, particularly at senior level, the importance of a wider than merely professional involvement in the affairs of the institution cannot be underestimated. This is not, as is sometimes interpreted, an ego trip, deserting the library for greater things, but a necessary part of the role in playing the institutional game on behalf of the profession and the library. Visibility in academic affairs, special managerial projects, and other university activities cannot, assuming a good contribution, do anything but good to the library image. This requires an understanding by library staff of the strategic involvement and implications; otherwise there can be resentment at lower levels of the apparent lack of presence of particular senior staff in the library.

Associated mention should also be made of national and international professional activities, and their role in promotion of the library. Everyone has to make their own assessment of the right balance; some perhaps virtually retire from the local scene, with deleterious effect; others eschew outside activities altogether, closing themselves off from new currents of thought and opinion. Somewhere between lies the activity which keeps the library in the minds of those who distribute special resources, research contracts and so forth. It also creates an image of the library in the external world, which is useful for recruitment of new staff. It can all be very exhausting, but it is fundamentally PR activity.

Outside activity is for others beside the librarian. However, it is not to be a play pen. There must be a plan of sorts, a justification, behind a request to absent oneself for meetings in London, and so on. Nothing demotivates the Marthas who choose to stay home minding the shop than a weak librarian who allows the Marys to establish an external position of no apparent value to the library.

The importance of these elements of personal involvement with the institution and externally, while perhaps rather nebulous, cannot be overestimated. Personal relationships and confidence built in the library through them are arguably the most important element of PR that the library undertakes. With this tenet, the moving of as many staff as possible into customer-oriented, front-line roles in the library makes absolute sense. The creation of teams of subject librarians, the presence of all staff in some form of public service, with appropriate training in communication and customer handling skills, becomes of paramount strategic importance, and a performance indicator of potential success.

Let us now move on to consider the more concrete examples of public relations and publicity techniques. Kies[1] classifies these activities in the following terms of communication:

1. printed communication intended for large audiences,
2. spoken and/or visual delivery to large groups, and
3. written and oral communication, on a one to one or small group basis.

Printed mass communication includes press releases, newsletters, annual reports, brochures, posters, give-away gimmicks, and so on. The advantage of this kind of promotional material is that it can contain clear concise messages that are designed to be read and understood, and that can have been carefully prepared in advance. Their disadvantages are that once released, there is complete lack of control over their use, and they lack any personal touch. Also they are essentially one-way communications, lacking any specific feedback loop. Nevertheless they can be cheap and effective, and are probably the most used forms of promotion by academic libraries.

Library newsletters can be useful, especially where there is a large audience to reach. Ideally, they should be issued frequently in an attractive format. They can act as an inexpensive notification of policy changes, alerting readers to new services or items of purchase of special interest, and so on.

Library annual reports offer again the potential for excellent promotion of the library's activities, but frequently they fail to be attractive and appear in a stuffy, prescribed format, with lengthy lists of donors, boring reports of the trivial, and so on. This is the case often because they are primarily addressed as formal reports of accountability to the Library Commitee, and then, perhaps mistakenly, circulated for external publicity purposes. To confuse the needs of two target audiences is not sensible. A summary report for the wider audience may well be preferable, and libraries have much to learn here from examples produced by private sector companies and such bodies as the British Council and the British Library. With desktop publishing it is possible to produce professional effects without the expenditure associated with the glossy productions of larger bodies.

Library guides and handbooks are a popular form of library promotion, but from examples seen, they are as likely to bore, confuse and alienate users, as to inform. This often stems from the traditional view of 'educating the user', a librarian's perspective on what the user needs to know, producing masses of irrelevant material, badly presented. Booklists, bibliographies of suggested readings on subjects, are also favourites of librarians, but again they tend to be rather dull. We should not forget that there are an increasing number of alternatives to using print to get across our messages, ranging from video through to the promising developments in hypermedia.

Additionally, the library can and ought to take advantage of whatever institutional printed communication forms are available. Commonly there is a university newsletter and a student newspaper. Again, the tone of entries will need to be different than in purely library produced material, but this route has the advantage of integrating the library into the wider context, and reaching people who would not necessarily see or read the library's own material. The institution will also have developed relationships with the local press and advantage can be taken of that form of communication to gain greater community awareness of the library, probably in relation to the wider institutional picture.

A second form of communication is that of spoken and/or visual delivery to large groups. This can include television, radio, speeches and presentations. These media present formidable challenges of technique but can reach a mass audience. Libraries do not often have news which on its own merits such widespread attention, but special events, such as the opening of a new building, inauguration of a new service, a visit of an eminent person or international group, the opening of an exhibition, the start of a series of lectures, can justifiably attract media attention. Press releases, local radio and television can all be used to advantage, but care has to be taken not to be misunderstood, and preferably training should be undertaken in handling the media before any significant exposure to this form of communication.

On a smaller scale, presentations to various groups can be an effective part of a public relations strategy. This might include receptions in the library for various groups, such as Convocation, lay members of Council, local businessmen, Friends of the Library groups and so on. Again much detailed preparation is required and messages must be professionally presented and relevant to the group in question. Careful consideration needs to be given to venue and timing of such events.

The third area of communication, that of one to one and small group communication, has already been touched on, and forms, often unwittingly, the core of any library's promotional efforts. It has the distinct advantage of informality and fast feedback. It requires that all library staff are trained in notions of customer relations, how to handle people, and communication techniques. It requires guidance to staff on the interpretation of rules, so that they can say 'yes' as often as possible to users, rather than users being unnecessarily hampered by bureaucratic regulations. Training is needed in good telephone and correspondence manner, to create a friendly style and image, and in saying 'no' nicely.

A practical programme of public relations and publicity at Aston

Let us now move from the general to the particular, with some personal discussion and examples of some of the ways in which public relations and promotional activities are developing here at Aston, and particularly some of the lessons that might be learnt.

As relative newcomers to the University, the Director and Assistant Director have deliberately taken a high profile in University-wide activities, for example through committees, IT projects and staff development activities. It has been important for the LIS senior management to be participating actively in non-library matters.

We have chosen to exploit, consistently and frequently the University's own internal newsletter *Aston fortnight*, to promote LIS activities, in addition to producing *LIS newsletters*, often devoted to specific themes such as services over JANET. We have launched a well-produced and we hope readable and interesting variation on the usual library annual reports, called *The year in focus*, highlighting a few key issues.

Special presentations and events feature fairly regularly, such as open evenings or open days for special groups of users and potential users, showing them new service developments and learning about their particular concerns.

The library building itself is being subjected to major internal redesign and redevelopment to project an appropriately welcoming and accessible image, rather than the current rather forbidding atmosphere – for example, offices are being opened up with windows (a symbol of open management); there is a view from public service areas into the 'backrooms' (a symbol of taking down the barriers for customers; and a new, more open circulation desk is being created.

These initiatives have been supported enthusiastically by staff and assisted by training and development initiative such as Customer Care programmes and desk-top publishing activities.

Conclusions

The starting point for any library is an assessment of the current state of the library's public relations, including the image projected and user perception. Objectives can then be set within the aims of the library, and priority given to projecting the desired image, and promoting appropriately the collection and services. Feedback and evaluation methods are an essential part of any plan. Related activities, while needing to be led by senior management, must engage the enthusiasm and skills of all staff to be effective. This will almost certainly involve considerable training efforts. Promotional activities do not necessarily involve large budget commitments, but they need to be well considered, professionally presented and appropriate to the need. All of this should be undertaken in the context of a wider marketing plan.

Reference

1 Kies, Cosette, *Marketing and public relations for libraries*, Metuchen, N.J., Scarecrow Press, 1987.

Further reading

Harrison, K. C., *Public relations for librarians*, London, Gower, 1982.

Kotler, P., *Marketing for non-profit organizations*, Englewood Cliffs, N.J., Prentice-Hall, 1985.

Cronin, Blaise (ed.), *The marketing of library and information services*, London, Aslib, 1981.

32

Academic libraries: a new generation?

Maurice B. Line

From all the detailed presentations of particular aspects of academic library management in the foregoing papers, persistent themes emerge. This paper attempts to put these together and to present an outline formulation of a kind of academic library that is somewhat different from the past. I will call it the New Academic Library. This does not mean that some libraries have not practised some of the principles advocated, or that there is any sort of sudden change; rather, there is a gradual evolution towards a new style.

Purpose

The New Academic Library (NAL) has clear and precise objectives. These will differ according to the type of library, and the type of library will differ according to the function of the institution to which it belongs and the nature of the clientele it serves. The need for a clear statement of objectives, which are agreed by the staff (and agreeable to the institution), is apparent: without such a statement the library may have little sense of direction, or, equally bad, different members of staff may pull unconsciously in different directions because they have different ideas as to what the library should be doing.

People

The NAL is above all concerned with people: the people it serves, and the people who serve them. It is a *customer-based* library. This is an easy statement to make, but its implications, if followed through, are fundamental. No library I have ever seen is designed totally around customers, but that should be the aim. In order to serve customers, they must be understood; not only must their demands be met, so long as they are within the terms of reference of the library, but their *needs* must be met as far as possible. A library can readily satisfy demands by keeping them to a minimum, and it can easily keep them to a minimum by giving a limited range of services in a limited way.

The customer-based library not only serves customers but seeks customers. Even in a limited environment such as a small college library, there are almost certain to be a proportion of potential customers who remain potential. It may be that these have no needs that can possibly be satisfied by the library; but the number of people that this applies to is almost certainly very small. It may of course be that they are unaware of what the library might do; this is a matter of presentation, which is dealt with later.

Needs are not always expressed; the better the library, the more they are likely to be articulated, but it is easy to appear to give a satisfactory service because no-one complains. Admittedly, most libraries have some users who are very articulate indeed, but these are rarely typical, and they should not be the only ones who are listened to. It is the library's job to explore needs and then see how far they can be met by the library − as it is and as it might be, for the purpose of the NAL is *to serve the information needs of the academic community*. Exploration of needs can be a difficult exercise, though the needs of academic communities in general are now fairly well understood, and much can be learned from experience in other libraries where new services have been tried. What is needed in every library is constant sensitivity to customers − which means that library staff need to be in regular contact, if possible social as well as professional, with them.

Once customers and potential customers and their needs are understood, the library should consider what services might be offered. These should not be restricted to the purchase and supply of books, but extend to the provision of information. The question that should be asked is 'What information could assist and further the learning, teaching and research of customers, and how can the library help to provide this information?' Some of the services may be akin to those offered by industrial libraries, for example selective dissemination of information in response to interest profiles. The services might possibly go further than this and extend to the packaging of information: not merely the supply of references and documents, but distillations of the actual information that is wanted. How far the library can go in providing these services is a difficult question, but by careful use of staff resources and the use of staff at lower levels for routine and even some skilled operations it may well be possible to do far more than most libraries believe.

Services in most libraries depend to a great extent on the collections. Another question to be asked is how collections can be oriented to customers. It is easy for a library to have a stock and acquisitions that exist almost for themselves, paying relatively little attention to changing needs, so that material is retained that is no longer of interest while new fields are insufficiently covered. To orient collections to users once again requires knowledge of the customers and their needs; as far as possible, their needs should be anticipated before they are expressed as demands. Indeed, in many cases demands will not occur unless the needs are already capable of satisfaction; many customers use, and find useful, material that they would not have requested for purchase because they were unaware of its existence, or if aware of its existence unaware of its value.

Orientation of collections to users may require much more attention to students than is sometimes the case. Many university libraries give higher priority to research needs, though most of these can be satisfied by interlibrary loan, while many student needs which cannot remain unsatisfied. One reason for this is that research collections have a greater permanence than student materials − it is costly, and may seem wasteful, to acquire and process items that have only a short life; but I believe it is always a mistake to try to serve the unknown needs of the future while neglecting the known needs of the present.

This is not to say that future users should be neglected. However, I know of no evidence to suggest that material acquired for today's known users is likely to be any less useful for tomorrow's users than material acquired with the latter specially in mind; and while some academic libraries undoubtedly have a major responsibility to future generations (and should be clearly recognized as having it and funded to fulfil it), these are a small minority.

The building itself should be designed around customers. Persuading architects that libraries are for people and not for illustration in architectural journals may be no easy matter; but even in a building which is less than satisfactory a lot can often be done to arrange and guide the library so as to attract and serve people. It is not always easy to say precisely what constitutes a welcoming library and what constitutes an unfriendly library — but they are usually easy enough to recognize when one sees them.

The arrangement of the stock too should be customer-based. This may be a matter of open and closed access — not so much whether it should be one or the other, but what proportion of material, and what type, should be on open access, and how it should be arranged. A very detailed classification like UDC carried to its extremes can result in numbers that are unintelligible to the user and impossible to carry in the head from the catalogue to the shelves. In some cases it may be desirable to adjust a standard classification for the benefit of the local users, for example, to bring material on archaeology together which would otherwise be scattered.

The design and content of the catalogue should also be customer-oriented. Whatever generations of bibliographers may say, what users want is not detailed bibliographic description but better subject access. They also want catalogues they can scan and browse in — which rules out the card catalogue for a start. OPACs, if well designed, can greatly aid and encourage access to the user — as of course can printouts.

Library staff are nearly always courteous and friendly. However, their skills can be enhanced. For example, handling conversations over the telephone is a skill that can be developed; as can dealing with difficult customers over the counter. Everyone will have noticed how some shops have a far more friendly and helpful staff than others; and in the best it will usually be found that the staff have been specially trained and encouraged to help users. It is easy to forget what intimidating places libraries can be, and how easily potential users can be discouraged from pursuing enquiries.

The other half of 'people orientation' is concern for staff. Very few staff in libraries have had any training in managing or developing staff. Generally, they tell their staff very politely what to do, but this is not enough to motivate them. There is an enormous amount to be done in delegating work, giving staff responsibility, listening to them, understanding them, trying to help them compensate for their weaknesses and building on their strengths, consulting with them and working with them as a team, and so on. Bosses have to *care* for staff, and that means spending time with them. Showing a personal interest in staff is a powerful motivator. We all know this from our own experience when people show an interest in us, but we often neglect it in dealing with others at work, when there are always other things to be done. The increases in productivity that can be achieved by good staff management can be surprising, though perhaps they should not be: after all, a good proportion of most people's waking lives is spent at work, and they would much rather spend this time happily and fruitfully than otherwise. In any case, even if there were no increase in productivity the satisfaction of staff ought to be an aim of all senior management.

Vision

The 'new library' requires a compelling vision. Objectives can be clear and precise, and at the same time totally unimaginative and unadventurous. It does not require a very far-sighted look into the future to see that there will be increasing pressures, constraints, needs and possibilities. To approach such a future merely by continuing to do what has always been done, but perhaps a little better, will not work; resources will not permit it, new opportunities opened up by technology will be unused, and new demands will be unmet. Adventure for its own sake would be silly, but excessive caution and conservatism constitute a recipe for disaster. If the future is going to be such-and-such, what sort of library is needed to provide for it, and how can such a library be created, or re-created from the present library? Staff need to step aside from their customary framework of thinking and dare to conceive original solutions. 'Brainstorming' sessions, where the unthinkable can be thought and uttered, can be very productive. That many of the ideas will be impracticable does not matter; it is easy to weed out poor solutions from a range of options, much harder to create good solutions from a basis of conventional practice.

What should emerge from such a process, which should not be restricted to senior management, is a clear vision for the future, which needs to be followed by a plan for attaining it. This plan is often called a Strategic Plan, already mentioned in chapter 1 (p.5–6) (an example of a rough outline is given in the Appendix). This spells out where the library wants to be, and how it is going to get there. It may cover from three to five years; the latter is more common in the public sector. It will be a rolling plan, reviewed annually and totally revised perhaps every third year.

A Strategic Plan will constitute a valuable document for the staff, and for the institution; if there is an institutional plan the library's plan will obviously have to fit into it. Such plans may soon be demanded of academic libraries, and it is well to prepare them in advance of being obliged to, if only because they take time and hard work to construct. Typically 12 months is needed, depending on the amount of staff effort devoted to it; six months is the minimum if there is to be adequate discussion and consultation, and two years is not out of the question.

Efficiency

A Strategic Plan will be a fairly general document; to make sure that aims and intentions are translated into reality, more detailed annual Operational Plans are needed. These set out precisely what targets are set for the year immediately ahead, for the library as a whole, for departments or sections, and for individual staff at managerial level (and perhaps below). Wherever possible, performance measures will be agreed and used, and costs will be included. Since everything the library wants to do cannot be done, priorities have to be established. Staff are encouraged to set their own targets – perhaps surprisingly, they rarely under-set them – and these can then be used for an annual staff appraisal system (a much better basis of appraisal than the usual 'and how do you think you did last year?' sort of interview).

Operational Plans not only go into detail as to what is to be done, but they include target dates within the year for action. They are then reviewed by senior management every two months or so to assess whether progress is up to date, the reasons for delays (or early delivery), and what should be done about slippages. The process sounds very mechanistic, but so long as staff are fully involved they actually find it is helpful to them and a valuable discipline, far better than vague expectations with no time-

258

scale. The construction of the first Operational Plan is hard work, but after that it gets much easier.

Where a particular activity is new, and especially if charges are made and there is some attempt at cost recovery, a Business Plan is desirable. This too is likely to be an unfamiliar concept, and it may meet some resistance from staff. It must always be borne in mind that the aim is not commercialization of the library but a better service to customers and a more credible operation to present to the parent institution.

To produce the various indicators of performance, and costs, a Management Information System is needed. It is easy to produce a lot of figures that look superficially impressive (annual library reports contain some fine examples), but in fact do little to indicate how well the library is doing in comparison either with previous years or with other libraries. It is almost impossible to produce the level of detail that would be necessary to provide all the costs and measures one would like and to serve all possible uses, which in any case can never be precisely anticipated; often approximations have to be used. The work involved in preparing a good MIS should not be underestimated; it may take a few years to get right (and even then it will be modified from time to time as circumstances change).

Technology

Technology should of course be a servant and never a master. It should never be used for its own sake, and sometimes manual systems can be so greatly simplified that technology is not needed, but it enables possibilities to be envisaged that could not otherwise have been, and in so doing it can liberate the imagination. It can help the library to serve people better and more efficiently — with new services, faster services, better services, more tailored services.

Many computer systems, like computer manuals, have apparently been designed for efficiency in operation — by the people who designed them. Mercifully, systems that can be used by ordinary human beings are becoming much more common. Computer people need to re-learn what it is like to be an ordinary human being; and librarians need to be aware of what technology can do and also know a little of how it does it. We have heard a great deal of CD-ROMs in the last three or four years, but there are many other technologies that are potentially capable of application in libraries, and librarians should be aware of these. The same applies to new developments that are not technological, such as expert systems, which have tremendous potential.

Public front

A good service should be self-evident; but the days are long past when a librarian could take it for granted that his institution would appreciate the library and fund it as it deserved (in the past some libraries have probably been funded better than they deserved). A librarian needs political skills to present and push the library's case against the many other pressing cases competing for attention and money. This means that the librarian has to be credible and respected — and where need be forceful. He needs also to make clear his overriding commitment to the institution and to demonstrate that the reason he wants funds for the library is to enable it to support institutional aims. At times he may have to voluntarily sacrifice something he wants for the library because he recognizes that another case has priority.

He has also to 'sell' the library in more direct ways, by marketing and publicity

– to existing customers, to potential customers in the academic community, and to potential external customers, especially if they are expected to pay. Some more general publicity, aimed at the general public, is desirable, for it is through repeated exposure and messages that images are formed. Publicity raises expectations – which will help to keep the staff on their toes. It is at the same time vital that publicity reflects the reality.

Implementing change

How can the change from an inward-looking to an outward-looking library be achieved? It can only be done through staff; however clever and powerful the boss is, there is little he can do on his own. However, it is he who has to give the lead. If he has no vision, he cannot expect any vision of his staff; and his vision should be broader and look further ahead. It must be exposed to staff, criticized, developed, improved, enlarged and eventually agreed; the time spent will not be wasted.

The boss needs also to lead by enthusiasm. He should have a sense of excitement, which will communicate itself to staff as surely as a sense of defeatism or lethargy. He should lead also by example, showing (e.g.) his willingness to work long hours when necessary, to spend time on things he does not enjoy doing because they benefit the library, and so on. Only if he sets himself high standards can he expect them of others; experience shows that staff will accept very high standards if they are at the same time given massive support by the boss. If he is to support them he must know them; he should have some personal contact with them at all levels, and if there are no more than 100 he should know them all by name.

If a library is to be customer-oriented, staff – if possible all staff – must be exposed to customers, to their expressions of satisfaction, their complaints, their suggestions and their ideas. This may not be easy to achieve, since many library staff may work in back rooms; but if this is so it demands attention in itself.

The boss should be a *team leader*, and team leadership should be the management style throughout the library. The boss will have his senior management team, each senior manager will have his, and so on. Participative management has sometimes been portrayed as democracy gone mad, an opting out of responsibility by the boss, and it has been suggested that it is appropriate (if at all) only for easy times. On the contrary, the full commitment of staff is more necessary when times are hard, tough decisions have to be made, and more is likely to be demanded of staff; and it is by no means a soft option to listen to and encourage ideas and comments from one's staff and achieve a corporate sense of responsibility. Once a general understanding and habit of working and thinking together have been developed, most decisions can in fact be made very quickly.

Strategic planning has already been discussed. The Strategic Plan should be the main map of how to get from A to B. Its preparation can also be a very useful means of staff development, particularly team building at the upper level and consultation with middle and other managers.

As pointed out earlier, the boss has to care for his staff. But personal concern is not enough, and practical measures need to be taken to develop the kind of staff required if a first class service is to be given. A 'skills audit' can be conducted to identify the skills that are wanted in, say, five years' time. It has then to be decided how they are to be acquired – by developing existing staff, by bringing in new skills as vacancies occur, by using short term consultancies, or whatever.

Developing existing staff is not easy — turning academics and professionals, not into non-academics and non-professionals, but into managers who use academic ability and professional knowledge to serve people. 'Management' should be seen not as antipathetic to scholarship and professional knowledge, but as *using* them on behalf of the service. 'Sub-academic' professional staff deserve equal attention, for they constitute 'shop-floor' management. Means of developing staff include crash courses in skills such as performance measurement, statistics, and costing, all skills on which the preparation of Strategic and Operational Plans focuses attention. Staff may also need to be shown what business plans look like and how to prepare them. Most of these formidable-sounding commercial practices are not in fact very fearsome when they are understood, but 'fear-reduction' courses may be necessary.

The main means of developing staff however is by giving them responsibility and letting them 'own' their jobs. Job ownership is a very important concept; all it means is that staff, however junior, should have, and feel, personal responsibility for their work. This implies a great deal more delegation than is customary; my own experience is that much work done at 'academic' level can equally well be done at lower levels, and much 'professional' work can be done by 'sub-professional' staff. Staff at all levels consistently underestimate those below them. Care has to be taken not to delegate too much too quickly to staff who are not accustomed to responsibility; here again, personal knowledge of staff is essential.

A good communication system is vital. How often do staff complain that they do not know something that is important to their work, or show that they have little idea of what is happening on the broader front? Formal mechanisms like newsletters are valuable, but there is no substitute for informal communication, which is an integral part of a good manager's equipment.

The secret of managing change, if there is one, is to involve staff fully and to get them to do things for themselves — and take the credit for doing them. In brief, staff respond to care and attention, example, enthusiasm, responsibility and exposure to customers.

Envoi

The New Academic Library, then, is customer-based, concerned with and for its staff, efficient in its use of resources, imaginative in its use of technology, well-managed, and visibly and demonstrably a first class service. It cannot stand still; it is constantly awake to new circumstances, needs and opportunities, and it must be designed for continual flexibility.

Change is after all more fun than a static situation. Few people seem to get much fun out of their work; whereas work should be, if not constant fun (that it cannot be), a regular source of pleasure and satisfaction. The task of serving people well in concert with colleagues should certainly be satisfying and often pleasurable.

APPENDIX
Strategic plan − possible outline
(There are of course other possible structures)

AIMS AND OBJECTIVES
General statement
Relationship to parent institution
Constraints, opportunities and challenges

COLLECTIONS
Objectives − collection policy
Books
Journals
Other materials
Performance measures (e.g. use of parts of collection related to cost of acquisition)

PRESERVATION, RETENTION AND DISPOSAL
Objectives − policy
Preservation (including binding)
Retention and disposal
Performance measures (e.g. length of life per binding, cost per volume retained vs. cost of disposal)

PROCESSING
Acquisition procedures
Cataloguing (including subject access)
Performance measures (e.g. processing time from receipt to shelving)

SERVICES
Objectives − service policy
Various kinds of service:
    Lending
    Reference
    Information
    Other
Services to internal services
External services
Charging policy
Performance measures (e.g. loans per student, loans per member of staff, loans per volume of collection)

AUTOMATION AND ELECTRONIC TECHNOLOGY
Strategy
Equipment requirements
Performance measures (cost-effectiveness)

ACCOMMODATION AND EQUIPMENT
Requirements

PUBLIC RELATIONS AND MARKETING
Objectives − policy
Performance measures (e.g. volume of demand stimulated by marketing)

OTHER
Publications (if any)
etc.

STAFF
Staffing policy
Staffing requirements (to achieve objectives above)
Staff requirements audit (analysis of types and levels of staff required)
Staff recruitment
Staff development and training
Performance measures (e.g. productivity)

FINANCE
Estimated costs
Income generation (including income from other areas than services, e.g. facsimiles, publications)

APPENDIX 1: PERFORMANCE MEASURES (Summary)

APPENDIX 2: ANNUAL TARGETS
Year 5: e.g. to eliminate cataloguing backlog; to change books: journals, expenditure ratio from 40:60 to 50:50; to develop SDI services in all subjects; to achieve 15% cost recovery; to achieve 10 days processing time from receipt to shelving
Year 4: (each year becomes more specific in terms of targets)
Year 3:
Year 2:
Year 1: as precise as possible (e.g. to reduce cataloguing backlog by 25%; to change books: journals, expenditure ratio to 42:58; to develop SDI services in physics; to achieve 5% cost recovery; to reduce processing time from 30 days to 24; to reduce staff by 2; to acquire 3 more computer terminals; to instal CD-ROM player; to establish staff development programme; etc etc)

A SWOT analysis (Strengths, Weaknesses, Opportunities, Threats) can be integrated into this − e.g. Opportunities and Threats can be identified in the first section, and the elimination of Weaknesses should be incorporated in Targets.

Index

access to records 108–12
access to stock 125–6
accommodation 1–2
acquisitions 1
  books 64–77
  budget 3, 17
  costs 68–70
  grey literature 84–9
  interlibrary access impact 141–2
  journals 78–82
  national schemes 142–3
  policy 9, 65–6
  selectivity and specialization 21–3,
    150–2
  systems 68–70, 74–7
Aston University Library 24–5, 137, 254
audiovisual collections 2, 29
automation 1, 25, 29, 30, 40, 233, 259
  cooperation in 147–8
  impact on staff structures 169
  interlibrary access 140–1, 143–4

binding 93
Birmingham Polytechnic Library 135
Birmingham University Library 14–17
book
  acquisitions 64–77
  physical damage and perishability 40,
    92–3
  retention time by readers 123, 130
  selection 66–7
borrowers 124, 125
budget 3, 8
buildings 30, 257
business information 136–7

cataloguing 101–8, 152
CD-ROM 29, 143–4, 148
change, implementation of 260–1
chemical hazards to books 93–5
collections 188
  acquisition 151–2
  building and demolition 32, 51–61,
    152–3
  cooperation in 147–54
  orientation to users 256
  preservation policy 153
  profile sheet 72–3
  selection 150–1
commercial services 241–2
communication techniques 251–3
computing services 2
conservation 40, 90–9
Consortium of University Research
  Libraries (CURL) 148, 152
Conspectus 153–4
cooperation
  approach 158
  coalition 156–7
  in collections 147
  exchange 155–6
  marketing 157
cooperative schemes 4
cost benefit 191, 200
cost centres 32
cost-effectiveness 199, 200
costing 227–8
costs 39, 40, 56–7, 68–70
Council of Polytechnic Librarians
  (COPOL) 30–1
Coventry Polytechnic financial

management system 220−2
customer-based library 255−261

data
  collection 201−2
  presentation 111−12
  validity in performance measurement
    200−1
databases for reference and information
    services 116
disaster planning 99
discarding of stock 57−61
document exposure 130

educational role 47−9
entrepreneur, librarian as 228−9
equipment, investment in 225
external users 133−8

financial
  control systems 230
  management 211−13, 215−22, 228−30
formula funding 8
functional structure 167−8
funding 1, 7−8

Hatfield Polytechnic Library 28, 35
  library marketing 237−8, 243−8
  revenue earning 230−1
HERTIS Information for Industry Services
    245−8
Huddersfield Polytechnic Library 34

income
  generation 32
  sources 224−5
  see also revenue
information 256
  exchange 156
  services 114−21, 136−7
  systems 230
  technology 5, 25, 27, 232−6
interlibrary access 3, 139−46
  automation 140−1
  charges 145
  international 145−6
  schemes 139−40
interlibrary loans 21, 56−7, 117, 152

Joint Academic Network (JANET) 148,
    149, 152
journals 3, 39, 78−82

lending services 122−32
library committee 9, 10−11, 34
library goodness 185−94
  librarians' perceptions 186
  performance measurement 204
  users' perceptions 187−8
life cycle costing 47

management 11
  impact of IT 232−6
  resource constraints 164
  skills 6, 182−3
  styles and systems 160−5
  training 180−4
management information 206−14
  automated systems 210−11
  financial 211−13
  IT-based systems 235
  needs 208−10
  system elements 213−14
marketing 157, 237−48, 249−50,
    260
  Hatfield Polytechnic Library 237−8,
    243−8
  plan 238−42

new university library 18−23
non-book materials 29
non-conventional literature 84

online databases 29
operational planning 258−9
organization theory 170

performance
  indicators 203
  measurement 5, 32, 127−31, 189,
    196−204
photocopying 20, 21, 225
planning 5−6
policy objectives 130
political nature of chief librarian's post
    9−10, 12−13, 259
polytechnic
  library 28−33, 35, 135
  teaching methods 115
preservation 4, 90−9, 153
pricing policy 227−8
public relations
  and marketing 249−50
  promotion and 250−4
publicity 249−54, 260

publishing output 38−41

quality of library 185−8

records, acquisition and creation of
  106−8
reference
  librarians 118
  services 114−21
reports, acquisition of 85−7
research 15, 16−17, 20−1
  collections 21
  cooperative 157
  reports 84
resources 2−3, 3−4
  management constraints 164−5
  people as primary 166
retention policy 141−2
revenue
  earning 223−31
  retention 228

scholarship 16−17
SCONUL (Standing Conference of
  National and University Libraries)
  201−2
Scottish Academic Libraries Bibliographic
  Information Network (SALBIN)
  148−9, 156
security 56
services 1
  internal and external users 4
  polytechnic libraries 32
  to students 14, 15
shelf time period 59−60
SIGLE (System for Information on Grey
  Literature in Europe) 84, 88−9
skills
  audit 5
  management 234
Southampton University Library 71
staff 1, 4−5, 9, 117−20, 234, 257
  appraisal 173−4, 175−9
  automation impact 169
  Birmingham University Library 14
  development 173−5, 177−8
  exchange 156
  polytechnic libraries 32
  promotion and mobility 171−2
  skills 137−8
  structures 166−72
  subject discipline 168−9

training 157, 170−1, 175, 176,
  180−4
Standing Council of National and
  University Libraries (SCONUL)
  201−2
stock 15, 54
  concepts 36−49
  disposal 60−1
  feedback on use 129−30
  management and disposal 51−61
  policy issues 54−7
  relegation 57−60
  storage 55, 91−2
  weeding 57−60
strategic planning 5−6, 258, 262−3
students 14, 19−20, 48
subject
  access 108−12
  discipline 168
  librarians 17
supplementary publications 89
surrogate documents 98
Sussex University Library 18, 19, 21
System for Information on Grey Literature
  in Europe (SIGLE) 84, 88−9

technological university 24−7
technology *see* automation *and*
  information technology
tenure of appointment 9
tutor librarian 30

universities 11, 14−17
  reorganization 41, 41−4, 45−7
Universities Funding Council 12, 16, 39
use patterns 59
user
  benefits to 189−90
  customer-based library 255−7
  education 15, 30
  perceptions of goodness 187−8

value of library 185, 188−91
videodisc systems 29
virement 8

Warwick University Library 18, 19, 20,
  23
weeding *see* discarding of stock
working collections 43